D0205351

Defending the West

Defending the West

A History of NATO

William Park
*Senior Lecturer, Royal Naval College, Greenwich
and Visiting Lecturer, The City University*

WESTVIEW PRESS
Boulder, Colorado

First published in Great Britain in 1986 by
WHEATSHEAF BOOKS LIMITED

© William Park, 1986

ISBN 0-8133-0408-3
    LC 86-50208

Published in 1986 in the United States by
    WESTVIEW PRESS
    Frederick A. Praeger, Publisher
    5500 Central Avenue
    Boulder, Colorado 80301

Typeset in Times 11pt
Printed in Great Britain

Contents

Preface   vii

Part One. NATO and the Nuclear Age: 1
    The Simultaneous Birth

1. NATO Born, Germany Reborn   3
2. The Roots of NATO Strategy: An Unconventional Beginning   21
3. Obviating the Necessity: Europe Enters the Nuclear Age   43
4. Nuclear Controversies   63

Part Two. NATO since the Early 1960s: 83
    Implementing Flexible Response?

5. Flexible Response: Washington Changes Direction   85
6. Extending Deterrence   94
7. The Nuclear Battlefield   127
8. Below the Nuclear Threshold   166
9. Conclusion   195

Notes   198

Bibliography   220

Index   235

Preface

Since its creation in 1949 the evolution of the North Atlantic Treaty Organisation (NATO) has been both punctuated and propelled by crises, so much so that the alliance has had to survive since birth against the background of an almost continuous death-knell. Crises, of all kinds, so often provide the impetus for human endeavour, and as a result there is no shortage of analyses of NATO's various tribulations. Curiously, however, there has been a tendency to disect each crisis, if not in a historical vacuum then at least with the historical background left unrehearsed and too readily assumed. This has been no less so in recent years, when heightened concern, not to say panic, concerning the West's reliance on a strategy seemingly dominated by nuclear weapons has brought into the arena of strategic debate participants whose ignorance of how NATO arrived at its present posture has too often been as profound as it has been self-evident. Nor can it honestly be claimed that the 'defenders of the faith' have been unvarying in their appreciation of context or presentation of overview. Although publications offering either broad analysis of NATO's dilemmas or historical reconstructions of some aspects of NATO's military preparations are more than adequate, both in number and quality, at least to this author's knowledge there has been no real attempt to incorporate within one set of covers an account of the development of NATO's overall military posture since the publication of Robert E. Osgood's indispensable book *NATO: The Entangling Alliance* in 1962.

The purpose behind this book is to bring the story up to date, hopefully in a way which stimulates as well as informs. There is no pretence here that this publication is anything other than an altogether more modest affair than Osgood's, not least because of the relative talents and experience of their authors. It seeks primarily to provide a service — to those in need of a 'refresher' and also to those new to the strategic deliberations of the Western Alliance. Although this book is not without argument and contention, it lays no claims to originality. Its preparation has consisted of little in the way of research into hitherto hidden official documents, memoirs or events, but instead has relied heavily on the footwork done by those more patient and more ambitious to further human knowledge than I can fairly claim to be. Indeed, it would not be amiss to offer pride of place in these acknowledgements to the innumerable works, referenced in this volume or not, from which this author has drawn both inspiration and substance.

In another respect, however, there is an excess of ambition contained within these pages. The chosen focus has been on the totality of NATO's force posture. This has required a consideration not only of its doctrinal deliberations but also of the way in which the Alliance has set about the construction of actual capabilities. It is, in other words, about what NATO says it would do in a confrontation with the Soviet Bloc, what it is physically capable of doing and what it is plausible or likely would actually happen. Thus it has been legitimate to delve into, by way of example, the positions the French — outside the Alliance's formal military structure — have adopted, or to rehearse some of the internal dissension which has taken place within NATO, or to identify any seeming incompatabilities between military capabilities and declared strategic intentions. There is great analytical complexity here and a morass of detail; as a result, depth has had to be sacrificed for coverage. The most crucial decisions the author has had to make have been to do with how lightly to touch upon some items, or even whether to omit altogether items which ideally ought to be included. Most crucially, the emphasis throughout has been on the central front in Europe and on the role of nuclear weapons. There is little in this book on NATO's flanks or on its maritime missions. If there is a justification for omissions such as these, it is that the concentration of forces and of contention has been related to Central Europe. I do not believe that the excluded regions are unimportant, uninteresting or even unlikely theatres of conflict. Another 'economising' measure has been to reproduce NATO's strategic debates from the stances taken up by its leading members — the US, UK, France and the Federal Republic of Germany. Again, this is not intended to imply that the smaller or geographically less central countries have no impact or nothing of importance to say. Clearly, however, their views and actions carry less weight, and it is partly upon this that I have based my 'editorial' decision to generally exclude them. It is also true, though, that the bigger countries have broadly represented the various strands of opinion to be found in the Alliance's capitals. Any errors of judgement in these respects, and the author is quite convinced there are some, are nevertheless entirely his responsibility.

Although this volume represents the fruit of 'library' rather than 'field' research, it remains true that it could not have been completed without the assistance, however indirect, of others. The help offered by the library staff of the Royal Naval College, and most notably that of Ann McGill, has been of the most direct, and laudably efficient, kind. My colleagues in the Deparment of History and International Affairs at Greenwich, especially Professor Peter Nailor and Dr Geoffrey Till for their encouragement, and Mr John Pay for the inadvisably generous access he has allowed me to his formidable private library and for the innumerable reading items and snippets of information he has passed to me, have had great influence on, though bear no responsibility for, this work. Indeed, any views expressed in these pages are entirely my own, and should not be taken to represent those of the British or any other government. Students are always a stimulant, and special mention is in order for the strategic studies students at the City University during 1983/84 and 1984/85. There is no shadow of doubt, however, that my deepest gratitude is to my wife, Pam, to whom this book is dedicated. It is a humbling experience to live with someone as patient, energetic, selfless and loyal as she is. Not only did she type the manuscript, but she provided a willing ear and words of encouragement whenever they were needed. Again, my thanks.

It is not entirely fanciful to mention our cat, Kozo, with whom we are both besotted. Kozo has not only allowed me use of her study from time to time, but she has also revealed an uncanny instinct for identifying which of my notes and jottings have most deserved being ripped to pieces. She has, by her constant presence, reminded me of how beautiful life, even in its simpler forms, is. On the other hand, her dealings with the local insect and bird life have reminded me that not all necessarily share such noble sentiments. In my immersions in the organisation of the means of mass destruction, I have found each of these observations useful.

William Park
London, December 1985

Part I
NATO and the Nuclear Age:
The Simultaneous Birth

1 NATO Born, Germany Reborn

It is almost obligatory for the author of any general work on the North Atlantic Treaty Organisation (NATO) to express some sense of incredulity at the durability the alliance has shown. The former Belgian diplomat Baron Robert Rothschild succumbed inimitably to this temptation when he launched an exposition of his country's role in the formation of NATO by reminding us that it is now the world's longest-lasting alliance since the Athenians organised the League of Delos in 477BC to repel the Persian invasion.[1] This geographically dispersed, somewhat ill-assorted and voluntary gathering of sovereign states has indeed displayed a remarkable collective ability to endure periods of tension, adjust to unprecedented change and respond to an evolving perception of threat. That the NATO enterprise should have remained afloat seems even more noteworthy when the nature of its birth is taken into account. Precisely which states should constitute the membership, and what that membership should commit them to, remained highly uncertain until almost the eve of the Atlantic Treaty's signature. Even after the signing, major differences of opinion, perception and interpretation persisted. Indeed, many of those who participated in the drawing up of the Treaty have forcefully expressed both the uncertainty which surrounded their work at the time and the unpredictability regarding the direction the Alliance would subsequently take. For example, a Canadian participant has since written that 'there might have been a better treaty, there might have been a worse treaty, there might have been no treaty at all'.[2] Charles Bohlen, counsellor of the US State Department and an important figure in the pre-treaty negotiations claimed that, 'At the time of the signing of the Pact, April 4, 1949, I do not believe that anyone envisaged the kind of military set up that NATO evolved into'.[3]

EARLY ATTITUDES

It is testimony to the clumsiness if not the wickedness of Soviet behaviour in the years immediately following the Second World War that the security concerns of Moscow's erstwhile allies should have so quickly shifted from their fiercely anti-German orientation to a primarily anti-Soviet one. This transition was often a reluctant one, less so in the case of the United States but especially so for the French. Even the British, whose recognition of a Soviet rather than a German threat came earlier than for the French, were only now belatedly facing up to the facts of post-Bismarkian Europe by signing the bilateral Dunkirk Treaty with France on 4 March 1947. This 'treaty of alliance and mutual assistance' was aimed specifically at the possibility of a renewed German menace and was to be of fifty years' duration.[4] The Brussels Treaty of 17 March 1948, which joined the Benelux countries to Britain and France, again specified the German rather than the Soviet threat in both its Preamble and its Article 7.[5] In France there was only one thing on which all political parties agreed, and that was that the Germans should be dealt with harshly.[6] In the years immediately following Germany's defeat, French objectives consisted of a lengthy occupation by the four victorious allies, substantial reparations payments, the detachment from Germany of the industrial areas of the Rhineland and Saar, and the internationalisation of the Ruhr.[7] Such was the obsession of the French with their German problem during these years that the US secretary of state, George Marshall, felt that the 'French preoccupation with Germany as a major threat at this time seems to us outmoded and unrealistic'.[8]

Although unease concerning Soviet intentions was growing in Washington throughout 1947 — resulting from the bullying and sinister nature of Soviet behaviour in Eastern Europe and elsewhere, from Moscow's maintenance of at least numerically formidable armed forces, from Stalin's increasingly uncooperative and sullen attitude, and from the activities of somewhat pro-Soviet communist parties in a number of West European states — the American response also remained rather vague in its target.[9] The Truman Doctrine enunciated in March 1947 was designed 'to support free peoples who are resisting attempted subjugation by armed minorities or by outside pressures'. Materially it consisted of the despatch of $400 million of aid and civilian and military advisers to Greece and Turkey. Although the Doctrine signalled that the United States was beginning to stir, it did not necessarily envisage sending American armed forces to the world's trouble spots. The European Recovery Programme, initiated by Marshall's Harvard speech of 5 June 1947, was directed 'against hunger, poverty, desperation and chaos', and as such the offer was open to the Soviet Union and what were becoming its satellites too. Indeed, Poland and Czechoslovakia sought to become beneficiaries of Marshall Aid but were prevented from doing so by Stalin. Policies such as these could be useful in combating any imminent collapse of political or economic systems, but they did nothing to directly confront the emergence of Soviet armed superiority in Europe — a possibility which in 1945 had already been identified by Winston Churchill[10] and of which awareness was to grow in the years immediately following the end of the Second World War.

TOWARDS SOME FORM OF UNION

It was with the collapse in December 1947 of the Four-Power Foreign Ministers' meeting, called to find a solution to the German problem, that the perception of the Soviet threat began to harden and the advisability of a firmer and more unified response to it began to be more seriously considered. Certainly it was this development which prompted Bevin to make a rather vague suggestion to Marshall on the evening the talks collapsed which was to lead directly to the signing of the North Atlantic Treaty over a year later. 'I am convinced', said Bevin:

that the Soviet Union will not deal with the West on any reasonable terms in the foreseeable future and that the salvation of the West depends upon the formation of some form of union, formal or informal in character, in Western Europe, backed by the United States and the Dominions, such a mobilisation of moral and material force as will inspire confidence and energy within, and respect elsewhere.[11]

Stalin very effectively came to the aid of the protagonists for an Atlantic treaty by instituting the Berlin blockade in June 1948, thereby prompting the famous eleven-month airlift of supplies into the city. As Attlee was to comment, 'it wasn't, I think, until the Berlin airlift that American public opinion really wakened up to the facts of life. Their own troops were involved in that, you see'.[12] Although the rapid succession of crises created a hostility towards the Soviet Union which was probably greater in the United States than in Europe, a widespread resistance to the despatch of American forces to Europe still prevailed. Sir Nicholas Henderson, a British diplomat who was a member of the working party asked to draft the North Atlantic Treaty, has noted 'how reluctant the Americans were in the first six months of 1948 to countenance the idea of a commitment to defend Western Europe'.[13] The immediate American response to Bevin's ideas had been somewhat negative, chiefly because Washington adopted a 'wait and see' attitude, desiring first to observe what the Europeans could do for themselves. This led Bevin to fear a 'vicious circle' of failure, in which the proposed Western European Union would be unable to get off the ground without American assistance, which would not be forthcoming because the Western Union had failed to get off the ground.[14]

It is one of the many ironies of the history of this period that it was a 'threat' to Norway, which had not yet materialised, and which may have been based on no more than a misunderstanding, that served as the immediate catalyst for American actions.[15] In response to a worried message concerning Norway from Bevin, and without consulting anyone in his department, Marshall arranged for tripartite talks to be held, in secret, between the United States, Britain and Canada on Atlantic security to begin by the end of March.[16] Hitherto, the State Department had been torn on the issue of an American commitment to the defence of Western Europe. Influential figures such as George Kennan and Charles Bohlen had argued that, as it was inconceivable that Washington would stand idly by in the event of a major Soviet action, a formal commitment was unnecessary and would be regarded as provocative by Moscow.[17] Events, and Marshall's response to them, had undermined though not yet destroyed their opposition. There was congressional opposition, too, and here Under-secretary Robert Lovett was able to use his friendship with the influential Republican Senator Arthur Vandenburg, who had initially been reluctant to accept a treaty, to draft the rather vaguely worded Vandenburg Resolution. Passed by sixty-four votes to four on 11 June 1948, it put the Senate on record as approving the 'association of the United States, by constitutional process, with such regional and other collective arrangements as are based on continuous and effective self-help and mutual aid, and as affect its national security'.[18]

THE MEMBERSHIP

In fact, the assumptions which the various Western governments made concerning the character of any future alliance were neither shared nor, for the most part, noticeably clear. Bevin's initial fancy, as expressed to Marshall following the collapse of the Foreign Ministers' Conference in December 1947, had been for a 'union, formal or informal in character' of the West as a whole. The Brussels Treaty, purely European, represented in effect a tight 'inner circle'. On the agenda now was the relationship between this 'inner circle' and an 'outer circle', presumably more loosely associated, which would include above all the United States.[19] The threat to Norway complicated British thinking, however, for the message to Marshall of 10 March which prompted the tripartite talks was concerned with Atlantic security. In this the United States and Scandinavia had a clear stake, yet Bevin was not in favour of inviting the Scandinavian states to participate in the negotiations for the Brussels Treaty but did favour associating Italy — not one of the states he linked to his Atlantic proposal — with it. An alternative possibility for Italy was some sort of Mediterranean pact.[20] In other words, which states were to constitute the 'inner' and which the 'outer' circles was unclear and open to discussion.

From Washington's perspective, the strategic significance of the Atlantic was clear and the membership of any alliance with which they were involved had to reflect this. Lovett had stated that 'Greenland and Iceland were more important than some nations in Western Europe to the security of the United States and Canada'.[21] American interest in Greenland required some sort of arrangement with Denmark, and the Azores, under Portuguese sovereignty, were added to what was known as the 'stepping stones' concept.[22] Participation was entered into by these countries only with some reluctance. Iceland joined only after it had obtained an American understanding that there could be no foreign troops or bases in Iceland in peacetime, that the decision on when developments required facilities to be made available would be Iceland's, and that Iceland had no intention of establishing any armed forces of its own. Even so, ugly scenes accompanied the ratification debate in Iceland.[23] The authoritarian Salazar regime in Portugal, on the other hand, was fired by anti-communist zeal, but was initially reluctant to join any new alliance without Spain and also let it be known that it would not regard itself as tied by an 'obligation of granting, in peacetime, military bases to a foreign power'. There can also be little doubt that from the Portuguese perspective the pact had an Atlantic rather than a European orientation.[24]

For the British and the Americans, the inclusion of Norway in an Atlantic security pact was indispensable, but a Swedish attempt to create a Nordic bloc offered Norway and Denmark an alternative option. Sweden, who in January 1949 turned down an invitation to join the Atlantic Alliance, sought to preserve her traditional neutrality, whilst maintaining the security of herself and her neighbours and avoiding the wrath of the Soviet Union. The stumbling block was her insistence that the members of the proposed Nordic alliance should not seek military aid or assistance from outside powers. It was the more Atlanticist inclined Norwegians who objected most to this precondition. History had left them with less faith than that of their Swedish neighbours in the benefits of neutrality. Furthermore, they had a 180-mile border with the Soviet Union and were again being subjected to political pressure from Moscow. In effect, the fate of Sweden's mission was sealed when, on 14 January, Washington publicly announced that those states willing to join the United States in a collective defence organisation would enjoy preferential treatment in the supply of military equipment. With Norway's loss of interest, it was the Swedes who rejected as unrealistic a Danish suggestion of a Swedish–Danish alliance, and Denmark followed Norway into the alliance.[25] It is interesting to note, however, that from a purely military point of view the British and French military authorities believed that a unified Scandinavia, even one detached from the Atlantic alliance, made more sense than the divided Scandinavia that resulted.[26]

As political circumstances precluded Spanish membership, and the Ulster question stood in the way of Irish membership,[27] it was left to the question of Italy to cause the biggest headaches concerning the geographic scope of the alliance; Italy, one of the Axis powers of the Second World War, was not properly an Atlantic state. It self-evidently occupied a strategically important position, however, particularly from the French point of view. In addition, internal communist-inspired disruption made it seem essential that the pro-Western elements in Italy receive external support. All the major participants in the negotiations waxed and waned somewhat on the Italian issue. That something should be done for Italy was something of a constant of American policy throughout the negotiations, though Dean Acheson — who had replaced Marshall as secretary of state in January 1949 — expressed some rather belated doubts on Italy's inclusion in a specifically Atlantic pact. American support reflected both a navalist perspective and a political concern. The Benelux countries and Canada tended to adhere to the British view that Italy could be invited to sign the Brussels Treaty, but that membership of the Atlantic Pact would be inadvisable. Italian membership would dilute the geographical coherence of the pact, would raise the issue of Greece and Turkey, and would impose a military burden on the other members as a result of the provisions of the peace treaty which had been imposed on Italy. The French, who tended initially to regard the Atlantic Treaty negotiations as a means by which the United States could be entangled in the defence of the Brussels Treaty powers, swung round to support Italian membership once they realised just how Europe-wide membership was going to be. Discussion of the Italian issue dragged on in this rather inconclusive way until the Italian government, hitherto no more decided about its membership than were the parties to the negotiations, made a direct request to participate on 12 January. It is difficult to assess the impact of the French tactic of February in refusing to acquiesce in an invitation to Norway unless one was issued to Italy too, but ultimately it appears to have been the American wish for Italy's inclusion that won the day.[28] This outcome paved the way to Greek and Turkish accession in 1952, which in effect confirmed the redundancy of the concept of a separate Mediterranean security arrangement, which had been the essence of the British position for much of 1948. When Spain became NATO's sixteenth member in 1982, the incorporation of the Mediterranean's non-communist European states was complete, barring Cyprus and Malta.

Combined with the absence of Sweden, Ireland and Spain, Italian membership diluted the Atlanticism which inspired Bevin's original conception and which the tripartite talks were initially supposed to consider. It remained, of course, to confront the much thornier illogicality of attempting to secure the Brussels Treaty powers against Soviet aggression whilst excluding West German membership and military potential. In short, the founding signatories of the North Atlantic Treaty did not wholly reflect any particularly coherent strategic logic. Rather, the nature of the membership reflected the gallant endeavours of the diplomats and statesmen involved to mould some acceptable shape out of the political possibilities which history had made available to them, and the conflicting demands and aspirations which they were tasked to revolve. The new alliance reflected both the Atlantic interests of Washington and London, but also the continental commitment to Central Europe which history and circumstances demanded of them. The terms of this continental commitment were still to be determined, and were initially accepted only with some reluctance, yet it has been around the central front that the debates about NATO's strategy and posture waged.

NEGOTIATING THE TEXT

In July 1948 the remaining Brussels Treaty powers — France and the three Benelux countries — joined the United States, Britain and Canada to negotiate an Atlantic treaty. The ensuing talks were long and arduous. As Theodore C. Achilles, one of the State Department enthusiasts for a pact, has since pointed out, 'The basic differences were due to the fact that the Europeans, particularly the French, wanted as binding and as long a commitment as possible, and the Americans, while agreeing in principle, were constrained by what the Administration and friendly senators thought the Senate would accept'.[29] In fact, this assessment is rather generous to the American negotiators and their friendly senators, for they too were by and large imbued with the traditional American hesitation towards excessively specific overseas commitments. The Inter-American Treaty of Reciprocal Assistance of 2 September 1947, or Rio Pact, represented the American view of the proper relationship between the 'inner' and 'outer' circles of the new pact. [30] Although the Rio Pact provided that 'an armed attack. . .against an American state shall be considered an armed attack against all the American states', determination of the appropriate response was left to each signatory individually, and there was no reference at all to military action. Predictably, the Europeans doubted the utility of so weakly worded a commitment, and pushed instead for a formulation based on the Brussels Treaty, Article 4 of which said that in the event of an armed attack against one or more of the signatories, the other parties will 'afford the party so attacked all the military and other aid and assistance in their power'. The effect of this would have been to abolish the 'inner' and 'outer' circle distinction, and it reflected in particular the French view that an American commitment to the security of Western Europe had to be guaranteed if the proposed pact was to deter any further aggression or defeat it should it occur. Again, predictably, the outcome was a compromise, proposed formally in a draft treaty by the Ambassador's Committee, which had conducted or supervised much of the spade work, on 24 December 1948. [31] This contained the words 'taking forthwith such military or other action, individually and in concert'.

The US negotiators had insisted that it would be pointless to devise a treaty which was too strongly worded for Congress to accept, and to this end leading members of the Senate Foreign Relations Committee had been consulted throughout. Dean Acheson, whose task it was to keep consultations with the senators in tandem with the deliberations of the Allied ambassadors, has written that he felt like 'a circus performer riding two horses — for one to move ahead of the other would mean a nasty fall. Safety required use of the ambassadors to urge on the senators, and the senators to hold back the ambassadors'. [32] The dismay, then, was deep when strong objections were raised in the Senate, most tellingly by Vandenberg and Connally, to the apparent automaticity of the response and the use of the words 'military or other action' provided by the draft treaty. [33] The senators were soon chastened, however, by the reaction to their debate, not only in Europe but also from the Canadian government and the US media. Connally, the chairman of the Senate Foreign Relations Committee, became altogether more amenable, and after discussions with Acheson and Truman the 'automaticity' which it was felt was implied by Article 5 of the draft text was left untouched and the words 'such action as it deems necessary, including the use of armed force' were substituted for the words 'such military or other action. . .as may be necessary'. As Acheson has since written, 'the negotiation of Article 5 became a contest between our allies seeking to impale the Senate on the specific, and the senators attempting to wriggle free'.[34] The Senate eventually ratified the North Atlantic Treaty on 21 July 1949 by eighty-two votes to thirteen, although the debate which preceded the vote was deservedly characterised by Acheson as 'long, often noisy and not a little ridiculous'.[35]

Before moving on to that creation of organisational substance and armed strength which ensured the North Atlantic Treaty was to be more than just another 'scrap of paper', it is worthwhile lingering just a little longer on the inauspicious origins of the Alliance which the story of the process of treaty formulation reveals. First, it should be noted that Article 11 of the Treaty says that the signatories are to carry out the provisions of the treaty 'in accordance with their respective constitutional processes'. Although the American negotiating team had been prepared to accept the European view that this clause was superfluous, it was finally incorporated at the insistence of senators anxious to retain a veto over future US entanglements.[36] Second, as against a French proposal for a fifty-year duration period, inspired by the terms of the Brussels Treaty and generally supported by the other European delegations, the Americans countered with, according to one version, a ten-year duration[37] or, according to another, a twelve- to twenty-year maximum,[38] owing to an assumed senatorial reluctance to accept a longer term. In fact, the final wording provides for unlimited duration, although since the Treaty's tenth birthday it has been collectively reviewable (Art. 12), and since its twentieth anniversary any member has been free to withdraw at one year's notice (Art. 13). This is superior to either of the original formulations. Miraculously, perhaps, no member state has yet exercised the right granted to it by Article 13.

MILITARY AID

For the Europeans in general and the French in particular, the North Atlantic Treaty represented a historical vindication. On publication of the final version of the Treaty in March 1949, Schuman felt able to say 'We have today obtained what we hoped for in vain between the wars: the United States have recognised that there can be no peace or security for America if Europe is in danger'.[39] Yet history had also taught the French and other continental states that 'a scrap of paper' is an insufficient guarantee of peace and security. Accordingly, during the Treaty ratification debates in the French National Assembly, the absence in French eyes (though not, as we have seen, in those of American senators) of an automatic assistance clause, cast doubt on the utility of the Treaty altogether.[40] More telling, however, were the comments made by rapporteur René Mayer during the same debates. Although he warned the deputies that the Treaty should not be regarded as 'a blank cheque on the American budget', it would nevertheless have 'no more value than the Locarno Treaty or the Briand-Kellogg Pact' if not backed by US military assistance.[41] As the US ambassador to France, Lincoln Caffery, reported in April 1949, signing the treaty was 'only half the battle to defeat [the] basic feeling of insecurity' in France.[42] The objective of French policy all along had been to entangle the Anglo-Saxons in the defence of France as much as possible. A treaty of preferably lengthy duration and promising automatic support, was simply one means to achieve this end. Better still would have been an Allied organisational structure and a physical military presence. To this end the French ambassador to Washington, Henri Bonnet, called on George Marshall in August 1948 and laid down firm conditions for a French acceptance of an Atlantic security pact: 'Unity of command at once; immediate movement of US military supplies to France; immediate movement of US military personnel to France'. This intrusive style irritated Marshall and provoked Lovett to utter, 'the French are getting in our hair!'.[43]

In fact, the US administration had already begun to consider seriously the military aid requirements of the European allies,[44] and by the summer of 1948 the National Security Council (NSC) had recommended and President Truman approved the outlines of a programme to that effect.[45] Furthermore, since July 1948 an American delegation with 'observer' status had been attending the regular meetings held by the Brussels Treaty powers to determine their military aid requirements.[46] The Truman administration was well aware, however, of the similarities between the reasons why isolationist senators opposed the North Atlantic Treaty and European governments supported it. Washington also appreciated that obtaining financial support for European defence efforts from Congress might be more difficult than obtaining ratification of the Treaty. This explains why it 'deliberately postponed'[47] submitting the Mutual Defence Assistance Bill until after it had obtained Senate ratification. It also explains why, during the Senate hearings on the Treaty, Acheson argued that the treaty and the issue of military assistance 'should be considered separately and on their own merits'.[48]

On 8 April 1949, agreement having been reached on the text of the North Atlantic Treaty, the five Brussels Treaty powers announced that their defence ministers had 'approved a plan for the defence of Western Europe', but that 'if this defence programme is to be effective, the material assistance of the US government is essential'. Denmark, Norway and Italy simultaneously made similar requests.[49] Out of the same process which had produced these demands emerged President Truman's request to Congress on 25 July, just hours after the North Atlantic Treaty had been formally ratified, for legislation authorising military aid to NATO and other friendly states. The congressional ruminations over the Mutual Defence Assistance Programme lasted until 6 October, when it became law after what have been described as 'long and trying hearings'.[50] Even then, Congress imposed the restriction that, before the bulk of the money could be transferred NATO would have to develop an organisational structure and a joint defence plan.

US TROOPS IN EUROPE

The Europeans now had what has appropriately been portrayed as a 'guarantee pact'[51] with the United States, coupled with access to American funds to finance their military re-equipment programmes. But, momentous as these decisions had been for the United States, for the Europeans it wasn't yet enough. Attached to the passage of the Mutual Defence Assistance Bill had been a demand that the Europeans, in effect, begin to take their defence tasks more seriously. Yet most West Europeans believed that it made little sense to try to defend what remained of their continent without the direct assistance of the United States. The American commitment was still too vague. American troops were needed in Europe, both for the physical contribution they would make and the psychological effect they would have. Many influential Americans understood this. In April 1949 the US Army chief of staff, General Bradley, argued that, 'Unless plans for common defence of the existing free world provide for the security of Western Europe, these people cannot be expected to stake their lives in the common cause'. The will as well as the means would be boosted by 'the assurance that they would be adequately helped in sufficient time'.[52] The US ambassador to Paris noted that there had to be some assurance that 'French soldiers would be dying for something that has a chance to survive'.[53] In other words, Europeans were unconvinced that it was worthwhile becoming corpses before liberation could be expected.

The deployment of US troops in Europe still seemed an unlikely prospect, however. In January 1950 President Truman approved a 'Strategic Plan' which had been drawn up by NATO's Defence Committee and which enabled the further release of funds under the military aid programme. The plan called for 'each nation. . .to undertake the task or tasks for which it is best suited. Certain nations, because of geographic location or because of their capabilities, will be prepared to undertake appropriate specific missions'. This clause reflected Washington's intention to confine its contribution chiefly to the strategic bombardment and naval missions. The implications of this were clear for, as the Plan noted, 'the hard core of ground forces will come from the European nations'.[54] For Washington, this included Germany.

American interest in German rearmament had been discussed in the Pentagon as early as 1947.[55] It stemmed not simply from a realisation that a German contribution was essential if any sort of numerical balance of forces in Europe was to be achieved, but also from an appreciation that 'forward defence', which meant the defence of Western Europe as a whole in West Germany, was a military necessity. In fact, this view was not confined to Washington. Even in French military circles there was a recognition of the logic of 'forward defence', and an acceptance that this implied a German contribution.[56] The Dutch foreign minister, Dirk Stikker, has recorded his realisation of the absurdity of a militarily necessary 'forward defence' which did not permit German involvement in its implementation.[57] However, the psychological hurdle which Germany's recent and bitter victims had to negotiate was still too great. Whilst approving ratification of the North Atlantic Treaty, the French National Assembly had added an amendment providing for its approval of the accession of any new member, which, of course, meant a veto over German membership,[58] and the French foreign minister, Robert Schuman, had spoken for many when he said in a speech to the Assembly in July 1949:

Germany has no army and should not have one. It has no arms and will not have any. . .It was therefore unthinkable, for France and for all her allies, that Germany could be allowed to adhere to the Atlantic Pact as a nation capable of defending itself or of aiding in the defence of other nations.[59]

Even as late as July 1950 the British government issued a statement declaring its continued opposition to German rearmament.[60] Yet the military balance, the requirements of forward defence, and American pressure, all pushed in the opposite direction. A *Le Monde* editorial was more prescient when it noted that 'The rearmament of Germany is present in the Atlantic Pact as the seed in the egg'.[61]

Given the belief widespread in Europe as well as in the United States that an armed Soviet attack on Western Europe was not imminent, there appeared to be few penalties for indulging in anti-Germanism.[62] The 'illusion' that Moscow's preferred mode of advance was political subversion was abruptly shattered by the outbreak of the Korean War on 25 June 1950. This was widely interpreted, however wrongly, as presaging a shift in Soviet tactics in Europe to that of frontal military assault. Unsurprisingly, the West German chancellor, Konrad Adenaur, was especially explicit in drawing out the parallel. 'I am convinced', he said, 'that Stalin has the same plan for Europe as for Korea. What is happening there is a dress-rehearsal for what is in store for us here'.[63] The issue of German rearmament was now firmly on the agenda.

The road to the eventual acceptance of German rearmament was a tortured and tortuous one. When Truman's August request to Congress for an additional $4,000 million of military aid was followed by his radio announcement in September that he had 'approved substantial increases in the strength of the US forces to be stationed in Western Europe', it looked as if Washington had accepted that it would take a major American commitment of troops to Europe to balance Soviet ground strength there. Yet Truman's announcement was coupled with the all-important condition that 'a basic element in the implementation of this decision is the degree to which our friends match our actions in this regard'.[64] Chiefly, what this meant was not only that a deployment of American ground troops to Europe would be contingent on a European willingness to accept their share of the burden, but it depended also on their readiness to acquiesce in the rearmament of Germany. This was made explicit at the North Atlantic Council meeting of September 1950.[65]

Out of the so-called 'great debate' on the commitment of US forces to Europe in the Senate, came Senate Resolution 99 of April 1951. This approved the appointment of General Dwight D. Eisenhower as NATO's first supreme commander and the despatch of the four additional army divisions to Europe, which constituted Truman's 'substantial' increase. This made six American divisions in all. The Senate resolution mirrored Truman's conditional offer when it insisted that 'the major contribution to the ground forces under General Eisenhower's command should be made by the European members'. Indeed, both Eisenhower and Defence Secretary George C. Marshall had stressed this point in testimony, and had speculated on the possibility of a future American troop withdrawal once Europe had acquired sufficient military strength of its own. In 1966 Eisenhower confirmed that the despatch of additional troops in 1951 had been a temporary measure. It was hoped, he said, that ultimately only air and naval units would be stationed in Europe, but this idea seemed to have been 'shelved or forgotten'.[66]

THE EUROPEAN DEFENCE COMMUNITY

If the promise of eventual withdrawal and greater European effort was the price the US administration had to pay Senate for the commitment of troops, then the commitment of troops was itself the price which had to be paid to the Europeans, and especially the French, to encourage them both to increase their own efforts and to accept a German contribution. It was to take another four years before the terms under which this contribution was to be made could be agreed. The American concept, forwarded at the September Council meeting, was to place German units in an integrated NATO force under an American supreme commander, and discussions to this end, involving a West German negotiating team, began in January 1951. In October 1950, however, the French put a plan before NATO's Defence Committee for a European army. It envisaged a European minister of defence nominated by signatory governments and ultimately responsible to these governments and to a European Assembly. With a common budget at his disposal, the minister would assume responsibility for raising, equipping and training a European army. This in turn would be made of national units, or combat teams, of between 800 and 1,200 men, thus ensuring no concentrated German armed strength would emerge. Whereas a proportion of those national forces with overseas responsibilities — France, of course, and Britain if she agreed to participate — could remain under national control, all German forces, without exception, would be incorporated into the European army.[67] The French, who had promised to raise twenty divisions — an effort which Pleven said could not be 'integrally borne by our country' and would depend on US assistance[68] — were also insisting that the rearmament programmes of the existing allies be completed before that of West Germany. In this they were supported by the Attlee government in London, but Washington was apprehensive about the pace of rearmament that would result.

In fact, under the closer scrutiny to which the Pleven Plan — now known as the European Defence Community (EDC) and which even much of Washington had come to support[69] — was subjected, its impracticabilities and incompleteness surfaced. The talks, held in Paris, began to stumble on a whole series of political and military obstacles. As a result, the proposed outline of the EDC altered quite drastically, so much so that it was paradoxically the French National Assembly which ultimately killed the idea in the summer of 1954. There were many reasons behind the French rejection. In the face of severe French pressure, the British had steadfastly refused to join the enterprise although they had, with the US, signed a treaty of association in April. Nevertheless, this meant the French would alone have to control a rearmed Germany within the EDC. Furthermore, many in France were suspicious of the extensive loss of French sovereign control over her own armed forces which participation in the EDC seemed to entail, yet were simultaneously concerned that the supranational provisions of the EDC were too weak to sufficiently contain the German units. French deputies were not alone in doubting the practicability of the whole concept, and this too served as a rationale behind its rejection. However, French rejection of the EDC did not imply the end of the pressure to rearm Germany. After all, the Pleven Plan had itself been devised only because Paris felt unable to resist American pressure for German rearmament, and turned instead to the attempt to control the form it took. It would be incorrect to assert that, following the French vote, the Allies had simply returned to their starting point of September 1950. Too many expectations had been aroused only to meet disappointment. Bitterness was the inevitable result. Washington, having invested so much emotional capital in the EDC project and now with an even greater determination to make full use of German resources, reacted especially badly. Frustration at the endless postponement of ratification had already led the United States to utter a series of warnings culminating in a statement by Secretary of State Dulles at the North Atlantic Council meeting of December 1953 in which he warned of 'an agonising reappraisal of basic United States policy' should the EDC fail.

THE WEST EUROPEAN UNION AND GERMAN REARMAMENT

Perhaps surprisingly, it was now the British who took up the torch. London's proposals took the form of an expansion of the Brussels Treaty to include West Germany (and Italy) [70] and were designed to get the Alliance off the hook. The West European Union (WEU) required no supranationality, no new organisations and no discrimination against Germany. The British were, of course, already associated as signatories of the Brussels Treaty, but at a conference held in London in September 1954 the British prime minister, Anthony Eden, held out a still greater inducement to the waiverers. The British were prepared to station four divisions and a tactical air force in Germany, to encourage the French and others that controls on the course a rearmed West Germany might take could be established. Furthermore, the British agreed 'not to withdraw those forces against the wishes of the majority of the Brussels Treaty Powers', except in the event of a major overseas emergency or a major strain on the UK's finances. In the circumstances these clauses could easily have been seen as, or have become, exit routes for the future; but the British forces are still there. This represents a quite remarkable turn of events. As Eden said in his closing speech at the Conference, 'my colleagues will realise that what I have announced is for us a very formidable step to take. You know that ours is above all an island story. We are still an island people in thought and tradition'.[71] In return, the occupation status of West Germany was lifted and the country attained full sovereignty; it was allowed to join NATO and to rearm. Bonn was required, however, to renounce the production on German territory of chemical, biological and nuclear weapons. By the end of the year the French had accepted this somewhat improvised package, and on 5 May 1955 the process of ratification was complete. To mark the end of this drawn out saga, the Soviet Union formed the Warsaw Pact.

During this first decade following the Second World War a number of shifts had occurred. Europeans had with some hesitation, particularly on the part of the French, come to accept that the Soviet rather than the German threat was the more immediately worrying. Germany, or at least the Federal Republic, had been reincorporated into the European family of nations, or at least the West European family of nations. The British and, more momentously, the Americans, had embraced a 'continental commitment' requiring the peacetime stationing of forces in Europe. In essence this meant a transfer of concern to a primarily continental rather than a specifically Atlantic conception of the new alliance, which was somewhat contrary to initial predispositions. This tendency was reinforced by what seemed to be the militarisation of the Soviet challenge signified by the outbreak of the Korean War. It is to NATO's response to this threat that we now turn.

2 The Roots of NATO Strategy: An Unconventional Beginning

THE FORCE BALANCE

With the outbreak of the Korean War, far more attention was focused than hitherto on the relative military force levels of the Soviet Union and its satellites, on the one hand, and of the West, on the other. Force, it was now more widely believed, might readily be employed by the Soviet Union to achieve its ambitions. The very nature of the Soviet system — its secrecy, its sullen hostility and its generally overbearing posture — served to both increase the fear and to encourage the time-honoured military tradition of worst-case analysis. Estimates of the adversary's military strength had to be made and they had to be based on whatever information was available, regardless of its reliability or finesse. This has, of course, been a difficulty under which, to some degree or other, the intelligence agencies of NATO powers have had to labour since the inception of the Alliance, but it is impossible to comprehend the evolution of NATO's strategy or force posture without reference to their findings. The complexities are particularly acute where the conventional (i.e. non-nuclear) force balance is concerned. Moreover, the problem is not simply one of determining precisely what exists. There are, in addition, questions such as of whether to count all that exists and how to count it. For example, should all forces, even those not normally based in Europe, be incorporated into any assessment of the European balance or, more difficult still, the balance on the central front? If not, what should be included, and according to what criteria and assumptions? Should all forces with some military training be counted (including, for example, internal security police and gendarmerie)? Alternatively, should the focus only be on combat troops in place? Are manpower counts more telling than division counts, or vice versa? What assumptions should be made about mobilisation rates and potential? And how should quality — factors such as superior equipment, better training and morale — be assessed? Comparisons between different types of force structure are still more awkward. How do we weigh off tanks against anti-tank weapons, or air superiority against ground preponderance?

Although some concern with questions such as these is unavoidable, the impact of perceptions of the force balance is of still greater significance. It is, indeed, with perceptions that we begin, for an undeniable feature of NATO's early force-structure considerations was its belief, indelibly marked right from the outset and never truly banished since, that the West was chronically and irretrievably inferior in conventional military strength to the Soviet Union and its new-found Eastern European satellites. This is a crucially important point for, as we shall see, this perceived weakness provided both motivation for and rationalisation of NATO's early drift towards a heavy dependence on nuclear weapons. It is, therefore, imperative that we look closely at the conventional force imbalance as it existed in the early years of the Alliance.

The Soviet Union had claimed a total wartime armed strength of around 12 million personnel; this is put higher by some Western authorities.[1] Like the Western Allies, Moscow set about demobilising these vast forces once the defeat of Germany had been completed. The fact of demobilisation alone should perhaps have suggested something less than a single-minded Soviet determination to commit further aggression. However, a number of complicating factors intervened, the most important of which was the differential rate of Soviet demobilisation when compared with that of the Western Allies, most notably the United States. It takes two to create an imbalance, and the extraordinarily rapid rate of Western demobilisation made its own contribution. A second, ominous factor was that this relatively slow Soviet force run-down seemed in any case to bottom out by 1948. Once again, rationalisations may be offered. The Soviet Army had certainly acquired extensive occupation duties in Eastern Europe, and it had long been Russian practice to maintain large standing armies even in peacetime. However, such explanations could hardly reassure a Western Europe living in the unprecedentedly proximate shadow of a large Soviet military presence. Furthermore, beginning in 1947, the Soviets began to engineer a rearming of the increasingly subordinated states of Eastern Europe. This included the unwelcome spectre of a thinly disguised East German 'police' force which was fifty-thousand strong by the time the Korean War broke out.[2] Moscow also embarked on a force modernisation and re-equipping programme of its own which, although it appears not to have begun in earnest until 1951 and thus could be presented as a response to the formation of NATO or to the rearmament associated with the Korean War — and Kruschev did subsequently claim that the Soviet Union had been provoked into rearmament by the West[3] — it nevertheless resulted in considerably enhanced naval, air and ground capability.[4]

From 1947 up until the 1960s, when American defence analysts challenged the veracity of the figure and the assumptions on which it was based, the number of Soviet ground-force divisions was constantly put at 175.[5] These were often described as 'active divisions', for example by the British defence secretary, Manny Shinwell, during a two-day House of Commons debate in July 1950.[6] Of the active divisions, the twenty-two which were in East Germany were on a war footing, and by 1954 it was officially estimated that there were a further sixty divisions elsewhere in Eastern Europe and the Western areas of the Soviet Union.[7] This did mean, though, that most Soviet divisions were some distance from Central Europe. In addition, the massive Soviet reservist system meant, according to US Army General Omar Bradley, that Moscow could organise 502 combat divisions within a few months of the outbreak of a war.[8] Moscow's East European satellite states were themselves credited with eighty divisions by 1954, although the threat they posed was not always taken too seriously. An American air-force officer, who was a member of the first US Joint Staff and NATO Standing Group in 1949 and a US military representative to the European Army Conference from 1950 to 1952, has since written that 'every knowledgeable observer knew that the satellite armies could not be counted on by the Soviets as either effective or reliable in the event of a European conflict'.[9]

In these early years, the NATO division count seemed hopeless by comparison. On the day the North Atlantic Treaty was signed the Alliance had a total of twelve ill-equipped divisions in continental Europe — seven French, two British, two American and one Belgian. [10] Furthermore, they were not deployed, equipped or trained for war but for occupation duties. In the wake of the outbreak of the Korean War in June 1950 the situation improved considerably, however, so much so that by December 1951 the Supreme Headquarters, Allied Powers Europe (SHAPE) could boast of approximately thirty-five divisions in varying states of readiness. [11] By June 1954 General Gruenther, Supreme Allied Commander, Europe (SACEUR), was able to declare to the English-Speaking Union in London that NATO now had almost 100 divisions in varying degrees of readiness. [12] If true, then NATO's resignation in the face of its 'failure' to reach a 96-division goal set in February 1952 is puzzling. It is worth noting too that the US Army chief of staff, General Collins, had calculated that 110 US divisions were equivalent in military power to 175 Soviet divisions. [13] There were improvements in NATO's aerial strength too. From a 1949 figure of fewer than 1,000 operational aircraft in Western Europe, [14] a total of almost 3,000 had been reached by December 1951. [15] Impressive as these improvements were, as with the ground force division count, they appeared to pale into insignificance when contrasted with the 19,000 aircraft which the British defence minister credited the Soviets with in 1951. [16]

Turning now to manpower counts, it has been noted how in these early post-war years, estimates of Soviet ground strength seemed to vary from 2.5 million to 4 million personnel. [17] Of these, only a million may have been located in non-Soviet areas of Europe. [18] Thus on 12 October 1949 General Bradley put Soviet Army strength at 2.5 million personnel, [19] even though four days later he was to inform a Senate appropriations sub-committee that Moscow had over five million men under arms in all — a figure which would seem to suggest unusually large air force, navy and internal security forces, even for the Soviet Union. [20] A British War Office appraisal, issued in March 1951 and which admitted to being 'unavoidably based on circumstantial evidence', gave a total Soviet armed-strength figure of over 4 million, lower than that provided by Bradley eighteen months earlier. [21] The British figures incorporated the internal security forces, as presumably did those offered by the British defence minister a few months later. He gave a ground strength of 3.2 million, an air force of 800,000 and a 600,000 strong navy. Furthermore, he added in excess of 1 million armed personnel which Moscow's East European satellite states could muster.[22] By 1954 official estimates of Eastern Bloc strength had grown to over 6 million, with 4.5 million in the ground forces.[23]

Clearly, then, Soviet force levels in the years following the Second World War were substantial, even though they had been massively reduced from the 12 million Soviet citizens under arms in 1945. The extent and rapidity of American, and to a lesser extent British, demobilisation following Germany's defeat was breathtaking by comparison. The United States, like the Soviet Union, finished the war with over 12 million under arms. By 1947, total American armed strength had plummeted to 1.6 million and was still falling.[24] In Europe, American armed strength had stood at over 3 million in 1945; within one year it was down to 391,000,[25] and by the time the North Atlantic Treaty was signed, it stood at around 100,000.[26] The British speedily reduced their armed strength in Europe too, from 1,321,000 at the war's end to less than half a million a year later.[27] Yet by 1950 NATO member states as a whole had a combined armed strength of 4 million; with the rearmament following the Korean War outbreak it was approaching 7 million by 1952. In 1954 NATO had no fewer and possibly more men under arms than did the Soviet Union and its 'allies'. Much of NATO's strength, of course, was not in Europe at all. For example, only 400,000 of the US total of 3 million was based in Europe.[28] The Americans were fighting in Korea, whilst the British, French and others maintained forces in various parts of their respective empires. On the other hand, over half of Moscow's armed strength was located within Soviet borders, and much of that outside Europe altogether. If the Soviet Union had begun serious preparations for war in Europe, then NATO would surely have redeployed its own substantial forces in response. The peacetime stationing of the armed forces of the various NATO allies, and the degree to which it underlined extra-European interests and concerns, presumably reflected the political priorities and threat perceptions then current. In other words, NATO collectively chose not to be weak overall, but to be relatively weak in Central Europe *vis-à-vis* the Soviet Bloc. What these admittedly crude comparisons reveal is that in 1954 NATO's total armed strength was numerically not inferior to that of which Moscow disposed, although the constant reiteration of the division comparison suggested an overwhelming NATO weakness.

The significance of this point for an understanding of the evolution of NATO's strategy and force posture cannot be over-stressed, and for two related reasons. First, NATO was born with an inferiority complex regarding its conventional force capabilities which was unwarranted in these early years, has been unwarranted at a number of junctures since, but which has persisted powerfully throughout the existence of the Alliance. For example, an official NATO publication has referred to 'the very marked inferiority of NATO conventional strength in Europe' in these early days.[29] Such inferiority as existed was not self-evidently marked; and if the force balance in Europe was unhealthy, this was largely because the chosen deployment of NATO forces made it so. Furthermore, the belief that some unbridgeable gap has existed (and still exists) in the conventional force balance has served to discourage serious efforts to close it. The task has seemed insurmountable. This brings us to the second point, which is that NATO's supposed conventional weakness provided both a rationale and a rationalisation for a shift, very early on in the life of the Alliance, towards a reliance on nuclear weapons of various kinds for the purposes of both deterrence and war-fighting should deterrence fail. This in turn tended to under-mine still further any effort aimed at building more credible conventional capabilities because in the nuclear age they were deemed less necessary and less effective. Nuclear weapons were supposed to offer a superior deterrent posture, combined with a militarily more destructive force with which to physically prevent any Soviet advance. We shall return to these arguments in due course.

CONVENTIONAL FAILINGS

In the context of his demand that Washington should offer military aid and assistance to its European allies, General Bradley had observed that 'the balance of military power is centred in the USA'.[30] In particular, the economic circumstances of the time should be borne in mind. By 1949 the European member states of

NATO were only just reaching their pre-war production levels, and all were engaged in major reinvestment programmes consuming between 20 and 30 per cent of total output. [31] Even by 1953 the 176 million North Americans were able to achieve a total economic output roughly three times that of the 208 million citizens of European NATO states. [32] With this remarkable imbalance in economic prowess coupled with the enormous prestige accruing in the US in the aftermath of the Second World War, in contrast to the demoralisation and shame war had brought to much of Europe, it was natural that many Europeans should look to Washington for leadership and guidance. We have already seen, for example, how keen the French were to obtain a concrete American commitment to the defence of Western Europe, and how central a tenet it was for the British to develop in peacetime the close links which had been forged in war. We should remember, too, that Germany — or, at least, its western portion — had not yet been accepted back into the family of European nations. A West German contribution to European defence was not agreed until 1954, and the first West German forces were not available until 1958. [33] Thus any attempt by NATO to offset the Soviet conventional force preponderance would for the time being at least have to be made without the benefit of German participation. The German absence, in addition to underlining the apparent hastiness of NATO's conclusion that it was doomed to conventional force inferiority, served also to enhance still further the power and prestige of the US in the Alliance.

However, as the Strategic Plan, President Truman's declaration of September 1950, and Senate Resolution 99 all revealed, the United States was keen to ensure that the bulk of NATO's conventional forces were provided by the Europeans, and any additional US contribution would be contingent on these efforts. It was Bevin's 'vicious circle' in a new guise, and it suggested too that the problem of burden-sharing was endemic to a voluntary alliance such as NATO. [34] On the other hand, all members were shouldering remarkable defence spending burdens. In 1952/53, the US, UK and France were each spending an estimated 10 per cent or more of their GNPs [35] on defence, and the NATO Council meeting of December 1953 was able to report that defence spending by NATO countries as a whole was 3.5 times higher than it had been in 1949, and 13 per cent up on 1952. For the US, the war in Korea accounted for a substantial proportion of this increase, of course. However, even the still war-shattered European economies had increased defence spending by a creditable 250 per cent since 1949.[36] Not surprisingly, such unprecedentedly high peacetime defence allocations took their economic toll, yet clearly the figures undermine, at least to some degree, the oft-repeated myth of NATO's unwillingness to make sacrifices in domestic spending in the interests of defence. Clearly, too, it is a myth which requires explanation, and much of this explanation seems to reside in the mismatch between NATO's force goals and the actual force levels attained, but also in the emergence of a sentiment which played down the urgency of the need to reach the targets.

In 1950 NATO set itself a force goal of thirty-six divisions in place by 1955.[37] Following the outbreak of the Korean War, new force goals were set at the North Atlantic Council meeting at Lisbon in February 1952. The new goals reflected the targets suggested in a report by a Temporary Council Committee which had been set up in September 1951 and tasked with reconciling NATO's military requirements with its economic and financial capabilities.[38] The goals also reflected a requirements plan which had been devised by military planners, which seems to have been used by the military as the basis for their force goal recommendations since at least 1950, and which was aimed at holding off, without using nuclear weapons, an enemy force two or three times as large.[39] The Lisbon meeting called for the establishment of ninety-six divisions to be available in Europe within thirty days of the order to mobilise (M+30). About thirty-five divisions were required in Europe, twenty-five of these on the central front. The new goals were to be achieved by 1954. Despite General Bradley's belief that NATO could call on a total of almost a hundred divisions in 1954, NATO gave up the Lisbon goals at the end of 1953 and chose instead to concentrate on qualitative force improvements. At this time NATO could dispose of around fifteen ready divisions in Central Europe, and another ten in Italy and Scandinavia.[40] The rest consisted either of reserve divisions in Europe, many of which would probably have taken over a month to mobilise, or they were deployed in Korea, the US or in various colonial trouble-spots and again would probably have taken in excess of a month to reach Central Europe. Whether this was adequate or not depended vitally on the assessments made of Soviet mobilisation requirements. Clearly NATO felt in 1953 that it would lose such a race. Later analysts were less certain.

One reason for NATO's failure to reach the force goals it had set itself was the lessening of tension which followed the rundown of the Korean War and the death of Stalin in March 1953. Just as a Soviet frontal assault was not deemed imminent before the war in Korea, so it was not deemed imminent after it. John Foster Dulles, during the presidential campaign of 1952, argued that 'When we analyse the Soviet military threat, we can find many reasons to believe that it may not be more than an unused threat, designed partly for defence but chiefly to throw the free world into panic'.[41] Following Eisenhower's election as president and his own appointment as secretary of state, Dulles justified NATO's abandonment of the Lisbon goals in December 1953 by referring to the lessening of the threat to Europe.[42] In fact, a prime feature of the security policies of the new administration in Washington was the shift away from the 'year of maximum danger' outlined in the National Security Council document NSC-68[43] to a 'long haul' concept of force planning, which implied long-term competition with the Soviet Union rather than a coming war.[44] Even as the Lisbon force goals were being agreed, defence programmes were being stretched out throughout the Alliance in response to the new mood. This is not to say that economic difficulties did not provide an additional motive, but such difficulties had not prevented rapid rearmament programmes when the atmosphere had been deemed more fraught.

TACTICAL NUCLEAR WEAPONS: THE ORIGINS

Any explanation for the failure to meet the Lisbon force goals or to match the presumed Soviet ground-force might would not be complete without a consideration of the impact of the emergence of an alternative, a military posture relying on the large-scale deployment and planned use of nuclear weapons. In particular, the development in the US of low-yield nuclear weapons for battlefield use encouraged many Americans to question the need for substantial conventional forces. America's initial monopoly in the nuclear field, rapidly succeeded by a still-impressive numerical superiority in both the weapons and their appropriate delivery systems, inevitably put the prospect of matching Soviet bloc armies with a nuclear counter on the agenda. Even so, NATO's perceived conventional-force weakness need not and should not be seen as the only stimulus to the new direction. Economic, bureaucratic, military and technological factors were at work too. To fully appreciate how NATO's strategy and capabilities originated, and to understand the present military posture of the Alliance, it is imperative that these additional motivations be teased out. In the process we may discover that the relationship between NATO's conventional and nuclear capabilities was not a straightforward one.

In October 1953 NATO formally embarked on a policy which was ultimately to lead to the deployment on land in Europe of over 7,000 tactical nuclear weapons (TNWs).[45] In that month the US government, on the basis of National Security Document 162/2 declared it would be prepared to use TNWs in any major conflict in Europe. Inevitably the North Atlantic Council followed the American lead when, in December 1954, it authorised its military commanders to plan to use TNWs in the event of aggression, conventional or otherwise.[46] Even before the October announcement, on 15 September 1953, the US secretary of the Army revealed that six 280mm cannon, which could be adapted to conventional or atomic ammunition, were to be deployed with US artillery battalions in Germany. The first of these arrived at Bremerhaven on 8 October 1953. Bound by restrictions imposed by the McMahon Act, and setting the precedent for what was later to become normal practice, it was neither confirmed nor denied that they would be accompanied by atomic shells.[47] This did not prevent General Alfred M. Gruenther, who had succeeded General Ridgway as SACEUR in July 1953, from announcing in January 1954 that 'We can now use atomic weapons against an aggressor, delivered not only by long-range aircraft, but also by the use of shorter range planes, and by 280mm artillery'.[48]

Few would dissent with the designation of short-range low-yield nuclear capable artillery as 'tactical' or 'battlefield', although arguably such concepts defy definition in the nuclear age. Nevertheless, few would argue either with the proposition that the 'tactical nuclear' category quickly became a somewhat broad and inclusive one. For example, it embraced the 700-mile range Matador guided missile. The US Air Force announced its intention to send two squadrons of these to Germany as early as January 1954.[49] In August 1954 a battalion of Corporal missiles was sent to Europe.[50] Although Corporal's range was seventy-five miles, its nuclear warhead had a yield of 20 kilotons, compared to the approximately 14-kiloton bomb used on Hiroshima.[51] Free-falling bombs of yields exceeding one megaton were introduced into the European theatre. So too were the low-yield Honest John surface-to-surface missiles (in 1954), with a maximum range of twenty-five miles; Nike surface-to-air missiles; and in the early 1960s, Atomic Demolition Mines.[52] The purpose here is not to list all the TNWs made available in Europe during the 1950s and later, but to suggest the wide range of nuclear weapons by yield, range and function that were regarded as 'tactical'.

Almost since NATO's inception, then, TNWs have played a part — indeed a major part — in the strategy of the Alliance. Yet the production and deployment of the weapons, and the determination of the circumstances of their use and control of that use, were, in the 1950s, essentially American. Not until the very end of the decade did Europeans begin to receive TNWs, and for them the real build-up took place in the early 1960s. The perspectives and preoccupations of its non-nuclear members were peripheral to the earlier phases of NATO's nuclear strategy. Furthermore, as has already been noted, concern over NATO's conventional inferiority was just one of a number of factors contributing to the establishment of a TNW arsenal and the despatch of part of that arsenal to Europe.

THE SCIENTIFIC LOBBY

The American scientific community contained an influential lobby favouring TNWs, and its efforts stemmed in some degree from excitement at the scientific and technological progress they had made. As early as 1948 Robert J. Oppenheimer, the famous nuclear scientist who, according to the former chairman of the Research and Development Board in the US Defence Department, 'did more than any other man. . .to educate the military to the potentialities of the atomic weapons for other than strategic bombing purposes', had argued in favour of the production of smaller, more usable nuclear weapons for tactical employment.[53] Scientists such as Oppenheimer, Enrico Fermi, I. I. Rabi, David Lilienthal, as chairman of the Atomic Energy Commission (AEC), and another AEC commissioner, Edward Murray, were additionally and particularly concerned lest Moscow's atomic bomb test of September 1949 persuade Washington to develop the H-bomb, or 'Super' as it was known. They regarded the H-bomb as immoral and militarily useless[54] and, assuming there would be a scarcity of fissile material, endeavoured to limit its availability for the production of H-bombs by increasing demand for the material for the production of smaller yield nuclear weapons for tactical use. As another of the nuclear scientists has since written, the scientists' advocacy of TNWs was, at least in part, 'an element in the struggle to contain the Superbomb'.[55] Thus the General Advisory Committee (GAC) of the AEC produced a report in October 1949, just weeks after Moscow's A-bomb test, recommending 'an intensification of efforts to make atomic weapons available for tactical purposes'.[56] The initiative for Project Vista, a study group set up in 1951 to consider ground and air tactical warfare with special reference to the West European theatre, seems to have come primarily from scientists.[57] The report of the Project, which was neither officially approved nor even released for publication, was submitted to the Service Secretaries in 1952. Its general thrust was towards 'bringing the battle back to the battlefield'. It concluded that 'the tactical employment of our atomic weapons resources holds outstanding promise' for defending Western Europe.[58] Vista advocated the production of TNWs with yields of between 1 and 50 kilotons for use against troops, airfields and supply lines; it urged the creation of a tactical atomic air force; and it developed a doctrine for army tactical use of nuclear weapons.

At the same time, low-yield warheads for TNWs were becoming a reality. During 1951 there were twelve test explosions of low-yield weapons.[59] One such test, in October 1951, was referred to in the official AEC report as of the first nuclear device in the sub-kiloton range — 0.1kt in fact[60] — and was described by an unofficial eye-witness as a 'baby' atom bomb. Gordon Dean, who had replaced David Lilienthal as the AEC chairman and who was to be a leading advocate of TNWs in the years to come, had in September told a House appropriations sub-committee that the AEC was developing 'literally dozens of different types and kinds of special purpose atomic weapons' which could 'definitely' be used against enemy troops from the outset.[61] Although a little overstated, there is clearly something in the observations of the eminent British scientist Lord Zuckerman, that 'before the strategists and formulators of military policy had even uttered a word, the idea that nuclear armaments could be used, given that a war broke out in Europe, had taken a firm shape in the minds of technical people'.[62] It is evident too that making up for NATO's conventional-force difficulties was not their only, or even major, consideration.

ARMY INTEREST

It would have been surprising if the US Army, struggling to find for itself a role in an American defence environment increasingly dominated by the Air Force and the concept of strategic bombing, had not taken an interest in these developments in the TNW field. The career of Lt General James M. Gavin, as described in his book *War and Peace in the Space Age*, affords a useful insight into the evolution of army interests in the new possibilities. Gavin noted, for example, how during 1949 Oppenheimer was already presenting his case for the production of nuclear weapons for battlefield use at gatherings attended by appreciative US Army officers. Gavin himself was given the task of 'studying the possible tactical employment of nuclear weapons' on becoming the Army representative on the Weapons Systems Evaluation Group in March 1949, and he rapidly became 'convinced that nuclear weapons had a tremendous field for tactical application'.[63] Although, having taken up a NATO appointment in June 1951, Gavin found General Eisenhower 'out of touch' with developments in the TNW field,[64] recent research has revealed that as SACEUR Eisenhower encouraged planning for the tactical nuclear defence of Europe.[65] In any case, Gavin and Eisenhower were able to discuss 'at considerable length' the utility of TNWs in the European theatre. Gavin was by now quite convinced of the 'essentiality of tactical weapons to NATO's future'. For example, during a spell with Southern Europe Command he observed how Greek and Turkish terrain offered 'excellent opportunities' for the defensive use of TNWs. He noted too how Admiral Carney, commander Southern Europe, 'had recommended, on a number of occasions, the static use of nuclear weapons in the Alpine passes'.

Gavin was far from alone among his Army colleagues in considering the tactical employment of nuclear weapons. Between 1945 and 1949, eight articles on the subject appeared in *Military Review*, the professional journal of the US Army. Between 1950 and 1954, thirty-two such articles were published.[66] Lively disagreements over the implications for the battlefield disposition of troops surfaced. For example, following an article by Lt General Leslie R. Groves, who had headed the Manhattan Project, in the July 1950 issue, a spate of articles appeared dealing with the problem of the dispersion of troops in the nuclear battlefield.[67] Elsewhere, the chairman of the JCS, General Omar Bradley, outlined in a newspaper article how the tactical use of atomic weapons would give a great advantage to a defending army pitted against superior numbers,[68] and in June 1950 General Collins, US Army chief of staff, stated that atomic weapons, and especially artillery shells and guided missiles, could be developed for army use. Two days later the Army secretary, Frank Pace, spoke approvingly of the tactical application of atomic weapons.[69] Inevitably, the Army took a close interest in the small-yield testing programme, and Major-General Kean, commanding officer US Army 3rd Corps, described the October 1951 test as the 'first step towards military tactical employment of the nuclear weapons'.[70] He went on to express his belief that the results would profoundly influence Army doctrine and training. The Army Command and General Staff College (CGSC) disseminated ideas of this kind to a much wider Army audience. As early as 1947 the CGSC curriculum 'introduced the hypothesis that the atomic bomb might by usable to support ground operations', whilst the 1948 curriculum 'offered the view that atomic weapons could be used in offensive or defensive roles'. In 1949 instructors at the CGSC were briefed that 'the entire field of the tactical use of the atomic bomb is definitely open to discussion'.[71] Also in 1949 the CGSC commandant appointed a study group, tasked with the construction of a doctrine governing the tactical use of TNWs.

The report, entitled 'Tactical Use of Atomic Weapons, FM 100-31', which stemmed from the work of this group and was published in November 1951 but classified 'confidential', has been described as 'a giant step foward' in 'developing an atomic warfighting doctrine for land combat units'.[72] At a more practical level, the JCS had as early as 1952 authorised General Eisenhower to begin planning for the use of a number of atomic bombs by already deployed navy and soon to be deployed air force tactical air units.[73] Gavin was given the opportunity to work on operational concepts for the use of TNWs by infantry organisations when he took command of the US VII Corps in southern Germany in December 1952.[74] War games, then exercises which simulated the use of TNWs, followed. In fact, it seems that some of his ideas were already being tested with smaller units. By the end of 1953, the US Army according to Gavin, 'was on the threshold of a revolution in tactics, weapons and organisation'.[75] It is worth noting too that Allied forces were being introduced to the requirements of a tactical nuclear battlefield. In April 1953, the US Defence Department announced the commencement of atomic warfare courses for NATO commanders at its Weapons School in Garmisch, southern Germany. This was to enable them 'to take into consideration the implications of atomic warfare in the defence of Western Europe'.[76] In September 1953 'the first instance of a NATO air–ground exercise in which atomic weapons were simulated for manouvre purposes' occurred. It was held along the east bank of the Middle Rhine and involved French, Belgian and American forces.[77]

TNWS AND FORCE LEVELS

Three observations are in order here. First is that it would appear that US Army interest was in the contribution low-yield nuclear weapons could make to the European battlefield. In this, their focus was similar to that of the interested scientists discussed earlier. However, the yields of many of the nuclear weapons eventually introduced into Europe could by no stretch of the imagination be described as 'low'. Second, how many nuclear weapons for tactical use in Europe were thought to be necessary at this stage is not clear. As we shall see, it may not have been the case that the numbers which were ultimately deployed were ever carefully tailored to any overall assessment of NATO requirements. Third, what is noteworthy about the interest shown by the Army is that it was largely, though not entirely, based on an appreciation of the inherent tactical utility of low-yield nuclear weapons, a utility that did not derive from a supposition of low conventional-force levels. Indeed, as we have seen, TNWs attracted interest before NATO was formed, and before the intractability of NATO's supposed conventional inferiority became apparent. Put another way, the introduction of TNWs into the Army's most valuable and perhaps most likely theatre of operations, Western Europe, may have been seen as desirable whether Soviet Bloc conventional forces were seen as markedly superior to those of NATO or not. For many of those soldiers who interested themselves in the application of TNWs to the battlefield, more rather than fewer troops would be required, especially in the context of a two-sided tactical nuclear war. As Gavin wrote, 'one over all conclusion stood out clearly, although for several years it was the basis of considerable argument; more rather than less manpower would be required to fight a nuclear war successfully'.[78] For Gavin and others like him, the 'New Look' policies of President Eisenhower's administration, with their emphasis on nuclear weapons of all types, were objectionable not only for the threat they posed to the size of the US Army but also for their inconsistency in envisaging reductions in conventional strength combined with an increased reliance on TNWs. 'Congress', wrote Gavin, 'was assured. . .that our combat strength was not being reduced, that as our atomic stockpile increased, fewer divisions would be required. . .That the contrary was the case few, outside of the Department of the Army, seemed willing to admit'.[79] He believed that TNWs could replace conventional fire-power, rather than manpower, owing to their superior military efficacy, their ease in handling and because of the financial savings they offered.[80] Brigadier General Robert C. Richardson III, who served as military planner at SHAPE HQ from 1952 to 1955, noted how the 'Ridgway Plan' devised during that period discovered that the lethality and destructiveness of atomic weapons used in battlefield scenarios would increase rather than decrease force requirements. The embarrassment these findings caused ensured that 'the Ridgway Plan never left SHAPE'.[81] It is more widely known that Maxwell D. Taylor, former Army chief of staff, believed that TNWs created a need for more rather than less manpower.[82] One analyst has observed that 'the popular view in military literature throughout the 1950s saw nuclear weapons not as a replacement for conventional ground and air forces but rather as a supplement'.[83]

The new Republican administration came to office pledged to cut government spending; as Eisenhower himself said, 'A bankrupt America is more the Soviet goal than an America conquered on the field of battle'.[84] In the defence field, nuclear weapons of all kinds were seen as a means to save money. As Secretary of State John Foster Dulles argued in January 1954, by depending primarily on nuclear weapons, 'it is now possible to get and to share more basic security at less cost'.[85] Obviously, a lower defence budget could not be achieved by adding TNWs to the existing conventional force levels; the point was to introduce TNWs to enable troop reductions to be made. Admiral Carney for the Navy and General Ridgway for the Army each publicly disputed the military validity of this equation,[86] but other professional soldiers could be found to support the thesis. As early as 1952, US Army Chief of Staff General J. Lawton Collins argued that TNWs would 'result ultimately in the ability to do the job with a smaller number of divisions'.[87] In January 1954 General Gruenther commented that 'If seventy divisions, for example, are needed to establish a conventional line of defence between the Alps and the Baltic, then seventy minus X divisions equipped with atomic weapons would be needed'.[88] On a later occasion, the same officer made a more precise reference to a study conducted in 1953 and presented to the NATO Council in 1954 which argued that the introduction of nuclear weapons would permit the ground-force levels in NATO's central sector to be reduced by two-thirds of the 1951 levels.[89] In any case, the administration, determined to cut the defence budget and to enhance the role of nuclear weapons, planned to reduce the total number of US military personnel from the June 1954 level of 3.3 million to a little over three million by June 1955 and to 2.8 million by June 1957. The Army was to bear the brunt of the cuts whilst the Air Force was to actually increase in size.[90]

THE NUCLEAR ADDICTION

Clearly, then, battlefield nuclear weapons were seen by an economy-conscious US administration as alternatives to the maintenance of expensively-high manpower levels. It seems too that both TNWs and, indeed, strategic nuclear weapons were valued not simply for their contribution to deterrence but also for their contribution to war-fighting. They were introduced into Europe to be used in the event of Soviet aggression. In addition, it is not clear that the numbers and types of nuclear weapons procured during this period were closely related to any precise military analysis of their utility. Rather, the numbers produced and the military reliance on them stemmed from a somewhat unspecific, generalised optimism regarding their suitability to war and, in the case of TNWs, to the battlefield, and from a procurement process driven by forces other than strict military need. The task of this section is to trace the impact on NATO's overall force posture these processes made. NSC-30, approved by President Truman on 16 September 1948, asserted that the military 'must be ready to utilise promptly and effectively all appropriate means available, including atomic weapons' in the event of war, and should 'plan accordingly'.[91] Although at this time there were only around fifty nuclear weapons in total in the American stockpile, apparently all of which were unassembled and too unwieldy to be used tactically; and although, too, Strategic Air Command (SAC) possessed only about thirty B-29 bombers modified to drop atomic bombs,[92] nevertheless the NSC-30 document represented an early stage in what one analyst has termed a 'nuclear addiction' first by the US but soon by the NATO Alliance generally.[93] The Truman administration approved three increases in the production of nuclear weapons material — in 1949, 1950, and 1952,[94] and this formed a foundation upon which the Eisenhower administration was able to build an age of nuclear plenty, and which gave the proponents both of strategic bombing and of battlefield nuclear weapons just about everything they could have wanted. What they wanted partly depended, of course, on what prevailing military and strategic doctrine indicated it was appropriate to have. NSC-162/2, approved as national policy on 30 October 1953, left no doubt on this score. 'In the event of hostilities', it declared, 'the United States will consider nuclear weapons to be as available for use as other munitions'.[95] The sentiments expressed in NSC-162/2, which formed the basis of the administration's nuclear-orientated 'New Look' strategy, were repeated on a number of occasions by government officials during the 1950s. In December 1953, for example, Eisenhower himself told the United Nations that 'Atomic weapons have virtually achieved conventional status within our armed forces', and in 1955 he said of TNWs, 'Where these things are used on strictly military targets and for strictly military purposes, I see no reason why they shouldn't be used just exactly as you would a bullet or anything else'.[96] His secretary of state, John F Dulles, threatened that should 'the United States become engaged in a major military activity anywhere in the world. . .those weapons would come into use because, as I say, they are becoming more and more conventional and replacing what used to be called conventional weapons'.[97] Of particular relevance to NATO was General Gruenther's June 1954 statement: 'We are working on a philosophy to have a force in being that is the smallest possible. . . In our thinking we visualise the use of atomic bombs in support of our ground troops'. If war occurred, he continued, 'our minds are clear that we must and shall use every weapon in our arsenal'.[98] In 1957, in a statement to Congress, the defence secretary, Charles Wilson, said, 'the smaller atomic weapons, the tactical weapons, in a sense have now become the conventional weapons'.[99] In short, there is precious little reason to doubt that the 'New Look' policies of the 1950s regarded nuclear weapons as instruments of more than simply deterrence. If deterrence broke down at whatever level, nuclear weapons were seen as usable military weapons, and this was particularly so 'on the battlefield'.

Requests for more TNWs by the military authorities became somewhat routine too.[100] In fact, it is far from easy to discover where, or what, the limits were to the production of TNWs and to their deployment in Europe. By January 1961, when Robert McNamara arrived at the Pentagon, there were 3,500 TNWs of various types deployed in Europe. By 1966 the figure had risen to 7,000 land-based TNWs intended for the support of NATO and stored on the territory of the European member states of NATO.[101] Interestingly, a scientific adviser to the Pentagon has claimed that it was at one stage planned that the figure should rise to 15,000.[102] A former Pentagon official, Morton Halperin, has testified that his impression was that the rate of TNW deployment was determined largely by the rate of construction.[103] This in turn may have been determined by the practice of the US Joint Chiefs of Staff (JCS) to project requirements designed to use up all available fissionable material.[104] Even James Schlesinger, former US defence secretary, has accepted that there was 'some measure of truth' in this — that, for example, production of the 8-inch nuclear shell 'reflected the availability of U-235 and that military requirement for the shells was adjusted to that availability'.[105] However, he denied Halperin's statement that there was 'only routine civilian approval of deployment levels' and that determination of these levels was 'by and large left to the military'.[106] Procurement processes are notoriously difficult to penetrate and disentangle, but the prevailing attitudes in the US during the 1950s towards the utility of TNWs, and indeed nuclear weapons generally, combined with the bureaucratic practices of the military and the laboratories, do appear to have created a momentum which was at best loosely supervised and which appears to have been unrelated to any overview of military requirements. Indeed, on coming to office McNamara noted how the services established their requirements quite independently of each other and without consultation.[107] Ideally, the last word on the deployment of TNWs in Europe should perhaps be left to Paul Warnke, the former assistant secretary of defence and arms control negotiator: 'I think it is characteristic of weapons systems generally. Once they have been developed they get produced; once they get produced they get deployed'.[108]

Certainly the rate of production increased to such a point that as early as 1956 Eisenhower felt able to comment that 'nuclear production is now so vast that it may be possible to have everything that is needed'.[109] This does indeed appear to be what happened. By 1957 the US had stockpiled over 5,000 warheads of various kinds; by 1960 the figure had reached around 18,000, and by 1967 it peaked at 32,000.[110] There are signs that Eisenhower himself grew frustrated with his inability to control this massive growth in the nuclear weapons stockpile. By 1959 he bitterly criticised the military for seeming to want 'enough to destroy every conceivable target all over the world, plus a three-fold reserve'.[111] It was presumably this sort of experience which led him to warn, in his 'Farewell Address to the Nation', of 17 January 1961, that 'In the councils of government, we must guard against the acquisition of unwarranted influence, whether sought or unsought, by the military–industrial complex' — thus coining a phrase, or, rather, a concept. He noted, too, the danger that government policy 'could itself become the captive of a scientific technological élite'.[112] To be warned against, a danger must be presumed to exist, and we can only assume that Eisenhower had felt his own administration had been threatened by it.

For the moment, though, our concern is with Europe. As we have already noted, there were around 3,500 TNWs of various kinds deployed in Europe at the end of Eisenhower's presidency. This number, and the make-up of the European TNW arsenal, including as it did a large number of very destructive bombs and warheads not obviously appropriate for the European theatre, does suggest a production/deployment momentum. There seems to have been little sensitivity to the level of damage and destruction which would inevitably result from the unrestrained theatre-wide use of TNWs. Nor is there any evidence that in the event of war in Europe, restraint in TNW use would have been attempted or was even possible. In June 1953 the US government began the process of transferring nuclear weapons from civilian to military custody, so that by 1961 less than 10 per cent of the total US stockpile of nuclear weapons remained in civilian control.[113] The purpose, and result, of this measure was to increase the operational readiness of this increasingly integral part of the US military arsenal. In 1956 the US Army begun reorganising its combat forces to meet the demands of a nuclear battlefield.[114] It is likely, too, that Eisenhower gave advance authorisation to the military to use nuclear weapons in certain circumstances without prior consultation.[115] It is not even clear that the fear of escalation would have induced caution in Washington. Thus, in 1956, Eisenhower expressed his belief that, 'The tactical use of atomic weapons against military targets would be no more likely to trigger off a big war than the use of twenty-ton "block-busters"'. He appeared to approve, too, of Henry Kissinger's arguments, outlined in his book, *Nuclear Weapons and Foreign Policy*, that not only might it be possible to keep nuclear war limited but that it could also produce less devastation than a conventional war.[116] As we have seen, towards the end of his presidency, Eisenhower began to have serious doubts about the direction US military policy had taken under his administration and he expressed a fear that the services had become so heavily dependent on nuclear weapons that it might in fact be very difficult to contain a limited nuclear war. Thus, in 1960, he dismissed a report advising the creation of a doctrine and capability for fighting non-nuclear limited wars by arguing that 'we were unfortunately so committed to nuclear weapons that the only practical move would be to start using them from the beginning without any distinction between them and conventional weapons'. [117] When in 1957 NATO decided to disseminate tactical nuclear delivery systems to the European allies, it seemed unlikely that America's allies would play a restraining role in the event of a European war. The NATO Council had in effect already adopted Washington's 'New Look' strategy in December 1954, when it authorised the military to plan to use nuclear weapons in any war in Europe — 'whether', in the words of Gruenther again, 'the enemy uses them or not'. [118] Even so, as has been noted elsewhere, 'no aspect of the New Look decisions. . .was cleared or discussed to any significant degree with the other NATO allies until after the decision had been taken'. Such decisions were then presented to the Europeans 'to a large extent as United States *faits accomplis*'. [119] The European allies, materially, psychologically and politically dependent on Washington, were left only to react to a situation in which US forces were moving towards a battlefield reliance on TNWs anyway. The next task, then, is to consider Europe's contribution, and reaction, to NATO's evolving nuclear strategy.

3 Obviating the Necessity: Europe Enters the Nuclear Age

A congressional report published in 1980 commented that 'Europeans have traditionally viewed tactical nuclear weapons as obviating the necessity for providing conventional capabilities sufficient for credible conventional defence'.[1] This is not an uncommon observation; indeed, it is probably the consensus view. Nor is it without foundation notably if applied to the period since the very late 1950s or early 1960s. The reality, however, is far more complex, far messier. Defence spending by the Europeans was at historically high peacetime levels throughout the 1950s, and for the Germans especially it was still rising at the end of the decade. During the 1950s, although less so in the subsequent decades, there was no single European view of the desirability or otherwise of a reliance on nuclear weapons. Governments, opposition parties and public opinion took up various positions, and official policies were often unclear, ambiguous or simply acquiescent. Even so, many Europeans, almost from the outset, did find the development of a TNW capability appealing. Particularly attractive was the presumed deterrent effect. By the end of the 1950s NATO had — or believed itself to have — little option but to escalate to the widespread use of TNWs in the event of a major war in Europe. If the Soviet Union ever did entertain any notion of a direct military threat against Western Europe, then the almost certain prospect of a nuclear devastation of their forces in Europe, and probably of their homeland too, must have served to cool their ardour a little. Furthermore, should war break out nevertheless, then some categories of TNWs in NATO's possession manifestly offered the opportunity to destroy massed Soviet Bloc force concentrations, perhaps even before they had left East European territory. The attritional quality of TNWs indeed appeared to endow the defending and perhaps numerically inferior forces with distinct advantages.[2]

What cannot be disputed, however, is that it was the United States which first came to regard nuclear power as a substitute for more conventional forms of military power on the battlefield, and it was Washington which first considered cutting its troop levels as a consequence. Moreover, this policy was pursued simultaneously with that of exhorting the Europeans to increase their conventional force levels. We must remember too that the decision to provide American forces in Europe with nuclear weapons for battlefield use, to base war planning in NATO on the assumption of the battlefield use of nuclear weapons, and even to stockpile such weapons in Europe for use by the European allies, were all made before a single West German division had been created. In other words, to assert that TNWs were introduced because Europeans alone would not or could not provide sufficient conventional strength is to present only one part of a much larger truth. They were introduced because the US too would not or could not provide sufficient conventional strength, and because Washington felt TNWs 'obviated the necessity' of maintaining high levels of conventional military capability. Once TNWs were deployed in Europe, and were accompanied by actual or threatened cuts in overall US force levels, they increasingly came to be a disincentive for the often still rearming Europeans to make further effort. If TNWs enabled the Americans to maintain a smaller army and to cut their defence budgets, why shouldn't Europeans reap similar benefits? Indeed, what was the point of marching in a different direction from that taken by the alliance leader? Many Europeans felt, with some justification, that they most certainly could not match the numbers the adversary could raise without a full American contribution. They felt too that even if Soviet conventional force levels were equalled, the new emphasis in US defence policy ensured that any war would quickly become nuclear anyway. In that kind of war, what possible role could large non-nuclear forces fulfil?

THE BRITISH LEAD

Considerations such as these were not only more prominent in the United Kingdom, and at an earlier stage, than was the case elsewhere in Europe; it is arguable that, where the efficacy of strategic nuclear weapons was concerned, the British were chronologically and doctrinally ahead of the United States too. This development had additional salience given the considerable status and prestige Britain enjoyed in the immediate post-war years. Despite the passage in the United States of the McMahon Act on 1 August 1946, which denied to other states information on atomic energy — in fact, in part because of the McMahon Act, which brought home to the British government the dangers of relying on allies even as close as the United States — the Labour government decided to proceed with the creation of an independent nuclear deterrent.[3] In addition to the atomic programme, which produced its first test explosion in October 1952, the Conservative government inherited from its predecessor an expensive and expanding conventional defence programme which had put over 800,000 men and women in uniform by 1951, and which was to reach over 900,000 by 1953.[4] This meant that according to the TCC, defence spending accounted for over 10 per cent of GNP, and was to continue to do so.[5] The pre-war peacetime norm had been 3 per cent.[6] This inevitably caused further strain on the economy, which with the beginning of ceasefire talks in Korea in July 1951 and the consequent relaxation of tension, seemed excessive and unnecessary. Thus the British government felt able to safely slow down the programme and went for a slower build-up, a British version of the so-called 'long haul'. This was announced on the day the Lisbon Conference opened, which set NATO force goals at ninety-six divisions.[7] In fact, defence spending and manpower continued to rise, as the 'cuts' largely hit procurement.[8]

More important were the strategic reconsiderations upon which the Conservative government, under Churchill's guidance, embarked. In 1952 the British chiefs of staff produced a document entitled the 'Global Strategy Paper', which argued that nuclear weapons had revolutionised warfare. Aggression could be deterred by the threat of massive nuclear retaliation against the homeland of the aggressor, and if the deterrent failed then 'massive retaliation' should be launched. Conventional forces need be maintained only at substantially reduced levels. The document reflected the enormous faith Churchill had in the efficacy of the nuclear deterrent as a deterrent. For example, he revealed to the

House of Commons in 1953 that he had 'sometimes the odd thought that the annihilating character of these agencies may bring an utterly unforeseeable security to mankind'.[9] Interestingly, the attempt by British Chief of the Air Staff Sir John Slessor (who was himself to write later that owing to the advent of nuclear weapons, 'war has abolished itself') to sell the concept in Washington fell largely on deaf ears.[10] There, the commitment to the build-up of NATO's conventional forces appeared to be still intact, and the suspicion developed that the British were doing little more than rationalising an intention to renege on their NATO commitments.[11] In fact, the Global Strategy Paper simply anticipated by a year the New Look policies of the Eisenhower administration. American policies too came to reflect an emphasis on massive nuclear retaliation both as the deterrent to aggression and the response to it. As one American analyst has put it, 'The New Look originated with Churchill and the British chiefs of staff in 1951 and 1952'.[12]

In any case, British defence policy under the Conservative administrations of the 1950s was based essentially on the ideas contained in the 1952 document. Research and development on nuclear explosives and their delivery systems — at this stage, the strategic bomber — had not been cut, and this emphasis was stressed in the 1954 Defence White Paper along with the government's intention 'gradually to reduce the total size of the army'[13] The 1955 White Paper, which announced Britain's decision to proceed with the development of the H-bomb, correspondingly argued that 'The knowledge that aggression will be met by overwhelming nuclear retaliation is the surest guarantee that it will not take place'.[14] Anthony Eden, who replaced Churchill as prime minister in 1955, made a similar point in a telegram he sent to President Eisenhower; 'It is on the thermonuclear bomb and the atomic weapons that we now rely, not only to deter aggression, but to deal with aggression if it should be launched'.[15] It was not until the 1957 White Paper of Defence Minister Duncan Sandys that the logic of British government policy was fully implemented. On expressing resentment at the disproportionately large share of the burden of NATO's defence which Britain had been bearing, the Paper announced that conscription was to be abolished in 1960, and that by 1962 the armed forces would have been reduced from 690,000 to 375,000. The British Army on the Rhine

(BAOR) would be cut from 77,000 to 64,000 within twelve months; and the nuclear deterrent was to be given even greater emphasis. In fact, a further reduction to 55,000 was announced in January 1958, and later in the same year the British and German governments signed an agreement envisaging only 45,000 troops by April 1961. The Berlin Crisis obstructed the implementation of this latter agreement, however.[16] The logic behind the White Paper was contained in its belief 'that the overriding consideration in all military planning must be to prevent war rather than to prepare for it'.[17] The 1958 White Paper expressed the same assumptions even more strongly. 'There is. . .no military reason why a world conflagration should not be prevented for another generation or more through the balancing fears of mutual annihilation. In fact, there is no reason why all this should not go on almost indefinitely'.[18]

The most significant word in this statement was 'almost'. What would happen if, and when, deterrence broke down, presumably at that point when indefinitely was indeed found to be preceded by 'almost'? Much would depend on the role allocated to TNWs in British thinking, and this, it must be said, was opaque. Although the British were unenthusiastic about the atomic cannon which the US Army was introducing into the European theatre, believing its range to be inappropriately limited,[19] British and American officers were, on the other hand, collaborating closely at SHAPE on the use of battlefield nuclear weapons.[20] Following NATO's 1954 decision to base war plans on the availability and use of TNWs, an agreement was signed with the United States which provided for an exchange of information on the implications of the nuclear battlefield.[21] Furthermore, the BAOR had conducted its own exercises based on the assumption of a tactical nuclear battlefield.[22] By 1958 BAOR was trained and organised to fight nuclear war and little else. Interestingly, it appears not to have actually been equipped for the proper fulfilment of this role until a few years later! The British themselves had not as yet made free-fall bombs available for battlefield use, and warheads for the American-supplied Corporal and Honest John missiles did not arrive until 1959 or 1960. Nuclear artillery shells were not readily available in Germany until the autumn of 1961 and until that date had been stored hundreds of miles away from the appropriate delivery systems and the likely areas of use. As Mr Fred Mulley, later to become a Labour defence minister, once remarked, 'we had a nuclear strategy some considerable time before nuclear weapons were available to implement it'.[23]

As regards the role TNWs were envisaged as having, Mr Sandys in defending his 1957 White Paper in the House of Commons, expressed his belief that in the event of a very limited incursion by hostile forces, TNWs could be used without necessarily inducing escalation to the strategic nuclear level. In the event of a massive Soviet attack, however, everything available would be thrown into the battle so as to stave off defeat.[24] The 1958 White Paper made a similar point. If Russia were to launch 'a major attack. . .even with conventional weapons only', NATO 'would have to hit back with strategic nuclear weapons. In fact, the strategy of NATO is based on the frank recognition that a full-scale Soviet attack could not be repelled without resort to a massive nuclear bombardment of the sources of power in Russia'.[25] In other words, it would appear that even TNWs did not redress the balance of forces in Central Europe, and an assumption such as this led inexorably to a policy of placing almost all the eggs in the massive strategic-retaliation basket.

The nominal role this strategy left for non-nuclear forces enabled the British government to reduce its force levels, as we have seen. Not everyone was happy with this. In fact, Mr Anthony Head, Sandys' predecessor at the Ministry of Defence, resigned from the government following the publication of the 1957 White Paper because he indeed feared that it went too far in its conventional strength reductions.[26] The leading British strategic thinker of the time, Liddell Hart, provided a sustained assault on these trends in government defence policy. In a letter to *The Times* newspaper in 1955 he argued that 'The value of armies lies in providing a non-suicidal defence against attack. To arm them with atomic weapons is to destroy the case for maintaining them'.[27] He was to be even more succinct in another letter to *The Times* in 1957 when he noted that 'The present plan of using nuclear weapons both "tactically" and "strategically" makes sense as a deterrent, but not as a defence — for put into use it means suicide'.[28] One might, in other words, threaten to use nuclear weapons, but it is unwise to leave oneself with no option but to carry out the threat.

So large a conventional force run-down and so extreme a reliance on nuclear weapons of all kinds inevitably had ramifications for the Alliance as a whole. Denis Healey for the Labour Opposition hit this nail on its head when he commented that:

> if the outbreak of war means thermonuclear destruction of Western Europe in the first few hours in any case, the European members of NATO will be tempted to rely exclusively on the thermonuclear deterrent to prevent war, instead of wasting men and money on building armies which will be irrelevant once war actually begins. [29]

Once Washington and London had moved towards reliance on nuclear deterrence, it was indeed not surprising that NATO's continental members should begin to think along such lines, but it is instructive to note that the Germans and the French joined together in criticising the British troop cuts and in querying the move towards nuclear reliance which had justified it. [30] The Defence Committee of the West European Union (WEU) also launched an attack on British policy, whilst the WEU's Assembly moved a censure motion to criticise the organisation's Council of Ministers for tolerating the cuts [31] — not, of course, that they had much choice in the matter.

In short, Britain had acted quite unilaterally in the decisions it had made, with, as one analyst has put it, 'relatively little consideration being given to their ramifications for the Alliance'. The same analyst, A. J. R. Groom, went on to accuse the British of being instrumental 'in creating an element of fatalism on the Continent' regarding the possibility of providing a viable non-nuclear defence force for NATO. [32] Even more strongly, he argued that British behaviour amounted to 'sabotage of all semblance of an attempt to provide a considerable conventional option in Central Europe'. [33] Denis Healey shared similar sentiments. He wrote at the time that 'Britain's desire to end conscription has already led to a greater reduction in her NATO forces than her allies believe justified. And it may also have influenced her views on the strategic concept NATO should follow'. [34] By reducing her land contribution to NATO, 'she has', he said, 'cast a doubt on the sincerity of her concern with European defence which has infected all discussions of NATO strategy'. [35] Britain was determined to establish an independent nuclear deterrent, in which it had great faith; it was determined too to end conscription, which it believed was expensive and which was in any case unpopular with the professional armed forces and the population at large.[36] As with similar American thinking, considerations such as these were independent variables, possibly associated with but still distinct from any assessment of the prospect of providing a full NATO 'conventional option' on the central front. The Anglo-American pursuit of these goals created an important part of the reality with which NATO's continental members were faced. Of these, by far the two most important were France and West Germany.

. . .WITH THE FRENCH NOT FAR BEHIND

In the absence of a rearmed West Germany, France was the continental state with the greatest responsibility for shouldering the burden of conventional-force provision. Initially, the French had actively sought this role, for it tied in well with the national determination to re-establish France as a major power. Perhaps, too, a respectable defence effort on the part of France would postpone or undermine the necessity of rearming West Germany. Thus in August 1950, as part of the response to the Korean War, the French Cabinet approved a three-year defence plan which envisaged the raising of fifteen army divisions by 1952 and twenty by 1953, half of them on a war footing; the formation of a tactical air force of twenty-eight groups by 1953; and an increase in the armed personnel total from the 650,000 1950 figure to 900,000 by 1953. In a memo to the US ambassador in Paris, David Bruce, in 1950, the French government had promised that 'her efforts, in relation to her resources will not be inferior to any of those agreed to by the other participating countries' in NATO.[37] The TCC Report put actual French defence spending in 1950/51 at 7.3 per cent of GNP, a little below that of Britain but above that of the United States; and estimated that it would exceed 10 per cent in the years to come.[38] It did, and army strength alone had reached 420,000 or twelve divisions, by January 1953. Ten of them were in Europe and active, though some were of uncertain quality.[39]

However, as elsewhere, so impressive an effort by a war ravaged country trying to rebuild its economy and society took its toll. The diversion of resources to the non-productive military sector and a substantial increase in the rate of inflation created enormous political pressure, which the fragile governments of the Fourth Republic could barely withstand. Furthermore, the French had always made clear the extent to which their exertions depended on military assistance from the United States; for example, the 1950 memo mentioned earlier asserted that 'the war effort cannot be accomplished without external aid in arms, raw materials and equipment and also without substantial financial aid'.[40] To this end, Washington and Paris arrived at an agreement in October 1950 that France was to receive 40 per cent of the total amount of aid voted by Congress under the Mutual Defence Assistance Act.[41] In the period 1951 to 1954 military aid constituted about 25 per cent of the total French defence budget.[42] The sensitivity of the French military build-up to the amount of military aid was revealed by Prime Minister Pleven's announcement in October 1952 that unexpected reductions in aid meant France would have to settle for the twelve divisions then in place and would not be able to meet the planned increase to fifteen divisions.[43] In fact, American military aid to France did not dry up completely until 1964, by which time France had consumed almost 50 per cent of the total aid Washington had made available to its NATO allies since the inception of the aid programme.[44]

Even so, these early years illustrated the willingness of highly fragile French governments to make domestic sacrifices in the interests of a strong defence capability. The French contribution to NATO's failure to construct sufficient military strength in Europe came chiefly through her overseas activities; first in Indo-China and then, at even greater cost, in Algeria. By 1953 the war in Indo-China was consuming between 40 and 45 per cent of the French defence budget. However, following the 1954 Geneva settlement of the Indo-China situation, the French government drew up a programme which would create an army half a million strong which in its bulk would be deployed in Europe. Then, tragically from all perspectives, came the conflict in Algeria. In June 1954 there were 117,000 French troops in North Africa; fifteen months later, another 400,000 had arrived, taken mostly from France and West Germany.[45] As Fred Mulley observed, the French Army was to have more men at its disposal in North Africa than SACEUR had in Europe.[46]

How serious a problem did this disposition of French forces pose to NATO? Clearly forces employed outside of Europe were not available to bolster force levels in Europe — there were just 50,000 French troops and one French tactical air force in West Germany in 1960 — and this worsened the European force imbalance. On the other hand, French forces in Algeria were hardly further from the central front than many of those oft-quoted 175 Soviet divisions; if Moscow had begun a major mobilisation of its forces in apparent preparation for an attack on Western Europe, it would seem reasonable to assume that the French government would have withdrawn its forces from Algeria to defend France itself. Perhaps more detrimentally, the war in Algeria required the Army to adopt different organisation and tactics than those suited to European conditions. The two already-created 'pentatomic' divisions were especially inappropriate for the Algerian task. [47]

The French tried to counter the dismay of their NATO allies at the absence of a more substantial French military presence in Europe by arguing that the threat to the West was a global one and was far more likely to manifest itself in more vulnerable and less stable parts of the world than Europe. Indo-China and Algeria were examples of this. Thus, according to Paris, the French were shedding blood and expending resources in Algeria on behalf of the West as a whole in what was a common struggle. [48]

The French case did have some substance. The Korean peace and the death of Stalin had been seen in both the United States and Britain as pointers to a relaxation in the level of Cold War tension, and as a justification for slowing down their own defence efforts. It is not clear that anyone in high office in the West truly believed a Soviet attack in Europe to be imminent. We have seen too that ever greater faith was being put in the efficacy of nuclear weapons. Many in France shared this faith, and, given the circumstances, it was inevitable that they too should begin to question the utility of high conventional-force levels in Europe. As Beufre noted, 'Conventional defence, on which we had been concentrating, lost much of its *raison d'etre*'. [49] The French were clearly prepared to make great sacrifices, but in what their allies regarded as the wrong places and the wrong ways.

For their part, the French too were becoming disillusioned. They were aggrieved that their efforts in Algeria were not appreciated by their allies, and the Suez experience in particular taught them how unsupportive a partner the United States could be, and how important it was to be able to act independently. In Europe, having fought hard to enmesh the 'Anglo-Saxons' in the defence of continental Europe, the French came to resent their dominance of SHAPE and of strategic formulation generally. About one-third of the entire SHAPE staff were Americans, English was the everyday language, and French officers felt — and were — excluded from much of the deliberation regarding strategic planning and nuclear weapons generally.[50] General Andre Beufre, one of the leading French military thinkers of the day, wrote of 'the enormous American preponderance' at SHAPE, which had expanded even more with the nuclearisation of NATO strategy, and complained of the unfair allocation of commands in the alliance.[51] Repeated French proposals to establish some kind of Anglo-American-French triumvirate, an idea later to be resurrected by de Gaulle, had been resisted,[52] and we have seen already how the initial French suspicion of German rearmament was overcome largely by American counter-pressures. Excluded from the more influential and prestigious nerve-centres of the Alliance, and witnesses to a slackening of the Anglo-American resolve to maintain substantial force levels in continental Europe, it became clear to the French that the Alliance was moving in a direction they had not intended for it and which they did not desire.

Nevertheless, it cannot be denied that many Frenchmen perceived nuclear weapons as providing the same opportunities their Anglo-American counterparts saw. There were signs very early on of a French interest in the tactical use of nuclear weapons. For example, Beufre, who participated in military planning in the WEU and in NATO before the arrival of Eisenhower as SACEUR, has since recalled that 'The more we studied the problem, the more essential the support of nuclear weapons appeared; they were the sole method of preventing the enemy concentrating in his usual way'.[53] In 1952 a small group of officers led by Colonel Charles Ailleret began to advocate a French acquisition of a battlefield nuclear capability. Their protagonism was based on an assessment of the efficacy of nuclear weapons used tactically, and on the view that TNWs were cheaper than equivalent conventional explosives. Although a French TNW capability was still some way off, by 1956 a French defence minister was suggesting that 'A number of years hence. . .an army not vested with atomic weapons will be an outmoded force. . . The option which we face is not between classic weapons and nuclear arms, but between the possession of the latter and the abandonment of the national defence'. [54]

As with Britain, though, it was the ramifications of strategic nuclear weapons which attracted the closest attention in France. French soldiers were very quick to perceive the dangers of excessive reliance on American nuclear protection once the American homeland became vulnerable to Soviet nuclear attack. [55] This sentiment was to grow until it became a part of the essence of General de Gaulle's security policies. It did not originate with his presidency, however. There was too a considerable awareness during the Fourth Republic of the political status which might accrue from the possession of an independent nuclear deterrent. The widespread feeling that France was not treated sufficiently seriously by her English-speaking allies, and the British pursuit of an independent nuclear capability, served to inspire this belief. As such, the independent French deterrent had its origins as much in a determination to impress allies as deter adversaries, or, as one analyst has put it, 'Military incentives were supplemental, rather than central, factors in the government's final choice'. [56] The trust the British were putting in the credibility of a nuclear deterrent was mirrored in France, however, and Paris too came to lose interest in the conventional defence of Europe, preferring instead to concentrate resources in the deterrent basket. In short, the French position was and is complex. In 1960, the year of the first French atomic test explosion, army strength was still around 750,000, although, as we have seen, it was not for the most part in Europe. [57] It has been noted elsewhere that British and French policies more closely resembled the 'massive retaliation' strategy that was more usually associated with Washington, and there is more than a grain of truth in this. [58] It could also be argued that in these early years France was shown the way by both Britain and the United States. NATO's strategy was coming to depend profoundly on nuclear weapons, a process which had been completed by the time France withdrew from Algeria in the early 1960s. Furthermore, this dependence was coming about in circumstances in which a non-nuclear France was being excluded from making a contribution — at least that is how the French saw it. Thus, as Osgood has noted, 'the principal effect of NATO's nuclear strategy upon French military policies was to intensify France's concentration upon developing a nuclear capability instead of collaborating with NATO's forces'.[59] In other words, French experiences taught them that nuclear weapons did indeed endow status and privilege. Furthermore, if an uncertainty concerning the extended nuclear umbrella of the United States coloured British thinking, then the French can perhaps be excused for believing themselves to be even more at the mercy of Washington's potential perfidy.

THE FEDERAL REPUBLIC: CAUGHT UP IN THE TIDE

Although the late 1940s had seen serious consideration being given to the possibility of a West German military contribution to the defence of Western Europe, it was not until July 1955 that Bonn eventually passed a bill authorising the raising of 6,000 volunteer troops. This delay, induced essentially by the interminable EDC proceedings, created a situation in which German military thinking and planning found itself badly out of phase with that of Bonn's new allies — not that their activities were noticeably co-ordinated. The West Germans embarked upon and proceeded with a rearmament programme after the British and Americans in particular had already begun their drift towards a conventional-force run-down and an enhanced reliance on the nuclear deterrent. As has been noted elsewhere, Germany's misfortune was that 'It began its rearmament at the height of the age of nuclear euphoria'.[60] It was not long before this lack of synchronisation within the Alliance produced quite serious strains.

The Germans were aiming at a total armed manpower target of 500,000, which incorporated the creation of twelve army divisions. This would eventually give the Federal Republic Western Europe's largest land army. In fact, a half-million-strong West German force appears to have been first mooted during the very earliest days of the EDC discussions.[61] It was incorporated in the Lisbon force goals of February 1952, constituting another reason why these goals were unmet, and seems to have been simply carried over into the 1955 arrangements. This in itself typifies the somewhat reactive and even inert character of German defence policy. Decisions were made elsewhere, and especially in Washington. For the government in Bonn, ultimately the task was to adapt to the designs of others. As another example, there had been little comment in Germany of NATO's 1954 decision to base its plans on the tactical use of nuclear weapons. The Federal Republic had not yet formally joined the Alliance, of course, but membership was just around the corner, and this was a decision which had implications more profound for Germany than for any existing Alliance state. [62]

Many factors contributed to the passivity of German military policy and thought during this period. The chancellor, Konrad Adenaur, was himself uninterested in military affairs *per se*, and tended to regard Bonn's defence policy as simply one more means to reintegrate West Germany into the West European family. There was, too, a prevalent anti-militarism which stemmed from the sense of collective guilt for the causes and conduct of the Second World War and which reflected the extent to which the 'military caste' had been discredited. This ensured that Germans interested in military affairs cultivated a self-imposed caution in their utterances, and it suppressed, too, any open display of military enthusiasm, which had the capacity to upset allies and enemies equally.

Perhaps for these reasons, when debates on defence matters did break out in West Germany, they tended to take on an emotive and dogmatic character. It was a feature of German political life which may equally have been imparted by the fact that the issue of nuclear weapons, and particularly nuclear weapons for battlefield use, provided much of the substance of these debates. Thus the Social Democratic Party (SPD) Opposition, which had been much tardier than Adenauer's Christian Democrats in reconciling itself to the fact of Germany's division, put up a spirited resistance both to the Volunteers Bill of 1955 and to the reintroduction of conscription by the Service Bill of 1956 — just a year, note, before the British announced they were to abolish it. This opposition was based largely on the belief widespread in the SPD that any future war in Europe would be a nuclear one regardless of Germany's conventional efforts. As the SPD spokesman Fritz Erler noted, 'The strategy of NATO leaves no room for doubting that an armed conflict in Europe — even with 500,000 German soldiers — will not remain a conventional conflict. The NATO plans are based upon immediate and direct employment of atomic weapons in the event of a conflict in Europe'. The Opponents of Germany's rearmament were understandably encouraged in their assessment by the revelations of the now famous simulated NATO air exercise of 1955, code-named Carte Blanche. During the simulation, 335 nuclear bombs were 'dropped', resulting in 1,700,000 'dead' German civilians, 3.5 million wounded and an unknown number affected by radiation.[63] The SPD Opposition was simply the tip of a much wider though not always articulated popular unease which combined with the effects of a manpower shortage stemming from a rapidly rebuilding economy, to slow down the pace at which German rearmament progressed. One eminent student of Germany's defence policy has laid the sluggishness of the rearmament programme firmly at the door of 'Bonn's increasing recognition of the consequences of its dependence on other's nuclear weapons'.[64]

Chancellor Adenaur's sensitivity to these consequences was enhanced by the leak of July 1956 that Admiral Radford, chairman of the JCS in Washington, had proposed a cut in American forces of 800,000 men.[65] Over half of the cuts were to be met by the Army, and they would fall primarily on US forces overseas. This, of course, meant Europe, and especially Germany, and it was based on the view that any future US–Soviet war would very quickly escalate to a nuclear exchange. Coming as it did just one week after the Bundestag had finally approved the half-million-man force concept, Adenaur's anger and embarrassment was understandable. Whilst the German Defence Ministry argued that the introduction of TNWs did not justify a reduction in the conventional force level, and that in any case a full-scale Soviet attack was not the only contingency to be considered, a communique was issued in the chancellor's name which declared he and the German Cabinet 'to be of the opinion that a one-sided emphasis on the development of nuclear weapons, accompanied by a reduction in conventional weapons and manpower, would increase the danger of atomic war in the event of conflict'. A scheme such as that associated with Admiral Radford was 'extremely dangerous, not only for Europe but for the whole of the human race'. Although Bonn reiterated its intention of raising a 500,000-strong force, the comments of the American secretary of state, Dulles, which supported the view that nuclear weapons did offer the option of cuts in manpower and that such cuts could not therefore be ruled out in the future, were hardly designed to dispel Bonn's suspicions.

Whilst persisting in its show of displeasure, the West German government was also to reveal within a few weeks of its explosive response to the Radford leak that a learning process was at work in Bonn, too. In September 1956 it was announced that there would be a reduction in the term of service for conscripts from eighteen to twelve months. Furthermore, the delicate question of a German access to a nuclear trigger was raised.[66] Adenaur's logic was more clearly revealed in a speech he made in March 1958, when he argued that NATO's reliance on TNWs was going ahead regardless of West German sensitivities. The only sensible course was to swim with the tide, for to refuse to do so would be to so isolate Germany within the Alliance as to render its membership meaningless, and this in turn could leave Germany at Moscow's mercy.[67] Nor can there be much doubt that Franz-Josef Strauss, who succeeded Theodor Blank as defence minister in October 1956, encouraged Adenaur's creeping conversion. Strauss largely shared the American view that a strategy based on TNWs was desirable both from the point of view of deterrence and because it offered opportunities for the maintenance of smaller conventional forces.[68] In this he differed not only from Blank but from those elements within the Germany Army who, whether from a sense of self-preservation, a professional concern with the requirements of an effective forward defence, or a genuine anxiety over the implications for Germany of a nuclear-based defence strategy, dragged their feet somewhat on the TNW issue until well into the 1960s.[69]

All this, however, is to leap too far ahead. When the British made their 1957 announcement of their intention to reduce their conventional strength by phasing out conscription, Bonn was prominent in a European-wide outcry.[70] The French and German ministers joined together in their criticism of the presentation of the cuts by the British foreign minister, Selwyn Lloyd, to the Council of the WEU. The Germans were particularly fearful that NATO was being left with little alternative to either surrender or all-out nuclear war. At Adenaur's suggestion, the Council of the WEU proposed that NATO conduct an overall review of its force levels and posture. In May the WEU Assembly joined the fray by adopting a report prepared by its Defence Committee which was highly critical of the direction British defence policy was now taking and which declared impeccably that 'If Great Britain were to withdraw troops from Germany, it could not in logic be possible to prevent other states from doing the same'. In fact, the first censure motion ever moved in the WEU Assembly was moved by delegates from Italy, France and the Benelux countries and was critical of the WEU Council for its weak resistance to the British force reductions. Although after a heated debate the motion won the vote of members present, it was not adopted owing to a rule which required the support of a majority of all Assembly members, present or not. During the same month the issue was raised at the NATO Council meeting in Bonn, at which the West German foreign minister, Dr von Brentano, resignedly declared himself to be 'not very happy' about British defence policy. In passing, such sentiments as these were widely held elsewhere on the Continent. For example, in Paris, two members of the Military Committee of the Conference of NATO parliamentarians, M. Gilson of Belgium and General Calmeyer of the Netherlands, produced a report which was highly critical of trends in NATO military policy. The land forces of the Alliance, they felt, were in a process of 'disintegration', and for this Washington and London were primarily to blame. These criticisms were not included in the final resolutions adopted by the conference, however.[71] All in all, Fred Mulley, who had served as vice-president of the WEU Assembly and as rapporteur of its Defence Committee, seemed to be rather accurate in his assessment that the British reductions, which amounted to 22,000 men in little over a year 'were extremely unpopular in Europe'.[72]

It is perhaps worth noting that, following the tension over Berlin in 1958, the period of conscription was again extended to eighteen months in the Federal Republic, and by 1961 West German armed strength stood at 337,000.[73] By 1965 the long-promised twelve army divisions were ready, and towards the end of the decade total West German armed strength was approaching the half-million target first set way back in the early 1950s.[74] By the early 1960s, too, the West German defence budget exceeded 6 per cent of the country's GNP. Although this figure was less than the 7 per cent the British were spending, and was about equivalent to the sacrifices the French were making at this juncture,[75] it must be remembered that all German armed forces were NATO-dedicated. The Germans were not engaged in the construction of an independent nuclear deterrent but in the creation of NATO's most powerful conventional force in Europe. It is worth noting too, of course, that the levels of spending which Western democracies then felt were compatible with democracy and economic well-being, were substantially higher than the levels which many of those democracies now feel is compatible with democracy and economic well-being!

It was the Germans who — denied the nuclear option, committed to forward defence, the host (and potential target) for the majority of battlefield nuclear weapons and constrained in their ability to argue their case as forcefully as could their allies because of the bitter memories of the still recent conflict — experienced the biggest dilemmas as a result of NATO's drift towards nuclear reliance. The American commitment, vital psychologically and materially for German security, had the constant threat of force withdrawals hanging over it and was bedevilled by the often loose talk in Washington of early and massive use of nuclear weapons, including at the tactical level. The reduction of BAOR to 55,000, a figure itself under scrutiny in London, was difficult to construe as a convincing manifestation of a major shift towards an acceptance by the British of a 'continental commitment' as the centrepiece of their security arrangements. Furthermore, in abolishing conscription, Britain was additionally denying to itself a large body of militarily-trained personnel on whom it could call in any future emergency. As for the French, they had perhaps gallantly, but certainly wastefully and irrelevantly, committed their quite substantial military resources to meeting what they had come to perceive as the more immediate and likely challenges to Western interests outside Europe. Although Paris had remained doctrinally more committed and for longer than had the Anglo-Americans to the maintenance of large conventional armies in Europe, by their actions they too had undermined the efforts of those, and especially the Germans, who had continued to make the attempt. By the late 1950s and the early 1960s the French, too, through a fatalism in the face of the Anglo-American loss of interest in conventional forces, and because they had come to share the faith in the efficacy of a nuclear-based defence and deterrence posture, began running down their non-nuclear forces and devoting an ever-larger share of their defence budget to the independent nuclear deterrent.

In short, then, the explanation for NATO's early reliance on TNWs is more complex than is sometimes supposed. There is clear evidence in the American case that TNWs were seen to have an inherent military utility which was independent of the presumed cost of matching Soviet conventional force levels with similar forces. It appears, too, that the large numbers of TNWs simply emerged from a Byzantine procurement process unguided by any strong sense of military necessity. It is true that the Eisenhower government sought to reduce the overall size of the federal budget, and defence spending provided an obvious target. Governments often do like to control spending and cut taxes. This too, however, was seen as something desirable for its own sake, and did not spring from any easily identifiable strains in the American economy caused specifically by the maintenance of large conventional forces in Europe. The British were no less slow than the Americans in developing a fascination with the efficacy of strategic nuclear bombardment as a deterrent and, if need be, as a means of war. So convinced, though, were the British by the power of nuclear deterrence that they really did appear to come close during the 1950s to regarding almost any other kind of military capability as redundant. The British were beginning to experience severe economic problems, but not so much that they were not prepared to make considerable sacrifices in the interests of developing their own strategic bombardment capability. Indeed, British defence expenditure was high throughout the 1950s, and has continuously been set at a percentage of GNP in excess of that of its major NATO allies in Europe. Unfortunately, it was not only the British who had difficulties in coming to terms with their rapidly deteriorating economic status, for it is probably fair to say that continental Europeans expected more from Britain than it was becoming possible for her to provide. Nevertheless, politics is about choice, and the British chose to stress a nuclear rather than a conventional force emphasis in their defence posture. This was not unavoidable; it was what the British preferred to do. Although, as in France, there were influential figures who favoured the development of a TNW-based war-fighting strategy, both London and Paris were more interested in the strategic mission. Such interest as there was in TNWs mirrored American assessments of their military utility. If TNWs promised financial savings, then that constituted an additional incentive rather than the prime motivation.

4 Nuclear Controversies

THE EUROPEAN STOCKPILE

Despite the Alliance decision of 1954 to base war planning on the assumption that nuclear weapons could and would be used, the European forces were not even in a position to receive nuclear weapons until the adoption in 1957 of a five-year plan known as MC-70.[1] This called for the stockpiling in Europe of nuclear warheads which, although they were to remain under US custody, were for use by both European and American armed forces. For the most part the Europeans were to purchase the appropriate delivery systems from the Americans. This system, whereby the US controlled the warheads whilst Europeans owned the delivery systems, was the essence of the 'dual key' arrangements which governed, and still govern, the control of TNWs in Europe. The training and organisation of NATO's armed forces was already largely based on the presupposition of TNW availability and use. MC-70 also called for a standing force of thirty full-strength divisions in Europe, to be supported by ninety days' worth of supplies. Given that the Lisbon force goals had sought thirty-five ready divisions, this aspect of MC-70 was not the radically new departure it was sometimes credited as being. Nevertheless, the adoption of MC-70 meant that NATO had embraced the so-called 'trip-wire' strategy, which allocated to conventional forces the limited role of tripping the adversary over into a nuclear exchange.

The 1957 decisions represented a response to a number of pressures. In particular, the NATO Council meeting twelve months earlier had witnessed requests from a number of European allies that Washington make nuclear weapons available to them.[2] West Germany was among them, although the French and British were reportedly reluctant to contemplate a German finger on a nuclear trigger.[3] In addition, General Lauris Norstad, who had replaced General Gruenther as SACEUR in November 1956, was sympathetic to the idea that NATO's members should be equipped with a nuclear capability. He had become associated with the so-called 'pause' concept of war in Europe, which itself appears to have emanated from SHAPE, where the West Germans were becoming increasingly influential.[4] At the heart of this somewhat nebulous concept was the view that NATO forces could find themselves confronted either with a limited aggression or with an aggression which the Soviets might be prepared to curtail if the battle did not go well for them in the early stages or if it threatened to escalate to a full-fledged nuclear exchange. The point was that NATO forces should be sufficient to force a 'pause' in the attack, without the use of TNWs if possible, but with them if necessary. Difficult to pin down in practice, it nevertheless represented a shift away from the purer forms of 'massive retaliation'. In fact, it overlapped with the concept of 'graduated deterrence', which seems to have originated in Britain and which had found favour around Europe, not least in Bonn.[5] Like the 'pause' concept, this also incorporated the notion of intra-war deterrence, that it was not only the outbreak of war that had to be deterred but its escalation by the enemy. The costs to the aggressor of pushing on towards a hoped-for victory had to be raised the more he pushed.

The stationing of a British tactical missile regiment in Germany in 1958, armed with a nominal number of seventy-mile range, surface-to-surface, US-supplied Corporal missiles,[6] constituted, once warheads for the missiles were available too, the first European force equipped with a battlefield nuclear capability under the new arrangements. Apart from the dual-purpose howitzers supplied to some allies during 1959, other NATO members did not receive their first TNW systems until 1961.[7] These included atomic cannon, with a range of fourteen miles; the 15–20-mile range Honest John missiles; the 300-mile range Pershing I; surface-to-air missiles; free-falling bombs; and atomic demolition mines. Of the 7,000-warhead total reached by 1966, 3,000 is probably a better figure for the number of less ambiguously battlefield nuclear weapons,[8] given the range and yield of some of these systems.

The build-up in Europe during the 1950s of nuclear weapons of all kinds reflected a number of objectives. They could deter aggression, save money, enable wars to be fought more effectively, reassure allies and close the gap in the conventional force balance. Given the multiplicity of rationales, it is difficult to assign specific roles (as opposed to military missions) to specific types of system. Any attempt at this task would be hindered by the loose (by present standards) terminology which was used to describe the weapons deployed in Europe. As Henry Kissinger has noted:

the definition of 'tactical' was such that the Supreme Allied Commander Europe (SACEUR) was able to destroy all Soviet weapons aimed at Europe,

and, given their range and destructive capacity, many of the TNWs deployed in Europe:

could be called 'tactical' only in the sense that they were stationed in Europe and not in the United States and that they were controlled by SACEUR rather than the commanding general of Strategic Air Command (SAC). [9]

The warheads for the TNW systems came to be stockpiled in over one hundred sites, about two-thirds of which stored warheads for use by the armed forces of European states. The procedure was that the US entered into a whole number of bilateral arrangements for the stockpiling of nuclear warheads with each of those allies who had agreed to stockpile. Norway and Denmark expressly forbade the stockpiling of nuclear weapons on their territory, and France would not permit the stationing on her territory of any nuclear weapons not under French control. The agreements referred only to broad categories of weapons, however, and it was not until 1967 that Washington agreed to inform each country, by means of an annual letter to the minister of defence, of the details of the weapons stockpiled on its territory or for use by its forces. [10] Of course, it would be safe to assume that, in the nature of things, knowledge of the contents of each stockpile was more widespread than the official arrangements suggested.

GERMAN SENSITIVITY

The 1957 decisions once again highlighted the extreme sensitivity of West German public opinion to nuclear issues, for the decisions were followed by a national furore which exceeded in intensity even that which had been provoked by the Carte Blanche revelations. In fact, in the interest of accuracy, it is more appropriate to date the outbreak of the debate from April 1957, when eighteen leading German atomic scientists published their 'Göttingen Appeal'. In it they stated that Germany would 'do the most to advance world peace by expressly and voluntarily rejecting the possession of atomic weapons of any kind'.[11] The moral authority of the scientists, who had also declared their unwillingness to associate themselves personally in any way with any nuclear weapons policy, was matched by that of the churches, and most particularly the influential Protestant Church.[12] Although the synod of the Evangelical Church failed to push through a resolution condemning the government's nuclear policy, church leaders were joined by others eminent in German public life — the writer, Heinrich Böll, for instance — in signing the manifesto of 'Kampf dem Atomtod' (Campaign Against Atomic Death).[13] The official statements issued by the campaign's working committee paid precious little attention to military, strategic or even political reasoning.[14] Rather, they claimed the moral high ground, appealing to the natural fears and to the simple moral instincts of the general population. Of greater import than the activities of churchmen, however, was the fact that the Opposition SPD took up the anti-nuclear cause. In this, the party was able to call on its deep reserves of pacifistic, neutralist and pro-reunification political sentiments. Parliamentary debates on the issue acquired a very ugly face and not infrequently degenerated into little more than angry exchanges of the most immoderate kind. Personal insults and accusations became the everyday meat of political life. The issue was also given a strong extra-parliamentary dimension as a result of the numerous rallies and protests which were organised chiefly by the SPD, or with their co-operation and participation. The SPD even attempted, quite unconstitutionally, to arrange referenda on the subject of German nuclear armament. However, with the Christian Democratic (CDU) victory in the July 1958 state elections in North-Rhine Westphalia — the first such victory since the establishment of West Germany's constitutional and democratic political system in 1949 — the debate lost much of its heat. [15] It did rumble on for a while within the SPD, but in time the Party came to adopt a more pragmatic approach albeit one which still aspired to reduce and, hopefully, eventually abolish German reliance on nuclear weapons. This was to be achieved within the context of the NATO Alliance, by gradualist and parliamentary means, and by the maintenance of a viable, conventional-force-orientated defence policy. [16]

One political commentator was later to describe this period as one of 'total division, a total tearing apart that revealed all the old wounds. There seemed no basis for consensus; it was impossible even to talk'. He continued, 'Nobody would ever want to go through something like that again'. [17] Unfortunately, the late 1970s and early 1980s was to reveal that this was a wish which would not be granted. The explanation for this German sensitivity, at least in the 1950s, was two-fold. First, many elements within the German political and military establishment, including Adenaur himself, were doubtful of the desirability of NATO becoming overdependent on TNWs, and the need for a substantial non-nuclear capability was more constantly reiterated in Germany than elsewhere. To take just one example to illustrate this point, the WEU Committee on Defence Questions and Armaments found that German military authorities were prepared to envisage a military confrontation in Central Europe, perhaps growing out of developments in East Germany, in which the Soviet Union would forego the use of nuclear weapons. In such circumstances the Germans felt it would be inappropriate for NATO forces to adopt a 'first-use' nuclear policy. By way of contrast, their British counterparts found it difficult to envisage any war in Europe staying below the nuclear threshold. [18] Obviously, the fact that any nuclear exchange would be concentrated on (East and West) German territory contributed a great deal to these differing perspectives.

Second, whatever Germans thought, NATO's other leading powers were taking the Alliance firmly along the nuclear road. The development of NATO's strategy and force posture, and the conduct of any war, could take place largely in opposition to German preferences. Adenaur had made this perfectly clear during the March 1958 debate on nuclear weapons policy in the

Bundestag: 'If the strategical planning of NATO — and we must naturally and will naturally test this — desires that we too, the Federal Republic, make use of this development of weapons technique, and if we hesitate to do so, then we automatically leave NATO'. [19] Germans had far less control in the 1950s even than they have today over the planning for and conduct of any war in Central Europe, despite the fact it would largely be fought on Germany territory. Stripped of the moralistic excesses, the strategic inarticulacy, and the dearth of political realism, these considerations underlined German unease both in the 1950s and more recently. The distinction in practice between defence and deterrence had, and has, an immediacy in Germany which it lacks elsewhere. As both debates revealed, the rhetorical, taunting question, 'Better red or dead?' can transform itself for many Germans into a sober, and sobering, choice. Paradoxically, however — and the German position remains replete with paradox — the desire to obtain a veto over, or at least a greater say in, NATO's nuclear policies, led Bonn to push for access to the nuclear button.

THE NUCLEAR BATTLEFIELD

It is not surprising that contemplation of the use of TNWs frightened many Germans, and other Europeans, whose territory would provide the battlefield. The yield of the atomic bomb dropped on Hiroshima was 14 kilotons. In Europe, free-fall bombs had yields in excess of one megaton, and possibly rose to 1.4 megatons. [20] The majority of the TNW systems deployed in Europe during the 1950s were artillery systems, however. These had a range of less than 20 miles, and a yield of just 2 kilotons. As we have seen, in between these two extremes were systems of various ranges and various yields, which if used were capable in aggregate of causing enormous devastation over a very wide area indeed. In considering the impact of a tactical nuclear war in Europe, comparable Soviet capabilities are a factor in the equation. Moscow may have possessed a few TNWs available for use in Europe as early as 1954, but the more usual date given is 1957. Certainly that is when their serious build-up appears to have begun, [21] most particularly of larger-range SS-4s and SS-5s, which would today be designated as 'theatre' systems.

The 'Carte Blanche' exercise was not unique in suggesting that the outcome to any TNW use in Europe could be quite disastrous. Thus the studies the RAND Corporation was requested to do during this period on the outcome of a battlefield nuclear exchange all produced similar results: 'one side or the other invariably lost almost all its capability in a few days'. For example, one of RAND's games gave victory to the NATO side which had 5 per cent of its forces remaining against the total annihilation of the Soviet side.[22] Lord Zuckerman, chief scientific advisor to the British Ministry of Defence, set up in 1960 a series of studies played by experienced Army divisional commanders operating without inhibitions on nuclear use. The result of one such game was between 200 and 250 nuclear strikes of an average yield of 20 kilotons, in just a few days and confined to an area 50 by 30 miles square. 'The effect', he has written, 'would have been indescribable and meaningless from the point of view of any continuing battle between opposing armies'.[23] Alain C. Enthoven and K. Wayne Smith, two former US Defence Department officials, have written that:

Studies and war games. . .showed that high casualty rates and a great amount of collateral damage were likely to result from a tactical nuclear war in Europe. Even under the most favourable assumptions, it appeared that between 2 million and 20 million Europeans would be killed, with widespread damage to the economy of the affected area and a high risk of 100 million dead if the war escalated to attacks on cities.

As they continued:

In the light of this, it was difficult to see how initiating a tactical nuclear war would satisfy the United States basic goal of defending the people and territories of NATO Europe. When the defence of Europe is seen to entail its nuclear destruction, the European incentive to permit the use of nuclear weapons on its soil diminishes rapidly.[24]

A EURO-STRATEGIC DETERRENT?

The communique of the December 1957 Council meeting also noted that 'intermediate range ballistic missiles will have to be put at the disposal of the Supreme Allied Commander, Europe'. Part of the explanation behind this move can be found in Norstad's view that there needed to be a NATO deterrent in Europe and under his, SACEUR's, control. Such a force would enable NATO to respond to a Soviet attack, conventional or nuclear, on Europe, without involving nuclear systems based in the soon to be vulnerable American homeland. There was, too, a need to match Moscow's growing arsenal of nuclear weapons capable of hitting targets in Western Europe but not of crossing the Atlantic. The force could also go some way towards correcting Europe's lack of control over the conduct of a nuclear campaign conducted on its behalf. Whether SACEUR — as an American national occupying the dual position of military chief of the Atlantic Alliance as well as subordinate to his own commander-in-chief, the American president — can truly be the repository for a European deterrent, is a moot point. Nevertheless, Norstad proposed a medium-range ballistic missile (MRBM) force of between 300 and 700 missiles to be located in Europe. They should be land-based, mobile and designed to enable a controlled nuclear war to be fought. This required the missiles to be capable of penetrating air defences and accurately hitting military targets. [25] The Germans were particularly keen on Norstad's proposal, and the issue was to drag on until 1962, only to be eventually eclipsed by the Multilateral Force (MLF) negotiations. [26]

A far more insistent motive behind the intermediate-range ballistic missile (IRBM) decision, however, was the growing awareness that the American homeland was itself on the verge of vulnerability to a Soviet nuclear attack. In addition to the claim that the Soviet Union possessed an intercontinental bomber force, Krushchev declared in August 1957 that the Soviet Union had successfully developed an intercontinental ballistic missile (ICBM). The credibility of this claim was boosted by the October 1957 launch of the Soviet Sputnik satellite, which did indeed show that Moscow had mastered the requisite technology to put an object in orbit. Meeting this challenge required a different kind of force than that which SACEUR was proposing, and in fact London and Washington had already outlined a purely bilateral agreement, outside the NATO structure, to station some US Air Force missiles in the United Kingdom. The agreement, formally announced in February 1958, provided for the deployment of sixty Thor missiles, distributed around four bases. Authority to launch the missiles, which had a range of 1,500 miles and were thus capable of reaching Soviet territory from their launch points, required the 'joint positive agreement' of the two governments. Although the Royal Air Force had the responsibility for manning the bases, the warheads for the missiles were owned, controlled and guarded by Americans.[27] Within a year, the first of these missiles had arrived. The Anglo-American agreement was followed in March 1959 by an announcement that fifteen Jupiter missiles, which had a range similar to that of the Thor but which had been developed under the auspices of the US Army, were to be deployed in Italy. Shortly afterwards it was agreed that a further thirty Jupiter missiles were to be placed in Turkey. Unlike the British-based Thors, the Jupiters were placed under SAC-EUR's control and thus constituted a strictly NATO-dedicated force.[28] Nevertheless, as the US defence secretary, Robert S McNamara, confirmed in 1963, 'In 1957, when the decision was made to install the Jupiters, they, along with the Thors, were the only strategic missiles NATO had ready for deployment'.[29]

The British, who were in any case firmly committed to a strategy based on the deterrent capabilities of nuclear weapons, were also keen not only to re-cement their 'special relationship' with Washington following the Suez debacle of 1956, but also to obtain greater access to American warhead and missile technology and know-how. Perhaps for these reasons London seemed to enter into the agreement to deploy US missiles on its territory in a routine, almost casual, manner.[30] The contrast with the approach taken by the French could hardly have been greater. The American failure to support its allies during the Suez crisis served to distance Paris from Washington, whilst the launching of Sputnik dramatically fuelled the growing appreciation in France that the imminent vulnerability of the American homeland to nuclear attack undermined whatever credibility the US nuclear umbrella over Europe was still deemed to have.[31] France had already served notice to the NATO Council in 1956 that it was to follow the path of nuclear independence, and with de Gaulle's accession in 1958 this ambition was strengthened still further. The pride and sensitivity of which the French deterrent programme was a manifestation, guaranteed that Paris would reject any American offer which denied French, independent control, or which was in some other way deemed ungenerous. Sure enough, the Washington offer to France was akin to those which were made to Italy and Turkey, rather than the special bilateral understanding which had been arrived at with the British. Accordingly, de Gaulle rejected the stationing of American missiles on French territory. [32]

There were obstacles in the way of a more extensive or dispersed deployment of IRBM's elsewhere in Europe. Neither the Norwegians nor the Danes would countenance the siting of any nuclear weapons on their soil; the Dutch and the Belgians each experienced widespread public opposition to the missiles; the Greeks were going through one of their periodic bouts of anti-Americanism; and Portuguese territory was too distant from any intended targets. [33] This left the delicate case of Germany. Although Adenaur supported in principle the basing of American IRBMs in Europe, he chose to make an exception of Germany. The Soviets were, he believed, bound to be especially provoked by the appearance of IRBMs on German soil, and the forward basing of these missiles which this would amount to could both encourage pre-emption by the Soviets in a crisis, and render the missiles particularly vulnerable to it. Given the debate on the 1957 decisions which were raging all around him, he was also able to cite with some degree of conviction and plausibility the fragility of West German public opinion on nuclear matters. [34] In the light of the more recent controversies surrounding the deployment of Tomahawk Ground-Launched Cruise Missiles (GLCM) and Pershing II missiles in Germany and elsewhere, Adenaur's observations seem profoundly apposite. So, too, do Helmut Schmidt's 1961 observations that 'everyone capable of objective reasoning must concede that the stationing of enemy IRBMs, so to speak, on its very threshold [Turkey], must produce the psychological effect of a provocation on any great power'. [35] It does indeed seem highly likely that it was this 'provocation' which was to prompt Krushchev to order the placing of Soviet missiles on Cuba, in a situation of comparable proximity to the United States, thereby initiating the Cuban missile crisis, which in turn arguably brought the world closer to the brink of a nuclear exchange than it has ever been. [36]

The IRBMs, then, represented a 'quick fix', paralleled by the Soviets Cuban deployment in 1962, and pending the acquisition and development of a full-fledged American intercontinental nuclear capability in the 1960s. What they also signified, however, was the involvement of European territory in American nuclear strike plans. [37] This meant the proliferation of targets of high value to Moscow throughout Western Europe, and the Soviets were indeed building up a substantial nuclear strike capability aimed at Europe. This, perhaps, was not overly-worrying if it could safely be assumed that American nuclear superiority was so overwhelming and that the American homeland was absolutely invulnerable, in contrast to the massive vulnerability of Soviet territory. As we have noted, though, this asymmetry in the nuclear relationship between the superpowers was on the verge of collapse. It was, in other words, only a matter of time before American cities, too, would be victims of a nuclear exchange, and this, so many Europeans began to think, changed everything. It gave an additional boost to British and French efforts to build nuclear deterrents under their respective national control. But it turned the minds of all Europeans, and especially those who did not have or — as in the case of the Germans — could not have, a nuclear option of their own. What they now sought was access, control or a veto on the use of nuclear weapons, and most particularly those with the range to reach Soviet territory.

These European ambitions came to focus on the concept known as the Multilateral Force (MLF), notwithstanding the fact that it actually emanated from Washington at the tail end of the Eisenhower administration.[38] Designed to head off a proliferation of independent European nuclear deterrents, by 1962 the MLF advocates envisaged it as a 200-missile, 25-ship-based force, each component of which would be manned by a mixed-nationality crew. De Gaulle explicitly rejected it, whilst the British, who could not indulge in such ostentatious flaunting of Washington's initiatives, sought instead to sabotage it by obfuscation. One method London adopted was the introduction of alternative schemes, such as the Atlantic Nuclear Force, which was described by Franz-Josef Strauss as 'the only fleet that had not been created that torpedoed another fleet that hadn't sailed [MLF]'.[39] Both London and Paris were already in pursuit of a superior option, of course, and the MLF degenerated into an increasingly embarrassing series of consultations between Bonn and Washington. Eventually, in 1964, the Americans in effect withdrew positive support for the project. It had come to threaten the achievement of a non-proliferation treaty with Moscow, and in any case was ultimately doomed by an American reluctance to transfer real control over nuclear decision-making in the Alliance. With the formation of the Grand Coalition government in 1966, it ceased to be the official policy in Bonn too.

In addition to shunting Norstad's Euro-deterrent idea sideways, the MLF saga represented the end of what has been termed the 'hardware' or 'possession' approach to nuclear sharing in the Alliance. Subsequent to the MLF's collapse, the emphasis has been on developing the 'consultative' approach; that is, on the elaboration of guidelines and procedures by which the various members of the Alliance could have some influence on nuclear-use policy even where they didn't own, as such, the weapons themselves.[40] This is a subject to which we will return in due course.

WASHINGTON FOR PARIS AND LONDON

Now that the American homeland was within the range of the Soviet nuclear strike capability, would Washington ever risk its own existence for Paris, London or Bonn? Could one nation ever commit suicide on behalf of another? It would probably be overstating the case to argue that French security policy in the nuclear age has been based on a categorical 'no' in answer to this somewhat rhetorical question. Rather, the French have been more inclined, certainly than the British, and more free, especially when compared to the Germans, to openly articulate their doubts and uncertainties regarding the credibility of the American nuclear umbrella. In fact, it is not even true to argue that French policy has been guided solely by considerations so purely strategic as these, for there has been a strong admixture of political reasoning and sentiment too. In this respect, at least, the French experience has some resemblances to those of their neighbours across the Channel. In other respects, the differences are marked. It is to France that we must return, because it has been French policies which have had the more controversial edge to them.

Although de Gaulle has often been held personally responsible for those trends in French policy which have been coloured by a pronounced resentment of American domination of the Alliance, and which have sought to express the French determination to enhance their independence and sovereignty through the construction of an independent nuclear deterrent, it was in fact a prime minister of the Fourth Republic, Felix Gaillard, who authorised in April 1958 the manufacture of an atomic bomb.[41] Crucial decisions relating to the delivery systems had been made even earlier, in 1956.[42] Although, as in so many other areas, it cannot truly be said that the successive governments of the Fourth Republic followed a clearly delineated nuclear path towards an explicitly articulated nuclear goal, they did nevertheless hand over to de Gaulle's Fifth Republic an active programme for the development of an independent nuclear deterrent. What the programme now needed was a policy.[43]

De Gaulle's assessment of the Atlantic Alliance was not a secret, and the general outlines of subsequent French policy were therefore known on his return to power in June 1958.[44] In fact, the broader contents of his ideas can be identified as early as the Second World War. The problem for those who had the task of dealing with, or simply understanding, the General, was to sort out the bluster from the inner logic. Thus, although just a few months before returning to power he apparently threatened to 'quit NATO if I were running France',[45] he never did go quite that far and took almost a decade to finally withdraw France from the Alliance's increasingly integrated military structure. It was from the outset quite clearly de Gaulle's intention to give priority to the nuclear programme, as well as to provide a justification for it. As one senior official of the programme explained:

The advent of the Fifth Republic transformed the character of French atomic development by the decision of the government to give priority and the necessary funds not only to the rapid completion of the first bomb, but also to a true programme of studies and, later on, to the production of perfected atomic weapons.[46]

Military opinion in France was still strongly in favour of NATO. Although there was widespread support for the acquisition of an independent deterrent, most marked in the Air Force, it was generally felt that a French deterrent would strengthen the Alliance, and that this was a proper and desirable objective of French policy.[47] De Gaulle's more political eye could hardly fail to notice the reinforcement by the 1957 White Paper of the trend towards a nuclear-based policy in Britain.[48] The mixture of references London was making to the efficacy of nuclear deterrence, the contribution nuclear weapons could make to the maintenance of 'great power' status, and economic factors, all applied equally to France. Nor was the symbolic importance of the Sputnik launch of 1957 any more lost on de Gaulle than it was on others.

All this may have served to bolster de Gaulle's determination to acquire for France an independent deterrent, but it does not explain his more wide-ranging disillusionment with the Alliance as a whole. In fact, notwithstanding the comment he had made before his re-occupation of the seat of power, his disenchantment with NATO had not yet run its full course. Thus in 1961 he could still explain that 'What I question. . .is not the Atlantic Alliance but the present organisation of the Atlantic Alliance',[49] and what particularly peeved him about this 'present organisation' was its domination, as he saw it, by the Americans — or, rather, the 'Anglo-Saxons'. Concerned to elevate France in status as well as in power, this assessment led him to propose, in September 1958, a 'Triple Entente' of France, Britain and the United States. This would, as he put it in his memorandum to Eisenhower and Macmillan, 'function at a world-wide political and strategic level' and 'would make joint decisions in all political questions affecting global security'.[50] So transparent an attempt to deny to the Americans the capacity to act unilaterally on behalf of the Alliance as a whole could not be complete without Anglo-French access to any decision on the use of nuclear weapons. That de Gaulle was seeking precisely this — in effect, a veto — became clear in the correspondence which followed the despatch of the memorandum.[51]

Communications on the contents of de Gaulle's initiative continued until President Kennedy omitted to reply to a letter of January 1962 from his French counterpart which reiterated the demand for a combined military staff to prepare 'common decisions and common actions'. There were numerous reasons for the failure of the tripartite idea — one of them was Washington's legitimate concern over the consequences of excluding other members of the Alliance. But for the French, the experience strengthened their view both of the unwillingness of Washington to share responsibility for the security of the Alliance as a whole, and of the enduring and seemingly unbreakable nature of the 'special relationship' between Washington and London. The bonds between these two countries were especially strong in that very arena which de Gaulle had chosen to express his demand for French equality, that involving nuclear weapons. In fact, this Anglo-Saxon 'special relationship' in the nuclear weapons field served to confirm to the French that they were indeed held undeservedly in lower esteem by Washington, and underlined too the weakened ability of NATO to protect their own security and, by the same logic, that of other Alliance members.

There is no room for doubt that the British were looked on favourably by the Americans. Although the Atomic Energy Act of 1946, or McMahon Act as it is often known, had been designed to obstruct the flow of American nuclear know-how to other states, it had already been amended in Britain's favour by 1954. Following meetings with Prime Minister Macmillan in March and October 1957, President Eisenhower announced his intention to endeavour to persuade Congress to relax the provisions of the Act still further to enable nuclear information to be shared with 'other friendly countries' which had already made 'substantial progress' in this field.[52] Not unnaturally, the French believed they qualified on both counts. As a carrot, the French indicated at the December 1957 Atlantic Council meeting that they would be willing to permit the stationing of US IRBMs on French soil in return for US aid to the French nuclear programme. Paris also angled for a dual-key arrangement to apply to any American nuclear weapons on French soil, at minimum along the lines of the 'double-veto' provision of the London–Washington agreement of February 1958.

However, when the amendments to the McMahon Act were finally passed into law in July 1958, Congress — under the guidance of the powerful Joint Committee on Atomic Energy, ever-jealous of American nuclear secrets — had ensured that US policy in this area would continue in its restrictiveness. By insisting that technical information and materials for the manufacture of nuclear weapons could be offered only to states that had already made 'substantial progress in the development of atomic weapons', Congress in effect ensured that Britain would continue to receive favoured treatment.[53] This was certainly its intention. France, after all, had not yet conducted its first nuclear test.

Indeed, as if to more fully convey Britain's status, Washington signed an agreement with London in July 1958 providing for the exchange of information relating to the development, construction and employment of atomic weapons. The agreement also authorised the sale to Britain of a nuclear submarine propulsion plant complete with ten years' supply of enriched uranium. By way of contrast, the only assistance the French were able to obtain from Washington was a supply of enriched uranium to fuel a submarine reactor which the French were to build themselves. In 1964 the Johnson administration ceased even these deliveries — in fact, France received less than half the uranium envisaged in the original agreement.

Although Eisenhower himself was later to complain that the prevailing legislation prevented the development of sensible and healthy nuclear relationships between the United States and its European allies, [54] this has to be set against the impression gained by Georges Pompidou from a meeting he attended between the US secretary of state, Dulles, and President de Gaulle. Replying to a comment made in the French National Assembly in 1966 to the effect that France could have obtained assistance from the United States under the terms of the McMahon Act once the French had, like Britain, acquired their own nuclear capability, Pompidou recalled that he had left the meeting 'with the firm and definite conviction, not without some surprise. . .that never would the American leaders ever permit the subject to be raised. Since that time I have never had occasion to change this view'. [55] There does appear to be some truth in Pompidou's recollection, for it was the French misfortune that they were seeking to become the world's fourth nuclear power at precisely the point when American national policy was shifting, in the words of one Washington official, towards 'not assisting fourth countries to become nuclear powers'. [56]

The extent to which the British had slipped through Washington's anti-proliferation net could not have been more strongly confirmed by the events which followed the American decision to terminate the development of the Skybolt air-to-surface missile, on which the British had pinned their hopes for the maintenance of their nuclear deterrent. Concerned to avoid a serious crisis in Anglo-American relations, and seduced by Macmillan's pleadings, Kennedy offered to make Polaris missiles available to

Britain. They were to be deployed on British-built submarines and armed with British warheads, although American technical assistance was to be available in these departments. A key feature of this highly ambiguous agreement, hurriedly made at a meeting between the two leaders in the Bahamas, was that Britain's Polaris-based deterrent was to be NATO-dedicated 'except where Her Majesty's government may decide that supreme national interests are at stake'. As one is bound to assume that the use of strategic nuclear weapons especially against a similarly equipped adversary would not be contemplated except when 'supreme national interests are at stake', the exact meaning of this clause was, and remains, obscure.[57] Certainly its terms were hardly in keeping with what had hitherto been seen as the central thrust of the Alliance policies of the Kennedy administration, although the communiqué issued at Nassau did refer to the importance of conventional forces,[58] and the commitment of the British force to NATO did represent an American attempt to obscure the centrifugal ramifications of the agreement.

The point here, though, is that Kennedy immediately determined to make an offer to the French on terms similar to those which the British were to enjoy. For de Gaulle, however, the break-down in the nuclear relationship with the US had already gone too far. In any case, the way in which the offer was made in itself confirmed de Gaulle's prejudices, for it looked from Paris like another example of Anglo-Saxon collusion which had been concluded and publicised before the offer to the French was transmitted. There was too some deliberately inspired vagueness surrounding the precise contents of the assistance on offer. The French did not expect to be capable of building their own missile warheads until 1970, yet the American ambassador to Paris, Charles Bohlen, had left de Gaulle with the possibly erroneous impression that Washington would be reluctant to help the French in this area.[59] Nor was France yet able, unaided, to construct the nuclear-powered submarines which could serve as the launch platforms for the Polaris missiles. Again, Kennedy had only recently rejected a French request to purchase both material and information relating to a range of items in the French atomic weapons programme and which apparently included information on the construction of atomic submarines. Furthermore, Kennedy also vetoed the sale to France of a submarine later in the year.[60]

For his part, de Gaulle suspected the degree of ultimate American control of the system which any agreement might contain, and he was wary of the association with the MLF concept which was then under discussion and which the British had apparently been required to accept.

In short, de Gaulle had now set his mind on the independent construction by France of its own national nuclear deterrent, and he took the opportunity of a press conference on 14 February 1963 to reject both the American Polaris offer and the British application to join the European Economic Community.[61] The furore which had followed Washington's recent 'flexible response' initiative only encouraged de Gaulle to continue along the paths of nuclear independence and of gradual disengagement from the Alliance which had already been chosen. His utterance made at the Ecole Militaire in November 1959 — which surprised, among others, his own defence minister — which consisted of those banal but apparently immortal words, 'It is necessary that the defence of France be French',[62] set the tone for a sequence of steps which were already being embarked upon. Having refused the stationing on French soil of US IRBMs not under French control, Paris also decreed in June 1959 that there should be no stockpiling of TNWs in France which were not under French control. This decision necessitated the transfer, chiefly to West Germany and Britain, of over 200 US nuclear-capable bombers to ensure their proximity to stockpile sites.[63] In the maritime field, in March 1959 the French withdrew from NATO command that part of their Mediterranean fleet which had been subject to it. The justification for this was that France had 'out-of-area' interests, in Africa especially, which demanded French national control over their own maritime assets. There were echoes here of the view in the 1950s that the chief threats to the West might by global rather than continental, but there can be little doubt too that the withdrawal was both a means to enhance French sovereign control over their own forces and a symbol of their attachment to that sovereignty. It was followed in 1963 by French withdrawal of their small contribution to NATO's Atlantic Command (SACLANT). The impeccably logical sequel to this was the removal of all French naval personnel from NATO staff positions, although Paris was careful to arrange procedures for continued close co-operation and liaison with NATO naval command. De Gaulle also obstructed the creation of what to

SHAPE planners was regarded as a militarily crucial integrated air-defence network for NATO-Europe. When the command was finally set up under SACEUR in 1960 most of France was excluded from its geographical scope and Paris explicitly reserved the right not to comply with SACEUR's instructions in a crisis. It seems that even this limited degree of co-operation was conceded only because of the French need for access to NATO's new early-warning system, which, under the terms of the agreement, was to automatically feed data into the French national air-defence system.

There was probably very little which could have been done to prevent France's slide out of NATO's military structure once Moscow had acquired an intercontinental nuclear capability. For the French, security in the nuclear age was synonymous with the possession of an independent deterrent. Possibly Washington could have been more open-handed in its nuclear assistance, but the French requirement for national control of nuclear weapons was absolute, and this inevitably percolated down to the non-nuclear levels of military power. De Gaulle's personality did not help, but there was a consensus around his security policies in France which had its roots in the period before his return to office in 1958 and which has since outlived the man. The doctrine of 'flexible response' did not improve matters either, and Paris had vetoed its acceptance by the Alliance as a whole. But the French had become enamoured of nuclear deterrence, and did not see the point of making enormous sacrifices to build up their conventional strength. This rejection of the need for meaningful conventional capabilities was symbolised by their non-anticipation in a 1965 exercise for Allied general staffs entitled 'Fallex '66', which was based on the possibility of a non-nuclear defence of Europe. The subsequent development of NATO's strategy and posture would take place in France's absence.

Part Two
Nato since the Early 1960s:
Implementing Flexible Response?

5 Flexible Response: Washington Changes Direction

The United States entered the 1960s with Eisenhower's 'New Look' doctrine of pronounced reliance on nuclear weapons looking increasingly battered and questionable. Not only had doubts developed within the administration during the last few years of the Eisenhower presidency, but throughout the 1950s Washington's military policies had been subjected to sustained analysis by a new breed of academic strategists, and they had invariably found it wanting.[1] A nuclear response to many of the challenges Washington was most likely to face around the globe was deemed militarily, politically and ethically inappropriate by many of these critics. They were especially critical of the administration's failure to develop at the strategic level alternatives to massive nuclear retaliation. As McGeorge Bundy, assistant for national security affairs, told the new president, John F. Kennedy, 'In essence, the current plan calls for shooting off everything we have in one shot, and it is so constructed as to make any more flexible course very difficult'.[2] Such an action, it was calculated, could result in the deaths of between 360 and 425 million people in Eastern Europe, the Soviet Union and China.[3] Thus, even where the critics of 'massive retaliation' were prepared to concede the necessity or military utility of the use of nuclear weapons, they were inclined towards restraint, limitation and control. This could mean the development of tactical nuclear war-fighting doctrines and techniques, as proposed by Henry Kissinger,[4] or an emphasis on counter-force rather than counter-city nuclear strikes, an idea in favour of which almost all critics expressed approval at one time or another.

Threatening, and planning for, a massive counter-city nuclear response to Soviet aggression may have made some sense so long as the American homeland was outside the reach of Soviet nuclear weapons, as was the case for much of the 1950s. Even then, Western Europe could be held by the Soviets as a sort of 'hostage', for it had become vulnerable to large-scale Soviet nuclear attack as early as 1954, with the deployment of the TU-16 Badger bombers.[5] This was followed in 1958 by the first deployment of the theatre-range SS-4 missile and in 1961 by the first appearance of the SS-5. This theatre capability could in itself quite plausibly provide an effective counter to any American strategic nuclear threat. What really underpinned the thinking of the strategic analysts of the 1950s, however, was their realisation that the happy circumstance of American invulnerability would eventually, indeed shortly, cease to obtain, and the threat of a massive nuclear strike as a response to any less overwhelming act of aggression on the part of the Soviets would appear to lose much of its credibility. Although the American presidential election of 1960 had been fought in part on the issue of the so-called 'missile gap', the accusation by the Kennedy camp that the Eisenhower administration had been so sluggardly as to allow the Soviets to catch up and soon overtake the United States in the development of intercontinental ballistic missile (ICBM) technology and deployment, in truth no such gap existed.[6] The Soviets had, in 1957, conducted the world's first full ICBM test, and in December 1959 had ominously established the Strategic Rocket Forces, as a separate army.[7] However, it seems that they countenanced severe difficulties in their ballistic missile programme, and took rather longer than expected to translate their perhaps surprising technical progress into an operational capability. Thus, apparently only four SS-6 ICBMs were ever deployed by the Soviets, and even these were not operational before the spring of 1961.[8] Deployment of the vulnerable and inaccurate SS-7 and SS-8 missiles did not begin in earnest until 1962. Thus, when Moscow endeavoured to close the emerging cap between itself and Washington by placing SS-4s and SS-5s on Cuba, thereby prompting the missile crisis of October 1962, there were just thirty operational ICBMs confronting over 200 of their American equivalents.

Nevertheless, the strategic context was clearly changing and would continue to do so during the 1960s. The task of the new Democratic administration was to fashion a credible deterrent posture for the age of American strategic vulnerability, for, as the defence secretary, Robert S. McNamara, put it, 'One cannot fashion a credible deterrent out of an incredible action'.[9] In the event of a major confrontation with Moscow, an American president ought to have a wider range of alternative options than either the 'suicide' which would result from a major nuclear strike on a Soviet Union capable of replying in kind, or the 'surrender' which would follow from an unwillingness to launch a massive strike and the unavailability of sufficient military capabilities of a lower order of destructive magnitude. In a speech made early on in 1962, McNamara enumerated the sort of alternatives he sought to create and what he hoped they might achieve:

We may have to retaliate with a single massive attack. Or we may be able to use our retaliatory forces to limit damage done to ourselves, and our allies, by knocking out the enemy's bases before he has had time to launch his second salvos. We may seek to terminate a war on favourable terms by using our forces as a bargaining weapon — by threatening further attack. In any case, our large reserve of protected firepower would give an enemy an incentive to avoid our cities and to stop a war. Our new policy gives us the flexibility to choose among several operational plans, but does not require that we make any advance commitment with respect to doctrine or targets. We shall be committed only to a system that gives us the ability to use our forces in a controlled and deliberate way[10]

MAD AND EXTENDED DETERRENCE

The new administration in Washington was perfectly aware that the provision of 'extended deterrence' by the United States to its allies, particularly when based on the threat of 'massive retaliation', had been complicated by the advent of 'mutual assured destruction' (MAD). A United States which believed itself less willing than hitherto to use strategic nuclear weapons naturally began focusing on the provision of other, less destructive and risky forms of military power. There was too a strong inclination on the part of the new generation of 'whizz kids' which had been introduced into the Pentagon by the Kennedy government to tidy up NATO's seemingly random military arrangements, which had resulted from somewhat unguided force procurement and from unfulfilled force targets and which have since been described by a former US ambassador to the Alliance as consisting of 'a mesh of contradictions'.[11] The US Army had, for good institutional reasons, been lobbying throughout the 1950s, largely unsuccessfully, in favour of more attention being paid to the non-strategic levels of military power. At the end of the decade, General Maxwell D. Taylor, who in 1955 had been made US Army chief of staff, published a book entitled *The Uncertain Trumpet*, which not only afforded an insider's insight into these doctrinal and resource battles but also proposed a new strategy to replace the 'New Look'. The new strategy, which General Taylor termed 'flexible response', called for conventional forces large enough to meet some forms of aggression without resorting to the use of nuclear weapons, and suggested too that, should nuclear weapons have to be used on the battlefield, their use should be at a later stage in a conflict than had generally been envisaged and should be conducted with restraint and limitation. Taylor's ideas made a strong impact on McNamara, and he was later to become the chairman of the Joint Chiefs of Staff in the Kennedy administration.

The raising of the nuclear threshold which a reduced reliance on battlefield nuclear weapons entailed became a strong feature of McNamara's ideas for a reformulation of NATO's strategy and force posture. One reason behind this was his belief that TNW's were often inappropriate for use in the overcrowded conditions of Central Europe. Thus in testimony before the House Armed Services Committee he expressed the view that 'Nuclear weapons, even in the lower-kiloton ranges, are extremely destructive devices and hardly the preferred weapons to defend such heavily populated areas as Europe'.[12] In other words, the use of TNWs by NATO could be self-defeating and almost suicidal. Second, even if TNWs were used, McNamara feared for the wider consequences. In comments he made to the Senate Armed Services Committee in 1963 he suggested that 'there is very little chance of limiting a conflict that has already seen the rather widespread use of tactical nuclear weapons'.[13] This scepticism, even pessimism, regarding the prospects of limiting and controlling a tactical nuclear war was widely shared within the administration, and is noteworthy for its apparent incompatability with the controlled and limited strategic nuclear war options which McNamara had initially extolled and which continued to guide the policies of US administrations throughout the 1960s. Perhaps more consistently, McNamara's deputy secretary of defence, Roswell Gilpatric, confessed that he had 'never believed in a so-called limited nuclear war. I just don't know how you build a limit into it once you start using any kind of a nuclear bang'.[14]

Such arguments as these led inexorably to the view that any use of nuclear weapons, even at the lowest level of destruction, was highly undesirable, because the uncontrollable processes of escalation which they could release could swiftly transform a limited TNW use into a full-scale nuclear war; or, more to the point, it could serve as the mechanism by which a war in Europe could lead to the nuclear devastation of the American homeland. It was not that escalation from TNW use was assured or inevitable; the point was that the employment of nuclear weapons on the battlefield represented 'a very definite threshold, beyond which we enter a vast unknown'. Therefore, the use of TNWs 'should not be forced upon us simply because we have no other way to cope with a particular situation'.[15] 'Other ways' had to be provided, and this meant, with General Taylor, the provision of enhanced conventional capability. Conventional forces were useful not simply because they offered a hope that the dreaded moment of nuclear use could be put off, but also because the very stability at the strategic level created by the situation of 'mutually assured destruction' might encourage aggression at lower levels. Conventional forces would not only reinforce deterrence but could also 'provide us with the means to meet a limited challenge with limited forces'.[16]

But how limited was limited? It was impossible to accurately determine the level of conventional strength which the Alliance should aim to achieve without deliniating, however broadly, the level of aggression it was required to confront and without agreement on the related problem of the location of the nuclear threshold. For the time being, McNamara was content simply to call for more. 'No one', he said, 'can put a precise figure on what the conventional strength ought to be, but we do know it must be more than what we had available last year'.[17] A deputy assistant secretary of defence, Alain C. Enthoven, was rather more precise when he argued that there was ultimately 'no sensible alternative to building up our conventional forces to the point at which they can safely resist all forms of non-nuclear aggression'.[18] More recently, McNamara appears to have confirmed that this was indeed the ultimate goal of his policies, for he has written that 'The strategy was based on the expectation that NATO's conventional capabilities could be improved sufficiently so that the use of nuclear weapons would be unnecessary'.[19] In effect, the Kennedy administration appeared to be hovering very close to adopting a strategy based on an undeclared 'no first use' of nuclear weapons, and McNamara has in fact since revealed that he recommended to each of the presidents he served, Kennedy and Johnson, 'that they never initiate, under any circumstances, the use of nuclear weapons'. Furthermore, he believes they accepted his advice.[20]

FLEXIBLE RESPONSE: PERSUADING THE ALLIES

McNamara, the secretary of defence, along with many of his contemporaries, including General Taylor, did not accept that NATO was seriously weaker than the Warsaw Pact at the conventional level, or that such 'gap' as existed was unbridgeable. The task, though, was not simply to convince the Europeans that they could afford to match the Soviets but also that it was desirable that they should do so. The Allies had already received an inkling of what was to come even before 1960 was out, when it was leaked to the press that Dean Rusk, the secretary of state, had apparently proposed that in the event of a conventional attack of any size on Europe, the response should be a conventional-only defence. Needless to say, this caused something of a stir in Europe.[21] In April 1961 Kennedy gave an address to NATO's Military Committee which was presumably based on a report, submitted in March and entitled 'A Review of North Atlantic Problems for the Future', which had been prepared at Kennedy's request by Dean Rusk, President Truman's former secretary of state.[22] In fact a whole series of hints, statements and initiatives emanated from Washington during these early months of the new administration which were designed to persuade the Europeans of the need for fresh thinking and, in particular, of the need for improved conventional capability.[23]

Meeting a somewhat cool response from the Allies thus far, McNamara decided to address NATO's foreign and defence ministers meeting in Athens in May 1962. There, in a speech which has been appropriately described as '. . .unprecedented in its candour, unusually blunt in its argument, and coldly logical in its structure',[24] McNamara laid bare for the Allies the direction of American thinking and Washington's expectations of the Alliance. He insisted that Washington was not only ready to respond immediately with nuclear weapons in the event of a nuclear strike against any of its NATO allies, but was 'also prepared to counter with nuclear weapons any Soviet conventional attack so strong that it cannot be dealt with by conventional means'. However, the US would clearly prefer to avoid 'being confronted with this choice'; as McNamara confessed, 'I would be less than candid if I pretended to you that the United States regards this as a desirable prospect'. Should the use of nuclear weapons nevertheless be imposed on Washington, an attempt would be made to exercise restraint both in the numbers launched and in the targets against which they were directed. If there was to be any likelihood at all that such restraint could be achieved, then 'unity of planning, executive authority and central direction' — thinly disguised code-language for American dominance of NATO's force capabilities and war conduct — would be essential. This applied equally to the TNW level too, although McNamara was quite frank in warning the Allies 'that local nuclear war would be a transient but highly destructive phenomenon'. The conclusion followed logically; better and bigger conventional forces were required, and furthermore, it was chiefly the responsibility of the Europeans to provide them. Washington had now recognised that 'the brute facts of technology and the realities of military power cannot be denied'. The Europeans must do likewise.

As we shall see, the European response to the quite radical new departure in American thinking manifested by Washington's advocacy of 'flexible response', was less than enthusiastic. What followed was a period of argument and consultation aimed at closing the gap in perspectives which had come to separate the two sides of the Atlantic, and it was not until December 1967 that NATO finally and formally adopted its 'revised strategic concept', or 'flexible response' as it has generally been known. Yet even then it could not truly be said that the decision represented the emergence of a consensus. Denis Healey reportedly once claimed, 'I got NATO to adopt a more realistic policy after 1964. This was tied to actual forces instead of just planning from force goals',[25] and it is perhaps fairer to say that the adoption of 'flexible response' in 1967 reflected the success of this approach rather than any particularly noticeable meeting of minds on a new strategic doctrine. The recent departure of the still-doctrinaire French assisted not only the adoption of the new 'concept' but also the pragmatic readiness to do the best with the forces available and to continue to debate differences in such a way as to not too overtly ruffle any feathers.

The 'revised strategic concept' had been submitted to the North Atlantic Council by the Military Committee following, in the words of the communiqué, 'the first comprehensive review of NATO strategy since 1956'.[26] The communiqué went on to describe the concept as being 'based upon a flexible and balanced range of appropriate responses, conventional and nuclear, to all levels of aggression or threats of aggression'. The communique nowhere used the term 'flexible response'. Indeed, NATO's SACEUR at the time, General Lemnitzer, strongly objected to the phrase on the grounds that it implied some flexibility about whether, rather than how, NATO would respond to aggression.[27] Some have preferred the expression 'flexibility in response'.[28] Many have argued that the variant of 'flexible response' adopted by the Alliance in 1967 differed so substantially from the original model proposed in 1962 by the secretary of defence, McNamara, as to be a different concept altogether. The basis of this argument has been that the capabilities necessary to pursue effectively a 'flexible response' posture (in its original formulation) have never been created. McNamara himself appears to be of this view. Writing in 1983, he noted that '"Flexible response" has remained NATO's official doctrine for more than fifteen years. Its essential element, however — building sufficient conventional capabilities to offset those of the Warsaw Pact — has never been achieved'. In other words, 'The substantial raising of the "nuclear threshold" as was envisaged when "flexible response" was first conceived, has not become a reality'.[29] Certainly it is hard to disagree with the assessment that the strategy adopted in 1967 'differed significantly from the more ambitious strategy which had — with the same title — originally been described by Secretary McNamara'.[30] In short, it was quite possible for the Allies to agree to adopt the 'revised strategic concept' even while disagreements about how it would be implemented and what was required to implement it persisted. 'Flexible response' is perhaps best seen as a declaratory rather than an action policy,[31] an expression of aspiration rather than of fact. It did not, or not necessarily and immediately, mean the provision of additional forces. The debate between the US and its European allies which led up to and followed the 1967 decision, focused in large measure on the rather ephemeral and immeasurable problem of the location of the nuclear threshold; that is, over the issue of when, and in what circumstances, and also in what manner, NATO would use nuclear weapons in the event of war in Central Europe. Their own vulnerability was a permanent factor in persuading Americans that the threshold should be high. Even General Norstad, who was then and has since been generally and loosely regarded as a 'Europeanist' SACEUR, asserted in his address to the annual conference of NATO parliamentarians in November 1960 that 'the threshold at which nuclear weapons are introduced into the battle should be a high one'.[32] This inevitably meant, Norstad continued, 'that our forces must have a substantial conventional capability. They must be able to operate where the military situation permits without using arms and weapons equipped with nuclear warheads'. Europeans, on the other hand, have throughout much of the period since 1967 favoured a lower nuclear threshold, a firmer commitment by NATO to use nuclear weapons and at an earlier phase of the battle, on the calculation that the presentation of such a posture to a potential aggressor before war breaks out should prevent war breaking out. Simplifying but not distorting these positions, Europeans have emphasised deterrence whilst Americans have emphasised defence. As the requirements for these two concepts, and indeed the concepts themselves, overlap at many points, so the positions adopted by each side have sometimes seemed inconsistent, and have not infrequently been less far apart than the rhetoric seemed to suggest. However we define 'flexible response', the remainder of this book is concerned with NATO's implementation of it, if that indeed is what has happened. This will be done by exploring in turn the policies the Alliance has pursued at the strategic nuclear, battlefield nuclear and conventional levels.

6 Extending Deterrence

Since the early 1960s, with the open recognition by the Kennedy administration of the implausibility of a nuclear posture based on the threat of an early and massive strategic nuclear response to a less than strategic nuclear challenge, successive American administrations have sought to provide credible, usable strategic options. Threatening to retaliate in the event of a nuclear strike against the American homeland is relatively uncomplicated, but, as McNamara had stressed, providing a credible 'extended deterrent' in an age of American strategic vulnerability constitutes a much greater test. Some, in Washington and elsewhere (most notably Paris), have doubted whether American strategic planners have met with success in this enterprise, and even whether it is possible to create a believable set of nuclear response options on behalf of others. The most significant voice which has been added in recent years to the long list of those who have questioned the credibility of 'extended deterrence' is that of Henry Kissinger, who caused quite a stir when he said at a conference in Brussels in September 1979:

I would say — what I might not say in office — that our European allies should not keep asking us to multiply strategic assurances that we cannot possibly mean or if we do mean, we should not want to execute because if we execute, we risk the destruction of civilisation. [1]

What Kissinger doubted is the resolution Washington would show if and when it had reached a point of decision which could put in jeopardy the survival of the US itself. This is not to argue that the US would not use strategic nuclear weapons on behalf of its allies. It is to say, however, that no one, not even the Americans themselves, can possibly know in advance whether they would or would not. Of course, no one can know either how much certainty there needs to be about the American use of strategic nuclear weapons in order to deter the Soviet Union. It could be that simply the prospect, however unlikely it may be, terrifies Soviet leaders.

Washington's European allies, on the other hand, have tended to show extreme sensitivity to even the slightest sign that Washington might lack some resolution. As Denis Healey so succinctly, if a little over-precisely, put it in 1961:

> Nearly all the strategic problems of the alliance are due to the fact that it takes a 5 per cent probability of massive retaliation to deter the Soviet attack; but none of America's allies would ever be happy in a situation in which there is a ninety-five per cent possibility that the Americans won't respond.[2]

ASSURED DESTRUCTION

Given the presumption that NATO has failed to provide sufficient non-nuclear capabilities, the US has had little alternative but to endeavour to provide nuclear response options which they believe themselves capable of carrying out, which seem adequate to deter Moscow, and which also serve to reassure Washington's allies. These endeavours have consisted over the years of the creation of a fuller range of nuclear use options. We have noted in the previous chapter how this development began with the Kennedy administration. Drawing in large measure on the language and ideas of academic strategists, McNamara, the defence secretary, sought initially to develop a strategic nuclear doctrine based on principles such as 'damage limitation' and 'controlled response'. This necessitated the provision of a capacity for precise, centrally controlled limited nuclear strikes which kept impressive amounts of invulnerable nuclear strike power in reserve as a warning to the adversary of the consequences of further escalation. Every incentive would be offered to the other side to refrain from all-out nuclear attack — in short, to reciprocate the restraint.[3]

Yet within a few years McNamara appeared to move away from this position and had replaced it with a stress on the notion of 'assured destruction'.[4] 'Assured destruction' was a deterrence-by-punishment rather than deterrence-by-denial doctrine which left unchanged the requirement for 'a highly reliable ability to inflict an unacceptable degree of damage upon any single aggressor, or combination of aggressors, even after absorbing a surprise first strike'.[5] It differed from McNamara's earlier considerations in that it took proper account of the transience of a one-sided second-strike capability. The Soviets too had programmes for dispersing, 'hardening' — that is, protecting — and otherwise rendering invulnerable their nuclear strike capability. Although the US enjoyed an undoubted lead in these fields — the first test-firing of a missile from a submerged Polaris submarine in July 1960 was a significant indication of this — again it would only be a matter of time before the Soviets had caught up. When both sides could hold massive nuclear firepower in reserve, then both the incentive and the ability to 'knock out the enemy's bases' would disappear. It is in fact somewhat surprising that McNamara did not incorporate this aspect of reality into his strategic thinking a little earlier, for it was a development of which many of the independent strategic thinkers of the 1950s were acutely aware. Indeed, the term 'second strike', and the drawing out of its implications, had been introduced in 1959 by Albert Wohlstetter in his influential article entitled 'The Delicate Balance of Terror'.

The underlying logic of Mutual Assured Destruction (MAD) was that any attempt by either side to disarm its adversary by a pre-emptive first strike was unlikely to succeed. Worse still, in the eyes of many, was that even insofar as it was ever a technically viable option for Washington, the strategic concepts which had initially fascinated McNamara had pronounced first-strike implications, both for the United States (for a counter-force strategy to make sense, Soviet nuclear forces had still to be in their bases, presenting targets) and for the Soviet Union (if Washington was to base its targeting policies on counter-force doctrines, Moscow could feel itself forced into a 'use them or lose them' syndrome). In other words, the strategic relationship could be 'destabilised', providing each side with an incentive in a crisis to pre-empt. 'Assured destruction', on the other hand, was 'stabilising', for it offered neither side any advantages in striking first, such was the 'second strike' capability of the adversary. As a result, 'assured destruction' came to be both a statement of technological fact and, at least in American eyes in the 1960s, a desirable state of affairs.

These were not the only reasons for McNamara's shift towards 'assured destruction', however. The development of limited, counter-force options imposed a very high requirement for survivable, duplicated nuclear strike systems which could be held in reserve. This gave the various parts of the defence establishment an opportunity and a rationale for making exaggerated demands for more and better nuclear weapons systems, which conflicted with McNamara's attempts to impose force-size limits on the

Pentagon. Nor was it clear that Moscow was attracted to or believed in the possibility of limited nuclear exchanges, and the potential absence of reciprocation could easily undermine controlled response — as a reply to its cautious and damage-limiting first strike, the United States might find itself devastated by massive uninhibited Soviet retaliation. Indeed, given the growth of urbanisation and dispersion of potential targets, the likelihood and enormity of 'collateral' damage to cities and civilians could be such as to make the distinction between a limited or counter-force nuclear strike, on the one hand, and a massive and unrestrained 'counter-city' or 'counter-value' strike, on the other, virtually unrecognisable and largely irrelevant. In addition, although during the 1960s, and subsequently, Washington invested substantial sums in the endeavour to protect the command, control and communications (C^3) systems necessary to manage a controlled nuclear exchange, there was little confidence yet that their survival could be guaranteed.

'Assured destruction' did not mean that, should a nuclear exchange take place, there would or should be no attempt to limit and control it. On the contrary, the massive damage which would result from any escalation continued to provide the most compelling incentive imaginable to make such an attempt, however distant any prospect of success seemed to be. There was, indeed, no guarantee that a nuclear war would not occur. In these new conditions, war was for McNamara 'no longer merely foolish, but suicidal as well',[6] so much so that he believed that 'no nation could rationally take steps leading to a nuclear war'.[7] It was this juncture in McNamara's logic that spread unease amongst America's NATO allies, for Washington now seemed to be saying that, even if the United States was still prepared to use nuclear weapons on behalf of its allies against the Soviet Union, it might do so in such a way as to guarantee the continued existence and viability of Soviet society, in the hope that Moscow would reciprocate where the United States was concerned. This, many Europeans felt, seemed to weaken deterrence, for it served to lessen Soviet fear of the consequences of its own aggression. Worse still, in pointing repeatedly to the obvious risks the United States would be taking with its own continued existence if it resorted to nuclear weapons, McNamara appeared to be undermining the extension of the American deterrent umbrella to Europe.

The Kennedy administration put into effect a strategic nuclear programme which by 1967 had created a massive strategic nuclear arsenal which, if released, would have caused unimaginable destruction to the Soviet Union. For deterrent purposes, McNamara assumed that it was necessary to construct an 'assured destruction' capability against one-quarter of the Soviet population and one half of its industry.[8] In fact, because of the conservatism in the method of calculation, the United States had by 1967 built for itself a destructive capacity which was substantially in excess even of those stringent requirements. The force consisted of 1,054 land-based intercontinental ballistic missiles (ICBMs), which included fifty-four Titan II missiles with warhead yields of at least 5 megatons each. The Minuteman III, capable of carrying three warheads on each missile, was also in the process of development. At sea, the US Navy had acquired forty-one ballistic-missile-firing submarines (SSBNs), each capable of carrying sixteen Polaris missiles. Again, a decision to produce the Poseidon missile for the SSBN force had been made, and each of these missiles too would carry three warheads. The American strategic 'triad' was completed by the long-range bomber force of over 500 B-52 aircraft. In addition to this strategic force were the land- and carrier-based medium-range aircraft, many of which also had a nuclear capability against targets inside the Soviet Union.[9]

Yet, in spite of the flirtation of both superpowers with anti-ballistic missile (ABM) technology, no amount of increase in the offensive nuclear capability of the United States (or the Soviet Union, for that matter) could yet hope to significantly diminish the vulnerability of either homeland to nuclear devastation. In other words, even as the United States was enhancing its own destructive capability during the 1960s, so Moscow too made a truly heroic effort to hold hostage more and more high-value targets in the American homeland. Hitherto, the Soviet nuclear effort had emphasised the medium-range theatre targets ringed around the Soviet homeland, chiefly in Western Europe but in the Far East too. Yet, incredibly, by August 1968 Moscow had surpassed the American figure for ICBMs and by 1972 had constructed 1,618 deployed ICBMs, including over 1,000 variable-range SS-11s, which had only begun to be put into service in 1966.[10] Clearly this represented a phenomenal effort on the part of the Soviet Union. At sea, however, the Soviet Union did not reach US levels of SLBM deployments. Whereas the American programme of forty-one SSBNs was completed in 1967, carrying between them 656 missiles with ranges of between 1,500 and 2,500 miles, it appears that operational Soviet sea-based ballistic missiles did not reach 100 during the 1960s, and these were of doubtful survivability and reliability, and possessed a more limited range than their American counterparts.[11] The Soviet government did, however, begin to attach greater importance to their SSBN force in the 1970s. In other words, despite the unprecedented resources poured into the American strategic force build-up during the 1960s, the vulnerability of American cities which lay at the heart of Washington's, and NATO's, strategic dilemma, had actually increased massively by the end of the decade. The emergence of strategic nuclear parity, codified by the Strategic Arms Limitation Agreement of 1972 (SALT I), served to intensify the search for alternatives to 'suicide or surrender' which had begun in earnest a decade earlier. If anything, the situation was now even more serious. As the US defence secretary, James Schlesinger, noted in his 1975 Annual Report, although during the McNamara years the rhetoric of assured destruction had been in the ascendant, he was nevertheless able to declare that 'several targeting options, including military only and military plus urban/industrial variations, have been a part of US strategic doctrine for quite some time'.[12] President Carter's defence secretary, Harold Brown, also noted the 'range of employment options — against military and nonmilitary targets' which had been a feature of US strategic nuclear employment planning 'for nearly twenty years'.[13] The problem for the Nixon administration, however, was that the available options which were the legacy of McNamara's years at the Pentagon were all 'large scale' and 'preplanned', thus offering little in the way either of flexibility or limitation. Schlesinger was more explicit still in testimony to the Senate Committee on Foreign Relations in March 1974, when he described the Single Integrated Operations Plan (SIOP) inherited by the Nixon administration as consisting of:

massive preplanned strikes in which one would be dumping literally thousands of weapons on the Soviet Union. Some of these strikes could to some extent be withheld from going directly against cities, but that was limited even then. With massive strikes of that sort, it would be impossible to ascertain whether the purpose of a strategic strike was limited or not. It was virtually indistinguishable from an attack on cities.[14]

Indeed, it seems that, according to one Pentagon expert, until 1974 the lowest SIOP attack option, excluding demonstration explosions, involved the release of at least 2,500 nuclear weapons and, because of its relationship to SACEUR's nuclear strike plans, would almost automatically have triggered another 1,000 or so NATO nuclear strikes.[15] This state of affairs seems to have arisen from the force improvements which took place from 1968 to 1974, which added many more warheads to the US strategic arsenal and which were simply incorporated into existing SIOP options.

LIMITED NUCLEAR OPTIONS

It is hardly surprising, then, that President Nixon should, in 1970, pose a question which has so often been quoted since and which echoed precisely the articulated concerns of President Kennedy: 'Should a president, in the event of a nuclear attack, be left with the single option of ordering the mass destruction of enemy civilians, in the face of the certainty that it would be followed by the mass slaughter of Americans?'.[16] Substituting the broader concept of 'challenges' for that of 'nuclear attack', Nixon reiterated the point in his Foreign Policy Review of 1971 when he insisted 'I must not be — and my successors must not be — limited to the indiscriminate mass destruction of enemy civilians as the sole possible response to challenges'.[17] In fact, it was the proliferation of available nuclear warheads for which the Democratic administrations of the 1960s should receive much of the credit which enabled Schlesinger to implement his own limited nuclear options strategy. The 'Schlesinger doctrine', as it was dubbed, outlined formally in the document designated NSDM-242, offered restrained options and strikes confined to specific theatres and regions, in addition to large-scale nuclear and non-nuclear counter-force and counter-city attacks. There was a distinct emphasis on military and strategic targets, however, both in the Soviet Union and elsewhere in the Warsaw Pact area. NATO's Nuclear Operations Plans were also altered so as to reduce collateral damage, and, within the Plan, the Priority Strike Programme was modified to incorporate lower-threshold and battlefield options.[18] In short, the 'Schlesinger doctrine' involved a shift towards the conduct of nuclear war in such a way as to render it both militarily meaningful and physically survivable, and it extended this thinking to NATO's nuclear use options too. Even so, some observers have felt that, from the targeting perspective, the distinction between the earlier postures of 'massive retaliation', 'counter-value strikes' and 'assured destruction' on the one hand, and the 'nuclear war fighting' and 'flexible and limited options' preferences of more recent years, has been overplayed. As Dr Desmond Ball put it in 1975:

> In terms of action policy there is little in the Schlesinger strategy that is essentially new. There is apparently to be some retargeting of missiles. . . The principal change is the greater emphasis on 'selectivity and flexibility', the drawing up of 'small packages' of targets from which a president could choose, some of which would involve strikes of 'down to a few hundred weapons'.[19]

However, the process of refinement of Washington's nuclear strike options has continued to the present day. Thus, for all the furore which greeted the publication in the summer of 1980 of the Carter administration's document known as PD-59, Harold Brown, the defence secretary, could nevertheless quite legitimately claim that it did not represent 'a new strategic doctrine; it is not a radical departure from US strategic policy over the past decade or so. It is, in fact, a refinement, a codification'.[20] PD-59 did envisage a change in targeting emphasis, from economic recovery targets to political and command targets, and there was, too, a rather more explicit recognition of a requirement for capabilities which would enable Washington to conduct a protracted nuclear exchange between the superpowers.[21] This objective has been taken further still by the Reagan administration, so much so that some have accused it of seeking superiority so as to 'prevail' in a nuclear conflict. Certainly Reagan's secretary of defence, Caspar Weinberger, has admitted Washington's desire to possess a 'margin of safety' in the strategic nuclear balance, although he has denied a quest for superiority. The purpose of such a margin is closely linked to the burden of extended deterrence, for Washington would seek 'to impose termination of a major war — on terms favourable to the US and our allies — even if nuclear weapons have been used — and in particular to deter escalation in the level of hostilities'.[22]

CONTINUING UNEASE

Many of the practical criticisms levelled against McNamara's initial fascination with limited nuclear war-fighting have been applied to subsequent attempts by Washington to create viable nuclear options. Although the survival of adequate command, control, communications and intelligence (C^3I) facilities is absolutely crucial if such a strategy is to be conducted successfully, and although the Reagan administration has been if anything even more generous than its predecessors in the resources it has made available for C^3I, arguably the most exhaustive independent study yet carried out on the feasibility of American strategic targeting and control policies was pessimistic. Published in 1981, it advised against 'pursuing the chimera of controlled nuclear war' chiefly because 'Command-and-control systems are inherently relatively vulnerable' and that 'the extent of their relative vulnerability remains enormous'.[23] It should be noted, too, that many Pentagon officials have themselves doubted the plausibility of controlled nuclear war. Let us consider the views of just two recent US defence secretaries, by way of example. Donald H. Rumsfeld in his 1978 Annual Report strongly suggested that the motivation behind attempts to control the actual conduct of a nuclear war was not a belief in the likelihood of success or a denial of the possibility of disaster, but rather was a determination to do whatever could be done to stave off the certainty of disaster.[24] Indeed, the whole drift of the report is in the direction of bolstering conventional strength so as to raise the nuclear threshold, and in itself it represents an eminent testimony to the unease and reluctance which has characterised Washington's endeavours to design deterrence and war-fighting options in the absence of adequate NATO conventional forces. In 1980 Harold Brown confessed that 'We know that what might start as a supposedly controlled, limited strike could well — in my view, would very likely — escalate to a full-scale nuclear war'.[25] Again, however, the reasons for making the attempt are not hard to find. In 1977 the Carter administration found that a major US–Soviet nuclear exchange would result in 140 million American and 113 million Soviet casualties — the disparity explained chiefly by the differing degrees of urbanisation between the two societies. Each superpower would suffer the destruction of about 75 per cent of its economy.[26]

That successive US governments have sought to create limited nuclear options chiefly because of the need to extend deterrence to Europe in the absence of sufficient conventional-force levels, and that they have not always had much faith in the technical possibility of controlling nuclear war and would prefer instead the provision of military options which did not so rapidly and unavoidably involve the American homeland, is a point not always appreciated in the literature on limited nuclear war doctrines.[27] Neither Washington nor a number of independent American observers have overlooked it, however. Not only has the American demand for greater conventional effort on the part of the Allies, or for a more usable nuclear capability based in Europe itself, become something of a ritual, but some Americans have argued for the withdrawal of the umbrella altogether.[28] There may be little reason to assume that the American threat to use its strategic nuclear weapons on behalf of its NATO Allies would not be sufficiently credible, or at least awesome, to deter any Soviet regime which might otherwise harbour aggressive intentions. On the other hand, there is no way of knowing and many reasons for doubting that Washington would be 'resolute' in a crisis. Too many senior American officials, people who might well have participated in any decision-making on the use of nuclear weapons if a crisis had erupted during their terms in office, have openly expressed their unease about the likelihood or advisability of American strategic nuclear use on Europe's behalf. The Reagan administration's Strategic Defense Initiative (SDI) notwithstanding — and, in passing, it is only logical for those Europeans who seek continued reliance on the American nuclear umbrella to support the SDI programme — the vulnerability of American cities is likely to be with us for some time. NATO's strategic posture cannot but be formulated with this dramatic fact as a backdrop. It is therefore pointless for Europeans to bemoan the reduced credibility of the American deterrent. If Europeans no longer believe it sufficient to deter Moscow, then there is no technological quick fix or more convincing form of political assurance which can restore its credibility. In such circumstances, the only alternative is to find an alternative, one which NATO can believe would deter the Soviets and which its members on both sides of the Atlantic would be prepared to implement if the deterrent failed.

THE NUCLEAR THEATRE

The arrival in Great Britain in July 1948, during the Berlin Crisis, of sixty US B-29 bombers, has conventionally been regarded as the hearalding, in physical terms, of the American nuclear commitment to Europe. Interestingly, recent research has revealed that, strictly speaking, this may not have been the case, for it would appear there were in 1948 only thirty nuclear-capable B-29s, and they were all based in New Mexico. Furthermore, as of July 1948 these bombers shared between them just fifty nuclear bombs, each weighing 10,000 lbs and requiring special facilities, presumably unavailable at British air bases, and enormous effort to load.[29] For the present purpose, the precise details matter less than the fact that the responsibility for implementing 'massive retaliation' against the Soviet Union rested in large measure on bombers based on or launched from the perimeter of the Soviet Bloc. Intercontinental reach had not yet arrived, and Europe provided the bulk of Washington's launch pads in the event of a nuclear strike. Thus, by 1955, American and NATO 'forward-based systems', as they have since become known, capable of conducting nuclear strikes against Soviet territory, exceeded 500 and consisted of carrier-based as well as land-based bombers and surface-to-surface cruise missiles.[30] Subsequent force improvements and additions included the deployment in 1959 of sixty Thor IRBMs in Britain followed by sixty Jupiter missiles divided equally between bases in Italy and Turkey and which 'should be looked upon as a modernisation programme', according to the then supreme commander of NATO, General Norstad, to replace some bombers.[31] This is curiously similar to a justification offered more recently for the deployments of Cruise and Pershing

II (PII) missiles. In 1960 there was also an arrangement whereby the United States was allowed to establish a Polaris nuclear submarine base at Holy Loch in Scotland, and in 1961 President Kennedy formally subordinated five Polaris submarines based at Holy Loch to the NATO command.

Moscow, because it too had not developed an international capability, focused much of its earlier nuclear build-up on targets in Western Europe. This meant that the explanation for the shape of Moscow's first generation nuclear capability was double-headed, in that the Soviet Union was both unable, for technical reasons, to target the United States and had an incentive to target a Western Europe which itself had come to house a large portion of the overall nuclear threat it faced. As a member of the Department of International Information of the Kremlin's Central Committee has more recently put it, 'The Soviet medium-range potential has never been trained on Western Europe as such. It was created twenty years ago as a counter-measure to the deployment of American forward-based systems'.[32] There is some mischief in this argument in that the sequence of deployments has not unambiguously supported the Soviet view, and the numerical levels attained by Moscow's 'medium range' nuclear arsenal has at various junctures appeared excessive if the purpose has simply been to counter the European-deployed Western capability. It is also highly doubtful that these earlier systems had the necessary accuracy to serve as effective counter-force weapons — if that, indeed, was what they were intended to be. Nevertheless, by the late 1950s the US alone had in excess of seventy nuclear-weapons facilities in the NATO—Europe area, and these were likely to have constituted Moscow's priority targets.[33] It is also likely that then, as now, Moscow incorporated high-priority but non-nuclear targets in Western Europe in its overall target-list just as Washington includes non-nuclear targets in non-Soviet Warsaw Pact countries in its SIOP.[34] Nor was Moscow's lack of an intercontinental capability a matter simply of regret and one which time would eliminate; it meant that Western Europe, and other American allies within reach, offered the opportunity to counter-deter the American nuclear threat to Soviet territory. Western Europe was a Soviet 'hostage'.

The first unambiguous manifestation of a Soviet medium-range nuclear capability against Western Europe appeared in 1954 with the deployment of the Tu-16 Badger bomber.[35] In fact, the Soviets already possessed a substantial number of nuclear-capable light and medium bombers. However, aircraft are notoriously difficult to define in mission terms; in this instance, they need not be used in their nuclear role, or as bombers at all, or in the European theatre in any capacity. In any case, there were over seven hundred Badgers by the late 1950s. The Soviet Union also introduced Bear and Bison bombers in the mid-1950s, which were intercontinental only in the sense that they could cross the Atlantic but couldn't return, and anyway were likely to be vulnerable over that range to air defences. It is likely, then, that a substantial portion of these weapons platforms should be regarded as earmarked for Western Europe. The 600-mile-range SS-3 missile was first introduced in 1955 or 1956, and by the end of the decade had reached a deployment total of around 100. But it is with the 1,200-mile-range SS-4 missile, which made its first appearance in 1959, and the 2,000-mile-range SS-5, unveiled in 1961, that the Soviets acquired a clear-cut and quite formidable medium-range nuclear capability. Of the approximately 600 SS-4s and 100 SS-5s which were eventually deployed (by 1964), all but about 100 were located in the western areas of the Soviet Union. As fixed-site missiles, their targets were in Western Europe. There were also sea-based variants of the SS-3, 4 and 5, although the mobility afforded by the submarine platforms which carried these and other nuclear missiles illustrates the awkwardness involved in categorising missiles by range and therefore by mission. It is likely though that, at least during the 1960s, the bulk of these sea-based missiles were also earmarked for the European theatre. Another example of the indefinability of missiles was the variable-range SS-11, first deployed in 1966. Of the 1,100 SS-11s ultimately deployed, 120 were so in a theatre mode.

Although today such weapons, on both the NATO and Soviet sides, would be designated 'theatre', as indeed are their replacements, in the 1950s and 1960s this designation did not exist. This is of more than merely semantic interest, for if a distinct theatre nuclear balance had been identified and addressed during the 1960s, it would undoubtedly have favoured Moscow. For Washington, however, there was no 'theatre nuclear balance' to maintain, only an aggregate American nuclear superiority to sustain. Thus, when the vulnerable Thor and Jupiter IRBMs were withdrawn from Europe in the wake of the Cuban missile crisis, in 1963 and 1965 respectively, it was not deemed necessary to replace them with similar systems because, as one analyst has noted, 'the US consciously adopted a strategy that sought to balance the Soviet nuclear threat to Europe with systems based outside Europe'.[36] 'Extended deterrence' depended on the maintenance of an overall American nuclear superiority which, it was thought, would be ensured by the vast number of SLBMs and ICBMs which became available during the 1960s as a result of the armaments decisions made during the Kennedy years. Geography determined that the Soviet Union did not need systems of intercontinental range to threaten many lucrative targets on the NATO side, even when technology enabled them to reach the American homeland too; geography combined with technology to offer Washington the option of reaching equivalent targets on the Warsaw Pact side from the far side of the Atlantic. Washington chose to take that option.

NUCLEAR PARITY AND THE THEATRE BALANCE

The 1970s saw a modernisation by the Soviet Union of its medium-range nuclear systems. First, in 1974, came the new dual-capable Backfire bomber, which begun to replace Moscow's ageing bomber force. Whether or not Moscow intends an intercontinental role for its Backfire force — and some have argued that this is unlikely[37] — its theatre utility is indisputable. Of greater impact was the new SS-20 medium-range missile, which the Soviets began developing in 1970 and began deploying in 1976, initially along the Sino-Soviet border.[38] With a range well in excess of 2,000 miles, and with three warheads per missile compared to the single-warhead SS-4s and SS-5s, and with the advantage of mobility and therefore invulnerability in contrast with its fixed-site and mainly unhardened predecessors, the SS-20 represents a substantial technological advance. It is less easy to pin down the degree to which it represents an increased menace to NATO. Whereas the 1979 Bonn Defence White Paper characterised the Soviet medium-range arsenal as 'a strategic threat to the North Atlantic Alliance in Europe' against which the West had no counter (p. 108), and argued that with the introduction of the

SS-20 and the Backfire Moscow had created 'a strategic threat of a new dimension to the North Atlantic Alliance in Europe' (p. 128), in 1981 former US presidential adviser McGeorge Bundy insisted that 'The SS-20 simply does not change the balance of danger in Europe'.[39] The invulnerability of the SS-20 should serve to reduce pressure on the Soviet Union to launch a pre-emptive strike during a crisis. Each SS-20 warhead has a yield of just 150 kilotons, whereas the SS-4s and 5s carried megaton range warheads. When combined with the greater accuracy of the SS-20, which has been credited with a Circular Error Probable (CEP) of 320 metres (which means that at least 50 per cent of SS-20 warheads should fall within this range of their target), the result could be that substantially reduced collateral damage would result from a full SS-20 strike. In fact, it has been calculated that collateral damage would be 25 per cent less than would have resulted from a full strike using SS-4s and SS-5s.[40] On the other hand, although there are and, it is expected, will continue to be fewer Soviet-range missiles than formerly as SS-4s and SS-5s are replaced, the Soviets will nevertheless acquire a higher warhead total.

At the time of writing, the Soviet SS20 programme seems incomplete — at least, according to Washington. When the Geneva arms control talks on intermediate-range nuclear forces (INF) broke down with the deployment of the first US ground-launched cruise missile (GLCM) in Western Europe in November 1983, Washington declared that the Soviet Union had deployed 369 SS-20s.[41] Although Moscow was insisting a year later that it had not deployed any more SS-20s since December 1983 (whilst declining to give the actual number in place) and that the United States was wilfully confusing missile sites with missile numbers, and although the Dutch defence minister also publicly disputed the American figures for deployed SS-20s,[42] Washington declared in March 1985 that the Soviet total had now reached 414. As at the end of 1983, the figure had not been broken down into western-deployed and eastern-deployed totals.[43] In June 1985, the US vice-president, George Bush, announced that more SS-20s had been deployed in Europe, and that the total now stood at 423.[44] Again, at the time of writing and to this author's knowledge, no precise breakdown was given, although it is said that about two-thirds of them are pointing towards Western Europe.

Even on the assumption that Soviet deployments remain at this general order of magnitude, with presumably two-thirds of the total deployed against Western Europe, it would appear that the following assessment offered towards the end of 1983 as a result of one in-depth study of Moscow's theatre capability still stands: 'The net effect of replacing SS-4s and SS-5s with SS-20s is marginal when the complete TNF [theatre nuclear force] posture — including peripherally targeted ICBMs — is considered and when the criterion for threat evaluation is NATO military assets destroyed'.[45] Yet NATO arrived at a rather more alarmist view of Moscow's theatre nuclear-force modernisation than this interpretation would warrant. This was because it was not the contents of Moscow's force improvement *per se* which caused the unease but rather the existence of weaknesses in NATO's overall posture which the new deployments drew attention to. More specifically, when the United States had enjoyed on overall nuclear superiority the theatre balance had not mattered. Now that the Soviet Union had attained strategic parity, its theatre superiority did seem to acquire new significance. Irresolution in Washington at the strategic level might mean a reluctance at the theatre level too. Interestingly, Helmut Schmidt had drawn attention to the significance of the European nuclear balance in an age of strategic parity in 1969, when he was Bonn's defence minister, and before the emergence of the Backfire and SS-20s. Observing that Soviet conventional superiority in Europe 'is further reinforced by about 750 medium-range ballistic missiles that have no NATO counterpart', he argued that 'there can only be an overall balance in Europe's central sector if strategic nuclear weapons are drawn into the equation'.[46]

MODERNISATION OF LONG-RANGE THEATRE NUCLEAR FORCES: THE ORIGINS

It has, too, become the received wisdom to trace NATO's more recent and emphatic concern with the theatre nuclear balance in the wake of the introduction to the Backfire and SS-20s to comments Helmut Schmidt made, this time as the German chancellor, in a speech at London's International Institute for Strategic Studies [11SS] in October 1977.[47] This is just a little surprising in that the speech was chiefly devoted to the non-military aspects of Western security and well-being, but what Schmidt did say regarding the military situation was endowed with great significance. He argued that the Strategic Arms Limitation Talks (SALT) process (SALT II had not yet been signed, of course) neutralised the strategic nuclear capabilities of both superpowers — or, in other words, undermined the credibility of the American 'extended deterrent'. 'In Europe', he noted, 'this magnifies the significance of the disparities between East and West in nuclear tactical and conventional weapons'. Thus, in parallel to the still desirable SALT process, and in response to it, Schmidt felt that NATO should make available the means to close these gaps in the non-strategic dimensions of military power between East and West. Although he dwelt on the need to establish conventional-force parity, and discussed the implications of the 'neutron bomb' for both deterrence and arms control, he did not specifically refer to the need to modernise NATO's theatre nuclear weapons — or, as they now became known, long-range theatre nuclear forces (LRTNF). That this was in fact Bonn's wish became clearer in the ensuing months. At this stage, two things stand out. One is that the reasoning behind Bonn's interest in the LRTNF balance had sources not dissimilar from their earlier interest in the MLF — a sense that the Soviets had to be deterred from using their European-targeted missiles by some kind of European-based deterrent.[48] The description of LRTNF as 'Euro-strategic' or 'grey area' weapons, less than full strategic systems but more than merely battlefield systems, neatly encapsulates this perspective. The second point is that it was the Germans, not the Americans, who were expressing the requirement. This was to change to some extent as time passed and, by some, was to be forgotten.

There were other, often overlapping, reasons for showing a renewed interest in NATO's LRTNF. There was, for example, a technological impetus, certainly where the development of the cruise missile was concerned. Richard Burt, who was then assistant to the director of the IISS, but who later became an official in the Reagan administration, wrote an article in 1976 extolling the virtues of cruise missiles as cost-effective and technologically effective replacements for strike aircraft and aircraft carriers.[49] This seemed to echo Schlesinger's concern, apparently expressed as early as 1974, at the growing vulnerability of the American

F1-11 nuclear-capable bombers based in Great Britain,[50] although it was announced in October 1976 that a further eighty-four F1-11 aircraft would be based in the UK. Indeed, in 1976 the US Air Force even initiated a study on the possibility of replacing the F1-11 force with ground launched cruise missiles (GLCMs)[51] Pentagon officials too had argued in favour of the suitability of GLCMs for theatre missions even before the system had begun development.[52] The 1978 Annual Defence Department Report also indicated an enthusiasm for cruise missiles.[53]

There was, too, a feeling that 'something ought to be done' about the burgeoning Soviet theatre capability. Fred Ikle, the director of the US Arms Control and Disarmament Agency (ACDA) was reported in 1976 to have referred to the SS-20 deployments as 'a towering cloud over Europe and Asia'. Why, he asked, 'are they adding to this arsenal? What must we ask with deep concern is the possible political purpose'.[54] Sentiments such as these naturally fed into an arms-control concern with creating 'bargaining counters' with which to trade down the Soviet force levels in any future arms-control negotiations. As such, the 'dual track' decision which NATO took in December 1979, which linked an LRTNF modernisation programme with an arms-control initiative, reflected one of the initial rationales behind the modernisation in the first place, although it must be said that the source of the 'dual track' decision has a rather more complicated lineage. In fact, the conduct of the strategic arms talks which were then taking place between the United States and the Soviet Union not only contributed to a general unease in Europe regarding the implications of strategic parity, as Schmidt's 1977 speech noted, but also created a more specific worry that Washington might be preparing itself to succumb to Soviet pressure to place constraints on cruise missile technology.[55]

It is possible, too, to identify military rationales for NATO's decision to modernise its LRTNF. We have already noted that Schlesinger regarded the vulnerability of the F1-11s in Great Britain as undesirable; indeed, he was reported to have referred to NATO's overall theatre nuclear arsenal as a 'pile of junk'[56] on completing a report on the arsenal for the US Congress.[57] His concern with providing more flexible and survivable forces and a greater range and variety of nuclear use options inevitably led him to question the utility of the nuclear force in Europe as it was then shaped. For example, in addition to describing how SACEUR's General Strike Plan (GSP) for the use of nuclear weapons in Europe is simply an adjunct to the Single Integrated Operations Plans (SIOP), Schlesinger made a number of general references to the need to improve the nuclear arsenal in Europe in his statement during hearings before a congressional sub-committee in 1974. [58]

THE LRTNF DECISION

NATO's response to the head of steam that was building up on the LRTNF issue was to establish, under the auspices of the Nuclear Planning Group, and in the very month Schmidt made his IISS speech, a High Level Group (HLG). That the HLG was the result of European pressure on a still sceptical Carter administration was made clear by remarks Vance, the secretary of state, made during hearings on the SALT II negotiations, again in October 1977. [59] Here he referred to the additional eighty-four F1-11 aircraft which had been based in Britain, and to the doubling to four hundred in the number of Poseidon warheads assigned to SACEUR. [60] In Vance's view, Washington's 'forward-based systems' were adequate. But with the formation of the HLG, a bureaucratic momentum was under way which came to drag the Americans along with it, and over which they eventually took the lead. Thus, by early 1978 and, it seems, in response largely to British and German lobbying, the HLG had agreed that there should be an 'evolutionary upward adjustment' in NATO's LRTNF. This position was supported by the Pentagon but, at least initially, not by the State Department and the National Security Council. [61] In August 1978 an inter-agency study group established by President Carter's Presidential Review Memorandum 38 (PRM-38) offered the White House the option of either supporting the HLG's view or, in essence, doing little. [62] Conscious, among other things, of the mess he and the Alliance as a whole had made of the neutron bomb issue, Carter opted for the 'evolutionary upward adjustment', following which the study group made an initial exploration of the physical means by which this preference might be implemented. A sea-based cruise missile (SLCM) option was rejected by the United States and its allies on the grounds that when its launch platforms were taken into account it would be expensive, that it lacked 'visibility', that it resembled the existing SACEUR-assigned SLBM force, and thus might appear to insufficiently link the nuclear capability of the United States with the defence of its European allies. An air-launched cruise missile (ALCM) option did not promise reliable penetration against Soviet air defences. The proposal to develop a completely new medium-range ballistic missile (MRBM) was ruled out because it would not be ready until the late 1980s. This narrowed the choice down to the Pershing II missile and the ground-launched cruise missile (GLCM). Both systems offered the advantage of mobility and thus, it was hoped, invulnerability. Both too were high on 'visibility'. The Pershing II, albeit initially in a shorter-range version, had already been under development with deployment in West Germany specifically in mind. Thus it was a relatively simple matter to replace the existing 108 Pershing I missiles deployed with the American Air Force with an identical number of Pershing IIs. This, of course, was what was eventually decided. The GLCM offered the advantage of cheapness, both with regard to the missile itself and the new bases which would have to be constructed. It was additionally agreed that a mix of systems complicated Moscow's calculations.[63] Also by the spring of 1979, the HLG had decided that a modernisation programme consisting of less than 200 systems would appear to be no more than a token and ineffective response to the SS-20 deployments. On the other hand, if a number in excess of 600 were deployed, it was felt that this would suggest an attempt to match Soviet theatre nuclear-force strengths. If this were the case, then a 'Euro-strategic' balance would be created which might 'decouple' the United States from Europe by providing the capability to conduct a nuclear exchange confined to European-based systems. The point, in other words, was to fill a gap in the spectrum of military capabilities possessed by NATO, so as to maintain the credibility of a 'graduated escalation' strategy but not mirror the Soviet-force structure.[64] The figure eventually decided on was, of course, 572, a number described by General Haig as representing 'only political expediency and tokenism'.[65]

Some other aspects of the December 1979 decision to deploy 572 LRTNF are also worth noting. The Germans had argued forcefully throughout the exercise that all NATO allies had a responsibility to accept risks on behalf of the Alliance as a whole. Specifically, this meant advocacy of the principle of 'non-singularity', which required that at least one other continental NATO state in addition to West Germany accept LRTNF deployments on its soil.[66] In the event, Italy agreed to accept 112 GLCMs, and Belgium and the Netherlands were to take 48 GLCMs each. In addition, Britain was to provide bases for 160 GLCMs, whilst Germany was to become the home of 96 GLCMs as well as the 108 PIIs which made up the programme. Of crucial importance for the aftermath of the December 1979 decision was the link to arms control which had been introduced. A 'special group' (SG) had been set up in April 1979 to examine the arms-control implications of any decisions to modernise LRTNF.[67] This represented a response to the emerging public unease which a number of European countries were experiencing. The Danish government, which in any case does not allow nuclear weapons to be deployed on its soil in peacetime, even attempted to persuade its NATO allies to defer their deployment decision. The Dutch, responding to even greater domestic pressure, suggested that the deployment decision be postponed pending progress in arms-control negotiations. The US, the UK and the Federal Republic refused these requests, ensuring that the decision reflected the view of the SG that deployment should go ahead as planned in parallel with the search for an arms-control agreement.[68] As the Americans put it, 'arms control should be viewed as a complement to, not a substitute for, force modernisation'.[69] Even though the decision to modernise was unanimous, the Belgians put off their own confirmation for six months, at which point they again refused to confirm whether they would comply with their part of the deployment programme. It was not until March 1985 that Brussels, expressing disappointment at the Soviet attitude towards arms control, agreed to take the first sixteen GLCMs earmarked for deployment in Belgium. Because work on the missile bases had been proceeding in the meantime, this meant that the missiles could be deployed almost immediately on schedule. The fate of the remaining thirty-two GLCMs to be deployed in Belgium will not be determined until the end of 1987 and again will depend on the progress any relevant arms-control negotiations have made by that date. The Dutch decision to confirm was also put off until November 1985 and made dependent on the level of Soviet SS-20 deployments. This added spice to The Hague's refutation of Washington's assessment of current SS-20 deployment levels. In the event, however, The Hague did agree to accept its share of GLCMs.

MILITARY IMPLICATIONS OF THE LRTNF MODERNISATION AND THE SOVIET REACTION

Both the GLCM and the Pershing II are accurate systems, with the latter also regarded as possessing a particularly high ability to penetrate Soviet air defences. With its high speed and short flight distance when compared to US-based ICBMs, the Pershing II does appear to offer the capability to strike time-urgent targets in the Soviet Union. On the other hand, the force is not at present large enough to offer NATO or the US such an option. As one observer has put it, the December 1979 modernisation decision was 'clearly not based on military analysis, or even judgements, of employment doctrine, pre-launch survivability and number of targets to be destroyed to meet an objective'.[70] The military options a larger force would offer presumably explains the US request made in late 1982 that Bonn deploy another 108 Pershing II 'spares' in addition to the 108 which formed part of the December 1979 decision — a request the Germans immediately rejected.[71] It should be noted, too, that President Reagan's defence secretary, Caspar Weinberger, has referred to the role both GLCMs and Pershing IIs play in providing 'a capability to attack hard targets while limiting collateral damage'. The Pershings, he noted, offer 'a high assurance of penetrating Soviet defences' and provide 'the capability to strike time-urgent targets', whereas the longer range of the GLCM 'allow it to attack deeper targets'.[72] The military role with which Weinberger seems to have endowed NATO's still-deploying LRTNF force — as ideal systems to launch against protected targets, which inevitably conjures up the prospect of first-strike missions — has been echoed in Moscow, where GLCMs and especially Pershing IIs have been seen as American rather than NATO systems, and where the distinction between 'theatre' and 'strategic' weapons is barely recognised at all. With faultless logic, a senior Soviet official told *Der Spiegel* on the eve of NATO's modernisation decision, 'We regard US weapons targeted on the Soviet Union — no matter where they are stationed, in the US or in Western Europe or in Asia — as a threat to the Soviet national interest'.[73] Given the capabilities, control and, it seems, the missions of NATO's LRTNFs, and bearing in mind the fact that their targeting is co-ordinated with the Pentagon's SIOP,[74] there is little reason why Moscow should regard the Pershing IIs and GLCMs as other than US strategic systems. Accordingly, it should not have been seen as especially surprising when, in a letter to *The New York Times* in November 1979, the director-general of TASS declared that 'the plans for deploying new American medium-range missiles in Western Europe intended for strategic purposes and capable of hitting targets in the territory of the Soviet Union up to the Volga, represent an attempt by the Pentagon to get around the strict SALT II limitations from the back door'.[75]

It would appear, too, that Moscow regards the new LRTNFs as having a first-strike mission — referred to as 'new strategic tasks' by another senior Soviet official, Victor Falin, in 1979.[76] His Central Committee colleague, Vadim Zagladin, first deputy chief of the International Department, utilised the pages of the Italian newspaper, *La Stampa*, in November 1979 to compare the (exaggerated) Soviet estimate of a Pershing flying-time of four to five minutes with the twenty to forty minutes it would take for an ICBM or SLBM to reach their target. He concluded that in the Pershing II case 'either one pushes the button right away or it is all over. As far as we are concerned, this is the change'.[77] Furthermore, Moscow has indicated repeatedly that its preferred solution might be to 'push the button right away' and launch a pre-emptive strike against NATOs LRTNF bases. As yet another official of the CPSU Central Committee has put it, 'One need not be an expert to see that this would practically reduce the warning time to nil for those European countries in whose territory American medium-range nuclear missiles are deployed'.[78] Brezhnev for his part indicated that Moscow would attempt to neutralise NATO's mobile LRTNFs by bombardment of the general areas in which they are located using high-yield nuclear systems. Brezhnev also highlighted Moscow's refusal to co-operate with the US in preserving the sanctity of the American homeland whilst undergoing nuclear bombardment of Soviet territory when he once more reiterated the Soviet view that any 'limited' nuclear exchange, including one which started in

Europe 'would inevitably and unavoidably assume a world-wide character. . .those who possibly hope to set fire to the nuclear powder-keg, while themselves sitting to one side, should not entertain any illusions'.[79]

Needless to say, there is a strong element of propaganda in these, and other, comments made by Soviet officials regarding NATO's LRTNF modernisation programme, much of it aimed at the European 'peace movement', which had gained unprecedented public support as a result of the decision to deploy GLCMs and Pershing IIs in Europe and whose activities at times seemed to threaten the cohesion and survival of the Alliance and some of its constituent governments.[80] This is not to say, however, that they lack logic or substance. NATO may well be creating for itself a 'seamless web'[81] of force capability stretching from the conventional right up to the strategic level, but it cannot re-establish its capacity for 'escalation dominance'. Indeed, the LRTNF programme continues to leave the Alliance in a position of relative weakness at the 'theatre nuclear' level. Only those fully absorbed by, and into, NATO's strategic theology can feel with any confidence that the necessary 'linkage' between the American strategic systems and the defence of Europe has been secured by the programme. Others may conclude that the constant Soviet reiteration of its view that NATO's 'theatre' systems are, in fact, American and 'strategic', will have the desired effect through the combined forces of repetition and plausibility. It is, perhaps, easier to appreciate how the LRTNF programme may shift Moscow towards the adoption of a 'hair trigger' strategy in the event of a crisis in Europe, than it is to envisage an American president feeling freer to launch strikes against Soviet territory with US nuclear systems based in Europe rather than with US nuclear systems based in the US. Only a larger LRTNF, and one with some more concrete element of European control over it, would be likely to adjust this assessment, and this brings us back to Europe's two nationally controlled independent nuclear deterrents.

THE EUROPEAN INDEPENDENT DETERRENTS

We have noted already how Washington's shift from the premises of the 'New Look' doctrine of the 1950s served, if anything, only to increase the determination of the British and French to persevere with their own independent deterrents. In neither case were there either the resources or the doctrinal necessity to develop more sophisticated nuclear response options as had become fashionable in Washington. In other words, the often unstressed strategy on which Europe's two independent nuclear deterrents were based amounted to a kind of 'mini massive retaliation', consisting of counter-value and ungraduated nuclear strikes against enemy territory. As a result, hardware has been more important than doctrine for both London and Paris, and the treatment of the independent deterrents in these pages reflects this concern. The problem has been not so much the development of plausible strategies — the mere fact of national control has, it has been assumed, guaranteed that — but the acquisition of deterrent forces of sufficient range and invulnerability to arouse a realistic expectation that they could achieve nuclear strikes against Soviet cities. Furthermore, although the non-nuclear states of Europe may have become relatively better disposed towards the British and French deterrents, and although there is now a much wider appreciation of the 'multiple centre of decision' argument by which their existence is generally justified, it is readily understood that neither London nor Paris can, or seek to, offer 'extended deterrence' to their European neighbours. This does not mean that their existence would not be taken into account by a Soviet government planning, say, an incursion limited to West Germany. They complicate Soviet computations, and in this lies their utility. This is perhaps especially so of the French system which, unlike its counterpart across the Channel, remains formally unintegrated with the Pentagon's nuclear strike plans.

THE FRENCH FORCE DE FRAPPE

Paradoxically, the concerns which led the French to develop a strategic nuclear deterrent under their own sole control had a great deal in common with those which propelled the Democratic administration in Washington to try to raise the nuclear threshold by persuading NATO to adopt the strategy of flexible response. In their different ways, each was motivated by doubts about the credibility of the American threat to use strategic nuclear weapons on behalf of its allies. Excepting the British, the remaining European members of NATO, however, lacked either the resources, the freedom or the sheer bloody-mindedness of the French, and had little option but to mould flexible response more to their liking. For Paris, however, flexible response offered neither a strategic solution nor an answer to the French aspiration for autonomy. With its de-emphasis on nuclear weapons and the greater integration and centralisation of NATO's force structure under American leadership, flexible response instead served only to encourage France along its already chosen path.

The most explicit critique of flexible response offered by the French was contained in a lecture given to former students of the NATO Defence College by the French chief of staff of the armed forces, General Charles Ailleret. [82] Ailleret expressed the firm belief in the efficacy of the strategic nuclear deterrent, which became so central to French strategy. Rejecting reliance on either TNWs or enhanced conventional strength, Ailleret argued that aggression should be destroyed at its root, by which he meant 'dropping strategic nuclear bombs on the war potential of the country unleashing the aggression'. The threat of such action, he believed, promised 'the best pledge of the elimination of external warfare as a political instrument'. In contrast, flexible response possessed only 'a rather illusory deterring power'. He went on to express his conviction that 'large-scale wars of the type involving the invasion of European countries from outside no longer have any political significance in our time. The Russians seem to realise this'.

As we have noted, however, the rationale behind the acquisition by France of an independent strategic nuclear deterrent was at least as political as it was strategic. This was revealed by comments made to the French Senate by de Gaulle's armed forces minister towards the end of 1959. The deterrent, he said, 'must be powerful enough to be feared at the international level, well equipped enough to be a sought after contribution in a coalition, and coherent enough to keep the autonomy that would on occasion permit it to act outside the framework of the Alliance'. [83] De Gaulle's outburst on hearing of the successful completion of France's first atomic test explosion of February 1960 was also revealing: 'Hurrah for France', he exclaimed, 'From this morning she is stronger and prouder'. [84] Such strength and pride was not to come free, however, for the impressive effort made by Paris in the nuclear field unavoidably choked the flow of funds and resources into the non-nuclear spheres. Government figures for 1967 suggest that a quarter of total national defence expenditure was being consumed by the strategic deterrent programme, a drain on resources never achieved by the British strategic deterrent. Unofficial estimates put it even higher, at 35 per cent. [85]

Although there were delays in the deterrent programme, the story here is altogether a more optimistic one. The deterrent became operational in 1963 when atomic bombs were delivered to six Mirage IV bombers. By 1970 the deployed French nuclear deterrent was still in its first-generation stage. It consisted of fifty-six Mirage IV bombers, each capable of carrying one bomb, which were available in yields of either 60 or 70 kilotons. Ironically, the strategic capability of the Mirage IV *vis-à-vis* targets in the Soviet Union was dependent on inflight refuelling from twelve American air tankers, which were the only significant fruits of France's 1962 shopping expedition in Washington. [86] France's second- and third-generation nuclear forces consisted of eighteen land-based missiles with a range exceeding 1,500 miles and a warhead yield of 150 kilotons. Budgetary problems had meant a reduction in the originally planned figure of twenty-seven, and deployment was put back from 1969 to 1972–73. The first of France's missile-carrying nuclear submarines (SSBNs) became operational in 1971, missing its original deployment date by three years. It carried sixteen missiles, each with a range of 1,500 miles. In 1980 the fifth such submarine was launched and, as with France's eighteen land-based missiles, warheads reaching a 1-megaton yield are now available.

In fact, in the years since the demise of General de Gaulle there has been little relaxation of the French commitment to its independent nuclear deterrent. Whatever wavering some may have detected during the Giscard presidency has firmly come to an end under the socialist government of President Mitterrand, and the deterrent force has enjoyed a constant modernisation programme. Thus, France's sixth SSBN, the Inflexible, will carry the new M-4 missile, each of which will have six 150-kiloton warheads, which means that the submarine will carry more warheads than the first five together. At least four of these early submarines will be retrofitted with the M-4 however. Furthermore, the Mitterrand government has allocated funding for a seventh, new generation SSBN, which should come into service around 1990, and which should enable France to keep three SSBNs on station simultaneously. A new missile, designated M-5, with which the seventh French SSBN will probably be fitted, will have at 4,000 kilometres a range advantage over its predecessors and will be fitted with improved penetration aids. The Mitterrand government has also made funds available for a triple-warhead mobile land-based IRBM, known as the SX, to eventually replace the existing eighteen missiles which, in the meantime, have been fitted with 1-megaton warheads. On the other hand, all but fifteen of the Mirage IV bombers are to be phased out, although those that remain will be fitted with a new generation air-to-ground nuclear missile.[87] Even before these improvements, a French parliamentary report found that the French deterrent could inflict twenty million deaths and twenty million wounded. Although some have doubted not only these figures[88] but the credibility of the French deterrent as a whole,[89] others have noted that by the late 1980s the SSBN force alone will be able to threaten over 200 Soviet cities or, supplemented by the other systems, over 400 targets.[90] There seems little reason to doubt, at least for the time being, the continued technical capacity of the French deterrent or, more importantly, its ability to 'proportionally dissuade' an aggressor from violating French territory.

The outlook which guides the French deterrent also seems to have altered little over the years in the important respects. Thus, in a speech delivered in September 1984,[91] the prime minister, M. Laurent Fabius, stressed the basic point that 'As far as our territory and vital interests are concerned, we have to rely on ourselves. . .This is why France spends much of her defence budget on acquiring an adequate nuclear capability'. For all the supposed 'Atlanticism' of the Mitterrand regime, Mr Fabius also argued that 'this deterrent strategy cannot be diluted into any Alliance system'. Above all, though, he confirmed the continued faith in strategic nuclear deterrence by asserting that 'France's strategy is a non-war strategy'. Yet it has also undoubtedly been the case that Paris under the socialists has been far more open in its recognition of the importance of the American commitment to Europe, and in particular its nuclear commitment, than is usually the case with French governments.[92] This has been most in evidence in the strong French support for NATO's LRTNF modernisation[93] (which, of course, did not and could not involve the deployment of American missiles on French territory!), which even led to Mitterrand appearing to lend support to West Germany's CDU in its election struggle with the left of centre SPD. The concepts of a 'coupling' of the two sides of the Atlantic and of the need for a balance between East and West have been recurring themes in France's analysis of the issue.

In fact, for all their endeavours, the French have been unable to isolate themselves from developments in the rest of the Alliance. It is probably true to say that Paris has never truly regarded its deterrent as a replacement or substitute for the American nuclear umbrella but rather as a link to it or an insurance against it failing. For the French, as for other Europeans, the extension of the strategic nuclear deterrent across the Atlantic has been a security issue of the utmost significance. Insofar as doubts about 'extended deterrence' have intensified in recent years, so Paris too has shared those doubts, as its policies towards NATO's LRTNF modernisation have suggested. This has also meant, however, that the French have been unable to insulate themselves from NATO's renewed interest in non-strategic deterrence.

THE MAINTENANCE AND UPGRADING OF THE UK DETERRENT

As the 1980s approached, the British found themselves faced with the need to decide whether there should be a decision to replace Polaris and, if so, with what. The Polaris deal arranged with the Americans back in 1962 had turned out to be a very happy one. The system consisted of four British-built submarines, all of which had entered commission by 1970. Each submarine carried sixteen triple-warheaded missiles, and at least one vessel was on station at any one time. Furthermore, it was believed that the Soviet Navy had met with no success in its attempts to detect and tail the Royal Navy's Polaris submarines. Aside from the capital costs of building the vessels and purchasing the missiles, the British contribution to research and development of the system had consisted of just 5 per cent of the missiles' purchase price, and the running costs had imposed minimal burdens on the British defence budget. Furthermore, whereas in the early 1960s Washington's readiness to assist the British pursuit of an independent deterrent had been inconsistent with the simultaneous American aspirations to wean the Allies from their nuclear dependence and to centralise NATO's nuclear strategy in their own hands, over the years Washington had more than mellowed. The US had come to support Europe's independent nuclear deterrents for the net addition they made to the overall nuclear posture of the West, and for the incalculability with which they confronted Moscow. Washington had also arrived at a more realistic and pragmatic assessment of what was possible in the way it approached the security policies of its European allies. London's European allies, not least both the Germans and the French, had also become firm supporters of the independent British deterrent, though for quite different reasons. [94]

In fact, on political and strategic grounds, there seemed little reason for London not to seek to maintain its nuclear deterrent in some form. Even the 'peace movement' in the country, vociferous and expanding as it was, focused the bulk of its activities on the deployment of US-controlled GLCMs and had relatively little to say on the Polaris replacement issue. The initial justifications forwarded by the British for their acquisition of an independent nuclear deterrent had essentially survived intact, although the emphasis on 'the multiple centre of decision' argument seemed the most significant of them. [95] It was not surprising that the British government should seek to arrive at an arrangement as similar as possible to the one that permitted the acquisition of the Polaris system, but it was perhaps less expected that Washington would again be so generous. Yet when, in July 1980, the government announced its decision to replace Polaris with the US Trident submarine system, it was able to do so on the basis of an agreement with Washington no less favourable than its predecessor. Although alternatives had been considered, there were persuasive arguments favouring the choice of Trident. [96] As an American system, the British would again be spared the cost of research and development, and would instead make a contribution similar to that incorporated into the Polaris deal. Furthermore, the invulnerability of Trident would exceed that of Polaris not simply because the submarines themselves would be less detectable but also because the larger range of the missile offered much wider areas of sea in which to hide and from where the missiles could reach their targets.

Nevertheless, the Trident decision has continued to be shrouded in some controversy, and for a number of reasons. First of all, that dependence on the Americans has its drawbacks was highlighted when in March 1982 Washington decided to discontinue the production of the C-4 missile, for which the British had plumped, and to concentrate instead on the more accurate and bigger D-5. The D-5 is capable of carrying fourteen warheads to the C-4's eight and, with its accurate delivery, will mean a British acquisition of a sophisticated counter-force system with a pronounced hard-target kill capability to provide a much cruder counter-value 'deterrent of last resort'. Not only will purchase of the D-5 be more expensive but the missile necessitates the construction of larger, and again more expensive, submarines. It was also announced in 1982 that servicing of the missiles will take place in the US. Chiefly as a result of this change to the D-5, but also because of fluctuating exchange rates, even the official estimates of the total cost of the Polaris replacement shot up.

Indeed, cost is the second and most compelling and persistent factor contributing to the controversy over Trident. Whilst the government has consistently expressed its confidence that costs can be kept under control, non-official observers have been less sanguine.[97] An additional factor, however, has been the coincidence of other major re-equipment programmes burdening the defence budget simultaneously with the Trident programme, leading to the fear that overall capital expenditure might be excessive over the next fifteen to twenty years. The defence review conducted by the minister of defence, John Nott, in 1981, although modified in the wake of the 1982 Falklands campaign, suggests that if further sacrifices are to be made, it is the Royal Navy's surface fleet that is most vulnerable. Given the preference expressed both by the Labour Party and the British Social Democrats that Trident be cancelled, quite how any future pressure on the defence budget will be met will depend vitally on the government in power. The current relatively high level of British defence spending and the country's continued economic difficulties both serve to undermine the proposition, forwarded by these two opposition political parties, that the cancellation of Trident would necessarily permit an enhanced conventional effort.

Third, the very sophistication of Trident has been seen by some as dangerous and unnecessary. Again, it seems very likely that the Trident force will consist of four boats. Although each will be capable of carrying sixteen missiles, it has not been confirmed that this number will in fact be installed. In addition, it seems unlikely that the British will fit their missiles with the full complement of fourteen warheads each, which the D-5 is capable of carrying, not least because there is a range trade-off. Eight or ten seems a more likely figure. Even so, whatever permutation is adopted, it will give the British deterrent a much larger number of warheads than that possessed by the Polaris force, and will enable the British to hit a greater number of targets. Although there are arms-control implications, this enhanced capability is by and large no more than a by-product of the decision to buy an SSBN system from the Americans. It hardly renders Trident a less-effective deterrent, and criticisms of the system on the grounds of its oversophistication tend to be part and parcel of a more broadly based disapproval.

In conclusion, the overall strategic nuclear posture presented by NATO is no less massive nor any more centralised than was the case before 'flexible response' was adopted. The British and French have both embarked on programmes to update their independent deterrents, which will remain the cornerstones of their respective security policies until well into the twenty-first century. For all the hand-wringing which has taken place in Washington over the years, the US has remained unable to free itself from the responsibility of extending its nuclear umbrella to its European allies. Nor, as we shall see, has it been able to reduce the dependence on that commitment on the part of those allies. Even the deployment of medium-range nuclear missiles in Western Europe has failed to lessen Washington's dilemma. On the other hand, the range of nuclear capabilities now arraigned against the Soviet Union can surely only be seen in Moscow as profoundly intimidating. It remains highly likely that the Soviet leadership is more impressed by the West's nuclear deterrent forces than is NATO itself, and these forces have become even more sophisticated and complex since the 1960s. Yet it has not been possible for the Alliance, or at least Washington, to fully convince itself that, because war is unthinkable, it will not happen. Hence we must trace the endeavours NATO has made to alter its force posture at the non-strategic level to render it more suited to the official doctrine of 'flexible response'.

7 The Nuclear Battlefield

If it was not already clear, then the response to McNamara's 1962 proposals left little room for doubting the extent to which European attachment to nuclear weapons as instruments of deterrence had hardened. So great was the confidence in deterrence that it sometimes appeared as if the actual conduct of war was simply not worth thinking about, and this mood was reinforced by a widespread feeling in Europe that war, any kind of war, would be so devastating to the area in which it was fought as to render it unthinkable. Talk emanating from Washington implying a readiness to contemplate war-fighting in the nuclear age seemed itself to undermine deterrence and was thus doubly unwelcome. Given the fact that most of NATO's battlefield nuclear weapons were located in West Germany and that any war could be expected to be fought there, the response from Bonn would be crucial, and it turned out to be a vociferous one. The Germans, however, were far from alone in their initial rejection of the contents of 'flexible response', and what followed McNamara's presentation was a transatlantic debate which in large measure revolved around the issue of the proper location of the nuclear threshold. Although the debate incorporated the adoption by the Alliance of 'flexible response' as its official strategy, this did not reflect any particularly precise agreement on the appropriate force structure, on the role of those forces, and in any case could only take place following the withdrawal of France from NATO's military structure. McNamara had expressed serious doubts about the utility of TNWs in NATO's overall posture, and it is with this central aspect of the NATO debate that this chapter is concerned.

THE GERMAN RESPONSE

Even before McNamara's Athens delivery, the defence minister of the Federal Republic, Josef Strauss, had inimitably described the contents of Washington's new strategic thinking as 'conceptual aids for the precalculation of the inconceivable and incalculable nature of the specific'.[1] This was an early indication of both the tone and the ingredients of the German response under the abrasive Strauss, and it was accordingly not too surprising when at Athens he publicly refused to countenance any further German contribution to stronger conventional forces for the Alliance. In fact Bonn even rejected the veracity of the more optimistic assessment of the state of the conventional balance in Europe which the Pentagon had produced.[2] In contrast to the new American position, Strauss's declared faith in the military and economic utility of TNWs remained high. For example, *Der Spiegel* reported him as declaring that 'An atomic bomb is worth as much as a brigade and costs less'.[3] Nor was he prepared to concede that the use of TNWs in Europe would inevitably escalate. Yet for all Strauss's bluster, Bonn extended the period of conscription in the Federal Republic from twelve to eighteen months and reinstated the original goal of achieving a half-million-man force. Although this move was chiefly in response to the Berlin Crisis, which began in 1958 and which uncomfortably brought home to the Americans and their allies the dilemmas involved in meeting limited challenges with what were thought to be inadequate forces, it showed too that the Germans were far from cavalier in their attitude towards NATO's conventional strength.[4] Another illustration of this was afforded by Bonn's comment on the transatlantic 'Big Lift' troop transport exercise conducted by Washington in October 1963. Congratulating the Americans on the technical competence with which the exercise had been carried out, the Germans nevertheless took the opportunity to reiterate their longstanding preference for US forces-in-being in Europe.[5] In fact there was not only ambiguity in the German position but positive disagreement within the German armed forces as to whether the process of escalation to nuclear war could or could not be prevented. But, in truth, this was not at the heart of German thinking. Even the German Army which favoured stronger conventional forces, regarded TNWs as indispensable. Although the

Germans were prepared to forward economic and military arguments in favour of a continued substantial reliance on TNWs,
their essential function was to enhance deterrence, and this
required confronting the Soviets with the prospect of an early and
possibly uncontainable use of them. As a German Army general
wrote, 'there is always the Damocles sword of atomic warheads
hanging over the battlefield'.[6] And as for strategic nuclear
weapons, even theorising about their use 'shook deterrence' in
Strauss's view.[7]

Clearly there were differences of perspective between Bonn
and Washington, and relationships between the two capitals were
probably as bad as they had been at any time since 1949.
However, towards the end of 1962 and as a result of a domestic
scandal, the ebullient Strauss fell from grace and power, to be
followed on October 1963 by the retirement of the increasingly
out-of-touch Adenaur. Adenaur's successor as chancellor,
Ludwig Erhard, was profoundly Atlanticist in his approach and
regarded the relationship with Washington as the cornerstone of
Bonn's external policies. These sentiments were fully shared by
the new West German foreign minister, Gerhard Schroeder.
Perhaps the most important new face, though, was that of
Kai-Uwe von Hassel at the Defence Ministry, who was as unlike
Strauss as it was possible to be. His preference was that military
and strategic matters should be removed from the public stage on
which Strauss had seemed equally determined to put them, and
this alone helped to ease the path of reconciliation with Washington.[8] In Washington, of course, McNamara remained at the
Pentagon in the wake of President Kennedy's brutal and tragic
death, but Lyndon Johnson's more resigned approach also took
some of the steam out of the atmosphere. As the decade wore on,
so the spiralling of America's Indo-Chinese involvement
switched not only Washington's preoccupations but some of its
forces too, which inevitably undercut the purity of Washington's
presentation of its case.

Yet, for all the changes in personnel in Bonn, doctrinally little
seemed to alter. The close resemblances that existed between von
Hassel's thinking and that of his predecessor was illustrated by an
article he published in *Foreign Affairs* in early 1965.[9] In this
classic statement of the European position as it then was, the
German defence minister rejected the doctrine of 'flexible

response' in its American formulation because it could mean that 'the so-called atomic threshold can be raised unduly high'. He preferred a varient of 'flexible response' which would resemble 'graduated deterrence', for this would enable the threshold to be kept 'very low' and would pose to the aggressor the risk of escalation to the level of 'his own self destruction'. The threat of an early resort to nuclear weapons was favoured by von Hassel not only for its deterrent effect but also because a viable forward defence, so essential to the Federal Republic, though not formally adopted by NATO until September 1963,[10] would be untenable without it. Not only might a prolonged conventional battle lead to the attrition of NATO's non-nuclear forces, it could also result in the nuclear forces themselves being overrun or destroyed. West Germany, and indeed Western Europe as a whole, was too narrow to allow such risks to be taken, and in any case a conventional war could also result in intolerable levels of destruction. As he put it in his article:

> To regard the Federal Republic, or even a larger part of Western Europe, solely as a battlefield, which NATO forces would have to liberate afterwards, would forecast the total destruction of Western Europe. This appears to me hardly a valid objective of defence policy.

It followed quite naturally from all this that von Hassel should reflect Strauss's studied inconsistency on the relationship between the dispersal of nuclear weapons and the process of escalation. Thus, wrote von Hassel, 'atomic demolition mines, nuclear air-defence weapons and, if need be, nuclear battlefield weapons must be ready for employment in an early phase of a recognisable attack on Europe'. Yet he also felt able to tell the West European Union (WEU) Assembly in June 1963 that 'Escalation is a possible but not. . .a necessary and automatic consequence of the limited employment of nuclear weapons'. In the same speech, and even more revealingly, and paradoxically, von Hassel argued that 'When both sides are afraid of the process of escalation into all-out war, this fear will counter the very process'.[11] In time, other Germans were to find themselves arguing that an excessive confidence in countering the very process of escalation, which in the early 1960s had been presented as an enhancement of deterrence, might result in a decline in the fear of war.

It would be incorrect, however, to gain the impression that there was no meeting of minds across the Atlantic, for von Hassel fell short of offering his support for an undiluted strategy of 'massive retaliation' when he conceded in his article that 'resort to a system of total nuclear defence, which would be tantamount to self-destruction, is not credible'. In practical terms — if matter as nebulous as this can ever be regarded practically — the doctrinal gulf boiled down to an exercise in locating the point at which NATO would first use its nuclear weapons on the battlefield, and determining the rate at which this first use transformed itself via the process of escalation into a strategic nuclear exchange between the United States and the Soviet Union. It was hardly the differential impact which these points on the spectrum of destruction would wreak which explained what one German officer characterised as Bonn's preference for the first use of TNWs 'as early as necessary' as opposed to the American predilection for delaying their use until 'as late as possible'. [12] Rather, it reflected the confidence Bonn felt in deterrence so long as Washington's strategic nuclear systems were brought into the account, coupled with a fear that all would be lost should deterrence fail, in contrast to the American suspicion that the deterrent might one day break down, coupled with a fear that all would be lost if their strategic systems were allowed to be brought into the account. For the Europeans, TNWs were the link between the theatre of battle and the deterrent; for the Americans they could become the chain.

BRITAIN, FRANCE AND FLEXIBLE RESPONSE

The circumstances with which the British and French were confronted in the early 1960s differed both from those of Bonn and from each other's. The path of nuclear independence was one which both London and Paris had taken but which for Bonn did not exist. The impact of the American pursuit of 'flexible response' was to encourage each of them to continue along this path. Otherwise, less dependent in at least this respect on the Americans than were their German neighbours, their reactions were perhaps a little less fraught. On the other hand, whereas the French had carved out for themselves a role as Alliance maverick, which freed them from the need to be polite to the Alliance leaders, the British had firmly hitched themselves, politically and materially, to the American nuclear star, and this had an inhibiting effect. Having been at least as quick off the mark of strategic nuclear deterrence as the Americans had been, the British now had to negotiate a situation in which Washington had moved towards a conventional-strength emphasis which London did not share. Of course, the low nuclear threshold which NATO's actual military posture on the central front made unavoidable had in part been brought into existence by the reductions in the size of the British Army. Although London was on record as willing to maintain the existing strength of the BAOR, numerically the German and American contributions were much larger, and it did not really cross British minds that the burden of increasing NATO's non-nuclear capabilities might in any large measure fall on them.

Insofar as the British thought at all in doctrinal terms about where NATO's nuclear threshold ought to be, their views were not dissimilar from those current in Germany and elsewhere on the Continent. Indeed, the 'graduated deterrence' concept to which von Hassel referred in his 1965 article had its roots in British critiques of 'massive retaliation' which had developed in the later half of the 1950s.[13] One of the leading adherents of this school of thought had of course been Denis Healey, and his became not only one of the most influential British voices but perhaps the major European voice during his spell as defence minister for the Labour governments of 1964 to 1970. His ideas were stated at their most concise in an article he published in 1969 — that is, after the formal adoption by NATO of 'flexible response' and as one of the allied defence ministers who had ratified the agreement.[14] Here Healey argued that 'it is far from clear that NATO would be acting wisely in seeking to achieve security in Europe through the building up of a Maginot line of conventional forces', and he enumerated a number of reasons why he believed this to be the case. Not only would it be unrealistically expensive in the circumstances but Healey also regarded the prospect of a massive Soviet conventional assault in Europe to be too remote to contemplate and to plan to resist — in other words, deterrence was working and would continue to work. Furthermore, should a large-scale conventional war actually occur in Central Europe, it would be so destructive in its effects, especially to West Germany, that it was nonsensical to plan to fight one. In any case, Healey went on to argue, there was every possibility that Moscow might simply respond to a NATO conventional build-up by so enlarging its own forces as to maintain its margin of superiority. Finally, it was quite likely that should a conflict occur, the Soviet use of nuclear weapons would render NATO's enhanced conventional forces largely irrelevant.

These were the ideas which guided British defence policy during this period, and they quite clearly reveal an affinity with the preferences of Bonn rather than Washington. NATO's strategy was not, and is not, purely a matter of doctrinal clarity but stems also from the capabilities actually deployed, and in this respect two important considerations need to be taken into account with regard to the British role. First, and in common with other NATO armed forces, the British Army was neither equipped nor trained to fight a non-nuclear war of any length, and would quickly have little option but to request permission to use those TNWs earmarked for its use but supplied by the US.[15] Second, the British, soon to be joined by the French, were able to 'nuclearise' the Central European battlefield on their own initiative with the use of air-dropped weapons of their own manufacture and under their sole control.[16] The ability to act independently of the US constituted the major reason for possessing such weapons, and explained, too, McNamara's unhappiness about them. The possibility that either or both of the European nuclear powers might unilaterally resort to an escalation to the nuclear level in the event of a war breaking out could make a mockery of any peacetime Alliance-wide adoption of a plan not to 'go nuclear' so early.

By and large, however, and certainly when compared to the stance adopted by Paris, the British fell into line in the sense that they did not reject 'flexible response' outright, and they did energetically involve themselves in the discussions which took place in the Alliance concerning the proper strategy to adopt and the forces which should be provided for it. As we have already seen, the French felt no such compunction. The application of French strategic logic, as presented by Ailleret, to the battlefield, is worth looking at, if only because it reveals the extent of the unwavering French attachment to what amounted to 'massive retaliation' or perhaps more accurately to the 'trip wire' concept.[17] Ailleret argued, not without plausibility, that although there was a good prospect that a conventional assault from the East could be blocked by the use of TNWs, they would either have to be used in large numbers or would require such high yields that the outcome would be a quite unacceptable level of destruction. In his own words, 'It is clear that even a purely tactical nuclear exchange would completely wipe out Europe over a depth of 1,800 miles from the Atlantic to the Soviet frontier'. On the other hand, Ailleret concurred with the assessments we have seen elsewhere that a conventional-only defence was not only expensive but was incompatible with the forward defence of a Western Europe that was too narrow to sacrifice territory and which would probably be destroyed in the attempt. As an example of the application of such thinking, a November 1968 directive sent to the armed forces by the French Defence Ministry reminded them that the 'basic role of the air and land forces does not consist in joining a battle they have no chance of winning in view of the balance of forces, but of obliging the adversary to face the risks of our strategic nuclear response'.[18] In practical terms, it could be argued that this was a fair assessment of the situation faced by NATO as a whole, and was simply a less cautious statement of attitudes which were quite widespread within the Alliance. Even so, in declaratory terms the French position remained an 'all or nothing' one reminiscent of the early 1950s, and showed little of the ambiguity which was creeping into the defence policies of some of France's neighbours.[19]

THE ROLE OF THE NUCLEAR PLANNING GROUP

Although it is difficult to trace and identify with any precision, the attitudes of Europeans towards the role of TNWs did appear to undergo a relaxation in the late 1960s and early 1970s. It is a shift which is perhaps best characterised as one away from the earlier rigidities rather than towards any clearly articulated and new stance, and had more to do with atmospherics than substance. It certainly did not lead to an acceptance of the American position as it had existed at Athens in 1962, so it was paralleled if not by a change in Washington's outlook, then at least by a greater display of patience and some readiness to submit to the realities imposed by the interests and dilemmas of its European allies. The chief forum for this process of compromise and accommodation was the Nuclear Planning Group (NPG), the deliberations of which provide a unique insight into the ambivalence, irresolution and inconsistency which coloured NATO's policies towards the role of its already-acquired TNW arsenal. Although the origins of the NPG are to be found in a suggestion made by Robert McNamara at the Athens meeting of May 1962, it did not finally come into existence until 1967, when it consisted of the US, UK, West Germany and Italy, plus one of the smaller NATO states in rotation (Turkey was the first of these). France refused to participate.[20] The motivation for the French absence may be gleaned from the NPG's first meeting, in April 1967. Here McNamara outlined the tasks he envisaged the NPG performing. In addition to analysing the threat from the Warsaw Pact, it could concern itself with 'the research and development programmes necessary to assure weapons will be developed to meet the threat effectively, the determination of the size of the force structure, the strategy to provide for the use of that structure and the tactical and operational plans contemplating such use'. What it would not do, however, was give the Allies actual control over any decision to use nuclear weapons. At minimum, Washington was to insist on the retention of its veto.

The manner in which this limitation operated was perhaps best revealed by the 'host-country veto' issue raised by Bonn at the NPG's first meeting and on a number of occasions subsequently. West Germany is, of course, the most important 'host country' for NATO's European TNW arsenal. For those TNW warheads in US costody for which West Germany owned the delivery system, Bonn could 'veto' their use although it could not, in the face of American unwillingness to release the warheads, ensure their use. However, there were, and are, thousands of TNWs in Germany for which neither the warheads nor their delivery systems are in German hands. Most notably the US alone owns and controls both parts of the weapon system of approximately half of the NATO TNW stockpile in Europe. The host country can neither prevent nor demand the employment of these systems. Although there was considerable sympathy in Europe for the establishment of some arrangement which would give the host country a veto, all that the Germans could achieve was a rather unsatisfactory promise by Washington in 1969 that it would consult with the host country 'time and circumstances permitting'. This arrangement is still in force, and it is not unreasonable to assume that 'time and circumstances' might permit very little in the event of a war in Central Europe. Washington's formal, and perfectly plausible, justification for adopting this stance was that any more genuinely participatory formulation would, given the multiplication of vetoes it would imply and the time it might take to obtain permission to release and use the warheads, be so inhibiting as to reduce the efficacy of the deterrent effect that the threat to use them offered. This meant too that the actual use of TNWs would become more problematic, and it is illustrative of German ambiguity on this matter that they should seek a veto on the use of TNWs whilst simultaneously warning of the dangers of too high a nuclear threshold. The explanation of this apparent inconsistency lay in the fact that Bonn was seeking the maximum deterrence effect from NATO's declaratory posture. Should the deterrent fail, then their concern would be to reduce the damage to Germany to the minimum achievable. In any case, the West Germans professed themselves to be satisfied with the American promise and, chiefly as a result of the arrival of a Social Democratic Government in Bonn in 1969, they withdrew the 'host-country veto' topic from the NPG's agenda. [21] This is not to say, however, that the issue has been absent from NATO's agenda more generally.

The saga concerning the role of NATO's atomic demolition mines (ADMs), largely played out in the NPG, has provided yet another example of the lack of clarity which surrounds the TNW stockpile, and again it has been the Germans who have exhibited the most glaring unease. ADMs, of which there are said to be around 300 in Europe, [22] have a low explosive yield, are purely defensive in their application and, in their very nature, presuppose early use. Not surprisingly, the Germans regarded them as ideal for their purposes, and von Hassel specifically approved of them in his 1965 article in *Foreign Affairs*. Indeed, the first detailed presentation of German thinking regarding the early use of TNWs was made by von Hassel and the inspector-general of the Bundeswehr, Heinz Trettner, during a visit to Washington in November 1964. The communiqué issued following the trip stated that 'Questions relating to the manner and timing of employment of battlefield and tactical nuclear weapons received close attention. The closest agreement was reached of any recent discussions by ministers related to NATO forward defence'.[23] If this was an accurate presentation of the contents of the discussions, then the American side would appear to have relaxed their attitude somewhat. On the other hand, as James Schlesinger, the defence secretary, was to point out a decade later, ADMs 'probably have lower escalation potential than most other theatre nuclear weapons'[24] and were thus less offensive to American sensibilities. Yet the US was to show that it had not completely lost sight of the command and control complexities which ADMs could create when, in 1967, Washington acted swiftly to smother speculation that Turkey had proposed the creation of an ADM belt along her border with the Soviet Union. Certainly, in a discussion paper presented to the NPG in April 1967 and on subsequent occasions, Ankara did appear to argue in favour of granting prior permission to SACEUR to release and to permit the use of ADMs, on the basis that the existing release procedures were too cumbersome for the Turkish scenario — which, of course, differs little from the German one. In fact, the *Frankfurter Allgemeine Zeitung* published what was apparently an inaccurate report of the proposals von Hassel and Trettner had forwarded in Washington in 1964, to the effect that they favoured the establishment of an ADM belt stretching along the inner-German border. This caused an intense, though short-lived, furore which once more revealed the extreme sensitivity of West German public opinion to even a hint of the use of nuclear weapons on their territory. Perhaps as testimony to their recognition of this fact, when a 1966 meeting of an NPG working group was followed by reports that the distribution of ADMs for limited but very early use had been discussed, the Americans quickly denied it.

It was not until the NPG meeting in Ottawa in October 1970 that draft guidelines for the release and use of ADMs, which had been drawn up chiefly as a result of the continuing interest Bonn and Ankara especially had shown, were adopted. Although an authorisation from the US president would still be required before the ADMs could actually be emplaced, the new guidelines reportedly aimed to speed up the implementation of a decision to use ADMs by permitting military commanders to plan to move them from their storage areas to the likely location of their use. If the adoption of these guidelines represented a victory for those

Germans and others who had sought to lower the nuclear threshold in this way and reduce the 'flexibility' with which NATO would be able to respond in the event of an incursion, then one would have thought that Germany would have at least agreed to the 'pre-chambering'; that is, the precautionary digging of holes in which the ADMs could be emplaced once their release had been granted. It seems, however, that although Turkey may have made such preparations, Bonn has never agreed to follow suit.[25] In fact, much of this evident incoherence in German policy can be explained simply by the change in government in Bonn, and indeed, the Social Democratic administration there did rule out the widespread use of ADMs on its territory in 1970.[26] Even so, subsequent changes of government seem not to have altered things, which has tended to undermine any rationale that could be offered on behalf of the continued presence of the devices in the NATO TNW stockpile.[27] Partly as a result of such reasoning, Schlesinger was in 1974 already considering their withdrawal,[28] but it was the Reagan administration which announced in 1982 that ADMs will not be replaced with newer nuclear systems when those currently available reach the end of their stockpile life.[29]

Following a decade of consultations and discussions along the lines of those we have discussed, it is perhaps not too fanciful to claim that a 'European' position on the role of TNWs could be identified, at least in outline, as the 1960s drew to a close. One of the more significant manifestations of this development was the production of a 65-page document containing draft guidelines for the use of TNWs in accordance with the NATO doctrine of 'flexible response', by the British and German defence ministers, Denis Healey and Gerhard Schroeder. Presented in May 1969, it did not result in any definitive action being taken, but did constitute a basis for further deliberation. Incorporating what was still at this stage a German requirement for a 'host-country veto' on any TNW employment, its more important recommendations suggested that the intitial use of nuclear weapons in the European battlefield should be early, limited and carried out in such a way as to demonstrate resolve and signal to the adversary the risk of escalation should he persist. It included, for example, the possibility of a 'demonstration' nuclear detonation, a kind of nuclear age 'shot across the bows'. In other words, Europeans had remained relatively unsympathetic to the American desire for a later first-use of TNWs or, better still, for a level of conventional strength which might offer the prospect of no resort to nuclear weapons at all. Nor were European strategists generally much enamoured with the notion that tactical nuclear exchanges could be conducted with their military utility in mind and with a view to their confinement to the battlefield. The reasons for the failure of these essentially American doctrines to cross the Atlantic and take root require little explanation. [30] On the other hand, Washington was not notably attracted to the 'demonstration shot' idea, and its status in NATO's nuclear use options guidelines remains unclear. [31]

CONTINUING DILEMMAS: NATO AND TNWS

Many, especially Americans, have been highly critical of the way in which NATO's doctrine with regard to the use of nuclear weapons on the battlefield has evolved, and not a few have laid the blame firmly at the door of Europe. As one former American official put it, in a somewhat colourful way in 1974, 'the NATO doctrine is we will fight with conventional forces until we are losing, then we will fight with tactical nuclear weapons until we are losing, and then we will blow up the world. . .indeed, that is what the Europeans think it ought to be'. [32] Even so, this does represent a shift away from an earlier preference for a doctrine which was based on a threat to 'blow up the world' at the first sign of any transgression. Europeans had reluctantly come to accept that an American promise to commit its strategic nuclear forces in an immediate and massive retaliatory blow was no longer on offer and in any case would be worth less than it had been in the 1950s. Yet opinion in Europe remained unreconciled to the possibility that European territory might in any future conflict provide the theatre for any major conventional or nuclear exchange. The result was an unwillingness to provide the conventional strength sufficient to defend Europe without recourse to nuclear weapons, coupled with an obstructiveness in the face of American endeavours to find some suitable military application of the TNW stockpile the Alliance had built up over the years. In short, Europeans hung on to their faith in deterrence, and dragged their feet when asked to think about the requirements of defence, for defence would take place in Europe. The outcome was the creation of an overall force posture which appeared to leave NATO with little chance of avoiding a resort to nuclear weapons. It was a formula which promised the maximum deterrent effect, whilst allowing the US to unhook itself from the dilemma which would otherwise be posed by the need to make gestures which nuclear parity had rendered unbelievable. [33]

A good and recent example of this sort of duality can be found in the reply given by four eminent Germans to the suggestion forwarded by four equally eminent Americans that NATO adopt a policy of 'no first use' (NFU) of nuclear weapons. [34] Having reiterated, quite predictably, that the aim of the Alliance must be to prevent war of any and all kinds, and having pointed out, quite properly, that for NATO to forego, publicly and in advance, the nuclear option, would be to lessen the deterrent, they then go on to present their view of the link between an attack on Europe and the American commitment. They criticise their American opponents for fatalistically assuming 'the impossibility of controlling a supposedly irreversible escalation', and go on to posit the possibility of a NATO response consisting of 'a limited use of nuclear weapons; small weapons in small quantities, perhaps even only a warning shot'. Yet they also believe that the prospect of a NATO use of nuclear weapons confronts an aggressor with 'an uncalculable risk'. Furthermore, although the four Germans do favour 'an energetic attempt to reduce the dependence on early first use of nuclear weapons', they also take their American counterparts to task for underestimating 'the political and financial difficulties which stand in the way of establishing a conventional balance'. What would happen, then, once the insufficient conventional forces began to be overrun and the limited use of TNWs has failed to stop the Soviets and their allies in their tracks? Here, although the language is coy, the message is clear. Not only would it be unfair for West Europeans 'to bear the destruction and devastation of war alone', but Soviet territory must not be accorded the status of sanctuary. More tellingly, the German team seek to establish within NATO 'the principles of equal risks, equal burdens and equal security', for deterrence rests on 'the indivisibility of the security of the Alliance as a whole and of its territory'. In short, once the seriousness of any attack on Europe has been clearly established, then NATO's posture should consist of an American readiness, in that graphic phrase we have already encountered, to 'blow up the world', including themselves. Given the reputations and careers of the four German authors — they include a former Social Democratic defence minister, Georg Leber, and a former commander-in-chief of Allied forces in central Europe — it is not unreasonable to regard their arguments as representing the mainstream of West German thinking on defence and deterrence, and indeed it remains the relationship between these two concepts and the role TNWs play in linking them which continues to divide opinion on the two sides of the Atlantic. Europeans seek to 'couple' the security of the United States and Europe so as to confront any likely aggressor with the maximum risk. This necessitates a plausible threat to cross the nuclear threshold and an ambiguity about what would happen thereafter sufficient to encourage Moscow to reconsider the balance between possible gains and conceivable losses.

Americans, not too surprisingly, find this approach both unappealing and flawed. Indeed, the four American authors of the NFU article — who also include among their number a former defence secretary, Robert McNamara — asserted, in complete opposition to the Germans, that,

no one has ever succeeded in advancing any persuasive reason to believe that any use of nuclear weapons, even on the smallest scale, could reliably be expected to remain limited. Every serious analysis and every military exercise, for over twenty-five years, has demonstrated that even the most restrained battlefield use would be enormously destructive to civilian life and property. . .Any use of nuclear weapons in Europe by the Alliance or against it, carries with it a high and inescapable risk of escalation into the general nuclear war which would bring ruin to all and victory to none.

Any faith Europeans may have that this state of affairs is acceptable because it makes for effective deterrence is resented by Americans who feel their own destruction could result, and refuted by them because they doubt their own readiness to implement it should war actually occur. Certainly some of the resentment shone through with Henry Kissinger's quite recent criticism of Europeans for insisting on maintaining 'a heavy dependence on nuclear retaliation, even while many of them are willing to invoke the American guarantee only so long as the consequences are confined to America and its population'. [35]

Nor can it be argued that any display of American unease concerning NATO's continued dependence on nuclear weapons has been confined either to former officials enjoying the luxury of freedom from the responsibilities high office imposes — not that it would enable their views to be dismissed, as their utterances out of power may simply reflect their likely behaviour in power — or confined to personnel associated with just one or a handful of past administrations. On the contrary, a succession of American defence secretaries have expressed their foreboding concerning the use of TNWs and the dangers of escalation. Thus James Schlesinger, who, as we have said, reportedly referred to NATO's European-based nuclear stockpile as 'a pile of junk' [36] and who was closely associated with a major attempt to inject some control and 'rationality' into Washington's nuclear options, argued in his 1975 Report to Congress that 'it is not clear under what conditions the United States and its allies would possess a comparative military advantage in a tactical nuclear exchange'. [37] It followed that NATO should recognise in its planning 'that the decision to initiate the use of nuclear weapons — however small, clean and precisely used they might be — would be the most agonising that could face any national leader'. Schlesinger made similar observations, and pleas for a raising of the nuclear threshold, during his testimony before a Senate committee in 1974. [38] Another of the Republican defence secretaries of the 1970s, Donald Rumsfeld, also expressed his belief that there was no way of knowing in advance whether a local nuclear war could be prevented from escalating, but felt that it was worth trying to establish control over the nuclear battlefield because 'the possibility of disaster is no reason to make certain that it occurs'. [39] Accordingly, he too stressed that 'the strategic and tactical nuclear thresholds must be kept as high as possible'. [40] If the Republicans of the 1970s lacked optimism, then President Carter's defence secretary, Harold Brown, positively exuded pessimism. Rejecting the use of the process of escalation as a policy, Brown found it 'difficult to visualise any nuclear exchange that could be kept from escalating to all-out attacks on cities'. [41] The Carter administration was certainly no less keen than its Republican predecessors to raise the nuclear threshold by improving the state of NATO's non-nuclear forces.

A PILE OF JUNK?

Despite the adoption by NATO of the strategy of 'flexible response' in 1967, it is evident from the record that there remained considerable doctrinal disagreement surrounding the role of the TNW stockpile, and widespread scepticism, notably in the US, about whether there are any circumstances in which it would be sensible for NATO to resort to the use of even a small portion of it. This scepticism, as we have seen, stems from an assessment of the likely damage which could result in Europe, but also from the fear that the escalation of the exchange could lead inexorably to the large-scale devastation of the American homeland. It is, understandably, not a posture which Americans are keen to put their trust in, and it has been Washington, not Europe, which has sought to reduce NATO's reliance on nuclear weapons. Furthermore, this has been US policy for over two decades now. The purpose has not been to withdraw the TNW stockpile in its entirety, for it is seen as serving as a deterrent to the Soviet use of nuclear weapons in Europe,[42] but rather to create conditions in which NATO has less need to rely on its TNWs in the event of an attack in Europe. This, of course, can only mean improving NATO's conventional forces, but as we shall see, this endeavour has met only with limited success. Should a major war develop in Central Europe, then it is generally believed that given the non-nuclear force balance between NATO and the Warsaw Pact combined with the military complexities imposed on a defensive alliance committed to forward defence, the West would have little alternative but to 'go nuclear' — or, of course, accept defeat or surrender! This is so regardless of the wishes of the American or any other Alliance government. However, as at the strategic level, it has burdened the American defence establishment with the task of finding some way of employing nuclear weapons on the battlefield in a militarily sensible — or at least survivable — fashion. This has not been easy, not least because their allies in Europe have not wished to encourage Americans in their pursuit of war-fighting doctrines which seek to 'decouple' the US from Europe for deterrence purposes and which could result in the devastation of the continent being defended. There are indeed some Americans who appear to be infected by an unhealthy enthusiasm for the development of such nuclear war-fighting doctrines, and some of these are associated with the Reagan administration.[43] But, contrary to the apparently dominant view held by Europe's 'peace movement', Americans have generally engaged themselves in the construction of nuclear use options because their friends in Europe have left them with few alternatives.

An additional obstacle in the way of devising credible nuclear use options for the European theatre was that the stockpile of TNWs which had been built up there since the early 1950s reflected little in the way of any military doctrine governing their use. As we have already noted, the yield of some of the bombs and warheads seemed to preclude them from deserving the designation 'tactical', for they could only be regarded as area weapons. Any attempt to use them on military targets only would inevitably result in massive collateral damage to civilians and their homes. The reach of the delivery systems varied from a few miles, as in the case of the nuclear artillery systems, to manned bombers which could hit targets deep inside Soviet territory. The shorter-range systems seem at first glance to be the most appropriate weapons from the point of view of their military efficacy and, as with ADMs, offer the best prospect of reciprocal restraint from the Soviet side. However, if such short-range systems were to be used to their maximum military advantage, the procedures governing their release to the fighting units on the battlefield would have to be relaxed and permissive to say the least. This, however, would be highly likely to result in their large-scale and uncoordinated application as the servicemen responsible throughout the theatre used them as military aids in their respective sectors, thereby creating substantial cumulative damage. Given the conventional imbalance in Central Europe, there would also be a danger that short-range systems which had been dispersed to the forces in the field but not used by them would simply be captured by the advancing Pact forces.

If the shorter-range systems threatened to destroy the countries supposedly being defended and required a decentralisation of the control of nuclear weapons in the battlefield which could pose its own risk of escalation, so the longer-range systems, such as the manned bombers and the 450-mile-range Pershing I missiles based in the Federal Republic, tend to carry higher-yield warheads and blur the distinction between 'tactical' and strategic.

Their employment would not only wreak nuclear devastation over a much wider area but would also require the Soviet side to locate the distinction between 'tactical' and 'strategic' at the same point on the spectrum as NATO adopted. There could be no guarantee of this, of course. In addition, the targets which most suited such systems would hardly be battlefield ones at all, for they would probably be some distance from any actual fighting. Ammunition depots, factories, communications centres and the like would constitute the destinations of these systems, and they are usually co-located with population centres. In other words, although these TNWs, if they can be called that, offer better prospects for centralised control and can be deployed at a greater distance from the 'front line', they bring with them their own contribution to the process of unwanted escalation. Also, many of the delivery systems for the nuclear warheads earmarked for the European theatre are dual-capable; that is, they can carry either nuclear or non-nuclear warheads. This too would pose a most awkward problem to the military commander faced with the choice either of holding back some of his delivery systems — most probably bombers — for later nuclear use, thus weakening the initial conventional effort, or committing them during this early non-nuclear phase and thus risking their loss or unavailability when the time to consider the nuclear option arrived.[44]

Clearly, then, the obstacles in the way of the development of usable nuclear options in the crowded conditions of Central Europe are legion, but probably the most insurmountable of these barriers is that of 'command and control', at which we have already hinted and which incorporates the procedures governing the release of the warheads from their storage sites to the use units in the field. During Senate Hearings in 1974, the US defence secretary, James Schlesinger, testified that there were over 100 TNW storage sites in Europe, and that although the Soviets probably did not know precisely what the contents of each site were, it was likely that they did know of their locations.[45] Furthermore, these sites were not militarily hardened, and were thus vulnerable to pre-emptive conventional, nuclear or chemical attack. Although Schlesinger, as part of his overall attempt to more closely tailor NATO's TNW arsenal to European conditions, insisted that these sites be afforded more protection, they appear to have remained considerably vulnerable to this day.[46]

The basic reason for the retention of the warheads in such storage sites is, of course, to keep them separate from their delivery systems. The procedure for the release of the warheads to their delivery systems was agreed at Athens in 1962, although these guidelines have been modified in relatively marginal ways since then. [47] Formally, as all the TNW warheads are American owned — except, of course, those which belong to the British and the French — and as the American president is constitutionally commander-in-chief of the US armed forces, and less formally because of the high stakes involved, it is his responsibility to authorise the release of TNWs. Before doing this, he would be expected to consult with Washington's NATO allies, although at each stage in the procedure consultation is subject to 'time and circumstances' permitting. The president's release authorisation would be transmitted, for the continental European battlefield, to SACEUR, who, although he is the commander-in-chief of the Allied forces as a whole, is also the commander-in-chief of the American forces in Europe (USCINCEUR), and therefore ultimately representative of the American interest and subordinate to the American president. SACEUR or, more accurately, USCINCEUR, would then be empowered to release the warheads either to the US-controlled delivery systems or to the American custodial units attached to European-controlled delivery systems.

Permission to release the warheads and join them with their delivery systems is not tantamount to permission to actually use them. Requests to use, which could come from a NATO commander or a member government, should be considered by the Atlantic Council or the Defence Planning Committee (DPC), both of which are political rather than military bodies. Again, this could only take place where 'time and circumstances' permit, and could conceivably be short-circuited by direct government-to-government contact. As we have noted elsewhere, those TNWs for which both the delivery systems and the warheads are American-owned could be used quite independently if 'time and circumstances' did not permit consultations to take place, as the lines of command are entirely American. Under 'dual-key' arrangements, on the other hand, US personnel maintain custody of the warheads. The precise form this custodianship takes depends very much on the physical context, but may consist of no more than a handful of American soldiers guarding the warheads on bases otherwise manned and owned by the host country. Certainly this situation has existed in Greece and Turkey, as has been revealed by an American serviceman in a letter to Senator Stuart Symington. [48] Not surprisingly, arrangements such as these have given rise from time to time to concerns for the physical security and US control of the warheads, most notably during the Cyprus crisis of 1974, when detachments of US marines were put on alert to remove nuclear warheads by helicopter from the proximity of Greek and Turkish Quick Reaction Alert (QRA) aircraft. [49] However, since 1962 the US has been fitting its TNWs with various forms of constantly upgraded electronic locks known as Permissive Action Links (PALs). It is not clear whether all TNWs have PALs, but their purpose is to make it impossible to fire a weapon until a coded electronic message from SHAPE is received. [50] Coupled with the requirement for at least two personnel, one American and one Allied, to actually fire the weapon, it is assumed that the likelihood of unauthorised use in normal circumstances is ruled out. However, as has been noted elsewhere, [51] the centralised retention of the codes presupposes the survival of the relevant HQs and their communications links to the often quite small and dispersed units scattered around what may already have become the very confused and chaotic theatre of war. This may not be a particularly wise assumption to make, and certainly was not in the mid-1970s when Schlesinger sought to improve the reliability of the command and control links. [52] In a crisis the military incentive to release the codes early could become irresistible. Indeed, there is an additional source of encouragement to the pre-delegation that this implies, for US Army Field Manual 100–5, issued in 1976, suggested that it could take twenty-four hours to obtain permission to fire a TNW. [53] QRA systems, chiefly aircraft which are kept in a high state of readiness and are loaded with warheads which need to be 'fused' or 'armed' by US servicemen obviously pose problems all of their own, but at least the introduction of PALs has improved the situation from that which pertained in 1960, when members of the US Joint Committee on Atomic Energy visited Europe and 'found fighter aircraft loaded with nuclear bombs sitting on the edge of runways with German pilots inside the cockpits and starter plugs inserted. The embodiment of control was an American officer somewhere in the vicinity with a revolver'. [54]

THE NEUTRON BOMB DEBACLE

For all Schlesinger's evident dissatisfaction with NATO's dependence on the use of nuclear weapons, he nevertheless believed that the 'pile of junk' needed tidying up in order that it might permit some possibility of rational, orderly use. Thus he sought 'improved doctrines for the tactical use of nuclear weapons' which would give the Alliance 'the ability to control escalation'.[55] Although when asked whether 'weapons of the yield which we now have in Europe could be used without catastrophic damage to civilians and civilian facilities' Schlesinger's answer was an unqualified 'yes',[56] he also believed that it remained necessary 'to continue to seek more accurate systems and more lethal effects from lower yields to improve military effectiveness and decrease unwanted damage'.[57] This was true even though he testified that the average yield of TNWs in Europe stood in 1974 at less than 4 kilotons, a considerable reduction from earlier levels.[58] It is probably fair to report that this 'miniaturisation' of warhead yields which had gradually evolved over the years, itself reflected a persisting American desire to create the sort of stockpile that Schlesinger was now specifying, and for the same reasons as he was now giving. Yet 'mini-nukes', as low-yield nuclear warheads are sometimes called, inevitably raise the spectre of nuclear war-fighting in Europe, and in doing so bring to the fore in a particularly dramatic fashion NATO's continuing uncertainty with regard to the role of TNWs in Europe. There has been no better illustration of this than the furore which surrounded the proposed production and deployment in Europe of the Enhanced Radiation Weapon (ERW), or 'neutron bomb' as it is more popularly known. In fact the political fallout from this debate could well bedevil and even undermine NATO's force posture and doctrinal modifications for some time to come. At a minimum, the 'neutron bomb' debate resurrected and strengthened Europe's — and North America's — long dormant anti-nuclear, pacifist and, in Europe, neutralist sentiments, and served as a 'practice run' for the comparable fuss which accompanied the LRTNF decision of late 1979. Similarly, NATO's governments and officials were so dismayed by the disunity and vacillation they had displayed during the events of 1977 and 1978 that their relatively high degree of determination to persevere with the LRTNF decision can only be understood in the light of these events. Nowhere was this impact more marked than in Washington, which not only overcame its inital coolness towards LRTNF modernisation but purposefully took the responsibility for leading the Alliance through this awkward period. In passing, it ought also to be noted that it was during the 'neutron bomb' debate that the Soviet Union discovered, quite possibly to its own surprise, how fruitful an active intervention in the security debates of its democratic adversaries could be, and they too used the experience they had gained from it to interfere in the LRTNF controversies.

The emergence of the public arguments surrounding the 'neutron bomb' which broke out on both sides of the Atlantic can be traced to the publication of an article by Walter Pincus in *The Washington Post* on 4 June 1977.[59] Here, Pincus claimed, incorrectly it seems,[60] that funding for the development of ERW warheads for the Lance missile and for the 8-inch artillery projectile was being 'hidden' in the Energy Research and Development Administration budget. This accusation of secrecy provided a provocative backcloth to the emotional tenor of a *Post* editorial on the same day, which declared that the ERW 'could be construed as another form of chemical warfare' and was 'the last thing anyone should want for the American arsenal'. What was to become a central tenet of the ERW's opponents was incorporated into the editorial when it asserted that the ERW would be 'regarded by the military as being sufficiently small, "safe" and controllable to be used without fear of starting a general nuclear war'.[61] In other words, it was being argued that the ERW threatened to lower the nuclear threshold by providing the military with a nuclear weapon they would be willing to use. NATO would be less 'self-deterred' from its use through fear of the collateral damage to its own side, and escalation would be less likely presumably because both NATO and the Warsaw Pact would recognise that a 'firebreak' existed between neutron and other forms of nuclear weapon. The 'neutron bomb' offered the prospect — or the risk, depending on one's point of view — of 'conventionalising' nuclear war in Europe, or indeed elsewhere. Along similar lines as these, the *Post* developed and extended its attack on the ERW three weeks later when it argued that:

By making a tactical nuclear response more feasible, it would sap the European allies' incentive to plug the NATO deficit in conventional forces; it would set NATO's nuclear forces on more of a hair trigger. . .and it would commit NATO more deeply to the dangerous premise that a small nuclear exchange can be conducted without serious risk of expanding into a general nuclear war.[62]

Senator Mark Hatfield, who was no less determined in his opposition to the ERW than was Walter Pincus at the *Post*, similarly argued that the 'precision' of the weapon, the ability it appeared to offer to discriminate between military and civilian targets, meant that 'there is more temptation to use it. . .and once we introduce nuclear weaponry into conventional warfare, we're on our way'.[63] As just one indication of the emotional tone which suffused the whole issue, Senator Hatfield saw fit to declare the ERW to be 'in the realm of the unconscionable'.[64]

Not surprisingly, feelings on the European side of the Atlantic were, if anything, even more intense and emotionally charged. Almost every country saw mass demonstrations, mass petitions and splits within the political parties of the democratic Left. In West Germany the editor of *Die Zeit* felt that the atmosphere resembled that ugly part of the 1950s when the country was similarly torn on nuclear issues;[65] it was certainly the case that reason and logic did not always enjoy a particularly high profile during the ERW debate. For example, Egon Bahr, the secretary-general of the ruling Social Democratic Party, said of the ERW that, 'Feeling and conscience rebel against it', and he went on to wonder, 'Is mankind turning mad? . . .Our scale of values is being turned upside down. The object now is the preservation of matter; mankind has become a secondary consideration. . .The neutron bomb symbolises the perversion of thinking'.[66] Willy Brandt, the SPD chairman and former German chancellor, and Karsten Voigt, an influential figure on the left of the Party, shared with Bahr a fear that the ERW would lower the nuclear threshold and make nuclear war in Europe 'thinkable'. With Chancellor Helmut Schmidt and other leading members of the Party if not quite favouring deployment then at least leaning in that direction, it was perhaps unavoidable that at its party congress in Hamburg in November 1977 the SPD fudged the issue somewhat and ratified by a narrow majority an ambiguous resolution which stated that 'There are not only overarching moral but also military. . .and arms-control arguments against the development, deployment and stationing of neutron weapons. . .We ask the Federal government to pursue a security and disarmament policy which would. . .make the stationing of neutron weapons on German soil unnecessary'. What the government was to do in the event that such policies failed to bear fruit was left open, it seems. In any case, the passion was not confined to the SPD, for members of both the Protestant Church and the burgeoning ecological movement joined the fray. Indeed, the unease was more widespread still, for a public opinion poll conducted in October 1977 found that only 28 per cent of the three-quarters of the population who knew of the issue declared themselves in favour of the view that the 'equipment of NATO forces with neutron weapons would make western Europe's defence more secure'.

After the Federal Republic, the next most seriously affected NATO member state was the Netherlands. A deeply Christian country with a history of neutralism and with a Labour Party both influential and long attracted to unilateralism, the Netherlands saw the numerically and usually politically insignificant Communist Party play a major role in its anti-neutron bomb movement. [67] In addition to the usual demonstrations, a petition opposing the ERW had apparently been signed by over a million people by April 1978. The position of the already vulnerable coalition government was weakened still further by the opposition of a majority in Parliament to the neutron weapon. Another blow came with the resignation of the Dutch defence minister, Rudolph Kruisinga, because of his moral outrage at the weapon and because of the government's refusal to reject the ERW outright. [68] In fact, the Dutch government eventually refused to commit itself to deployment until arms control had been tried, a position which was to find its echo in December 1979 with the decision to modernise NATO's LRTNF.

Moscow was neither slow nor unskilled in exploiting this widespread opposition to the ERW in the Western democracies. Just two weeks after *The Washington Post's* revelations of 4 June 1977, *Pravda* was sympathising with the technically quite erroneous view that the ERW was 'practically a chemical warfare weapon'. [69] In December 1977 Brezhnev extravagantly referred to the ERW as an 'inhuman weapon' and a weapon of 'mass annihilation'. Echoing, and perhaps prompting, some of the arguments put by the ERW's Western opponents, he suggested that 'attempts are being made to erase the distinction between conventional and nuclear arms' and that it was this that made the ERW 'especially dangerous'. Needless to say, Brezhnev went on to promise that if development was not halted, Moscow would answer the challenge, but he also adopted a more sophisticated approach with his attempt to establish a common cause with West Europeans whilst excluding the US by suggesting that 'Maybe this is an easy and simple matter for those who live far from Europe, but the Europeans, who live, figuratively speaking, under one roof, are of a different opinion'. In January 1978 Brezhnev followed this up by sending what were by all accounts very toughly worded letters to each NATO government individually. Other Soviet and Warsaw Pact leaders made similar points whenever the opportunity arose, and Moscow utilised a range of other devices to stoke the NATO fires. For example, the Soviet delegations to both the Geneva disarmament conference and the Conference on Security and Co-operation in Europe (CSCE) review conference in Belgrade issued denunciations of the ERW, whilst in March thirty-one very eminent Soviet scientists wrote to President Carter urging him to desist from any plans to produce and deploy the weapons. And it was not only in the Netherlands that the Soviet Union used front organisations to penetrate and lead Europe's 'peace' movements, although the Soviet ambassador in The Hague was unique in being singled out and honoured by Moscow for his efforts. [70]

Much was revealed by the 'neutron bomb debate' about Western attitudes towards TNWs generally, and not the least important of these revelations was the extent to which, albeit for entirely different reasons and unwittingly and unintentionally, those on the left of Western Europe's political spectrum had come to share with successive American administrations a scepticism regarding the role of NATO's TNW stockpile in Europe. This unlikely 'alliance' had in fact been immanent in the situation for some time, but had been, and continues to be, hidden from view by the Left's autonomous anti-Americanism and the fact there is precious little else on which the two 'sides' can agree. But it remains true that just as Washington has sought to avoid excessive reliance on TNWs through fear that their use might set in train a process of escalation, so the 'peace' movement in Europe cannot contemplate the use of TNWs in Europe through fear of the damage it would do to their homelands. It is not coincidental that both Washington and its European opponents sometimes display very vivid imaginations in their contemplations of the nuclear holocaust and are both prone to worry that the deterrent might fail. This contrasts with the general reluctance shown in Europe's capitals to consider the possibility that the nuclear deterrent might fail, and to ponder the aftermath of such a failure.

But what was it about the ERW that created so much emotion? Simply put, an ERW alters the usual balance between the heat, blast and prompt radiation effects of a nuclear detonation.[71] The heat and blast effects, which account for most of the physical, including collateral, damage created by a nuclear explosion, is substantially reduced. It is easy to see why the use of such weapons in the crowded central European theatre, where houses, villages and towns are never far away, would appear to be relatively advantageous to a defensive alliance quite possibly using nuclear weapons on or near its own territory. Two types of ERW warheads were under scrutiny. For the Lance surface-to-surface missile, which has a range of around seventy miles, a variable-yield warhead which could be set at less than or just over 1 kiloton was available to replace the existing fission warheads with yields ranging from 1 to 100 kilotons. For the 8-inch artillery shell, an ERW warhead offering a choice of three yields had been developed, ranging from well below 1 kiloton to two kilotons. Again, the degree of 'miniaturisation' was impressive, for the existing warheads ranged from 5 to 10 kilotons in yield. Even so, some of the claims that they offered a practically collateral damage-free battlefield were wildly overdrawn. On the other hand, the accusation levelled by the opponents of the ERW that it killed people and left buildings intact is difficult to answer in a rational way. Should such people be reassured by the revelation that, after all, the neutron bombs on offer destroy buildings too?

Stripped as far as possible of emotion, the possible introduction of ERWs into Europe served to focus on two basically overlapping sets of questions. One set was concerned with the uncertainty regarding the actual physical impact of the weapons. Would the collateral damage resulting from the more or less widespread use of ERWs be substantially less than that caused by use of the existing TNWs? Would the impact of ERW detonations be essentially confined to the tank crews and invading forces generally of the Warsaw Pact, or would such weapons in fact turn out to be hardly less indiscrimate than other types of nuclear weapons? In short, do ERWs combine military efficacy with a greater 'humanity'? The second set of questions even more explicitly spilt over into the whole issue of the role of battlefield nuclear weapons in NATO's strategy, and those considerations which were applied to ERWs could arguably be extended to cover the so-called 'mini-nukes' more generally. These questions swirled around the opposing views of those that believed that ERWs, and presumably other low-yield nuclear weapons, are more likely to be used, and used more freely, because they appear to be more acceptable, more discriminating, and others who insisted that precisely because ERWs seemed to lower NATO's nuclear threshold, they were thus less likely to be used, because they enhanced NATO's deterrent posture by making the threat to cross that threshold more believable, more credible. As the Supreme Allied Commander, General Haig, put it in March 1978. 'The utility of the weapon, its usability, its credibility generally in deterrence terms contributes to the reality that it will not have to be used'. The neutron bomb, he said, 'raises, not lowers, the nuclear threshold'. [72]

Let us take the questions relating to the physical impact, and thus the military utility, of the weapon first. The 'father' of the ERW, S. T. Cohen, has claimed that for bursts at 3,000 feet above ground level, 'significant urban structural damage from ER weapons essentially disappears'. [73] This, of course, is precisely the advantage the ERW is supposed to offer, but the picture is clouded when the impact of prompt radiation within the areas in which ERWs have been used is considered. It has been estimated that although radiation levels at distances in excess of 1.7 kilometres would not be sufficient to immediately incapacitate, about 10 per cent of people within this area could be expected to die within a few months, and for up to thirty years later there would be a high incidence of cancer of various kinds and of harmful genetic effects. The neutrons of the ERW are in fact more lethal in this respect than the gamma rays of fission weapons. Thus a former American presidential advisor, George Kistiakowsky, has concluded that:

Perhaps the number of prompt deaths of bystander civilians would be modest, but when delayed deaths following radiation sickness. . .are counted in, it ceases to be obvious that the use of ERWs will be much less disastrous to the civilian population in Western Europe, especially in the Federal Republic of Germany, than the use of fission warheads. [74]

Indeed, even the proponents of the neutron bomb concede this point, although they tend also to be more sanguine about the prospects for the protection of the civilian population against such effects. [75]

An additional problem with the ERW is that its upper yield limit is low. Put another way, a 1-kiloton ERW may have a radius of military effectiveness equal to that of a 10-kiloton fission bomb, but it simply cannot substitute for higher-yield fission weapons unless used in barrages. This is an important drawback in a number of ways, one of them being that Warsaw Pact tank tactics take into account the need to disperse in a nuclear battle-field and would concentrate only at the critical moment — when NATO defences are less than a kilometre away. A NATO use of ERWs at such a juncture would irradiate its own forces. In any case, any opportunity of this kind which did present itself to the defending forces would last no more than a few minutes, and we have already noted problems which could arise in obtaining permission to use TNWs in time. [76] Thus, a militarily effective use of ERWs — indeed, of any battlefield nuclear weapons — would seem to require prior devolution of the decision to use the weapons to the field commanders. And if they in turn are to use them effectively, they must use them early, before a Warsaw Pact breakthrough deep into NATO territory has been effected. [77] The alternative would be to launch barrages, or packages, of low-yield nuclear weapons, such as ERWs, to cover the whole area through which Pact tank forces are dispersed; in fact, the revised 1977 version of the US Army Field Manual did call for nuclear weapons to be fired in packages of fifty or more within short periods of time. [78] Given the inherent difficulties of target acqui-sition in a highly mobile battlefield, it would appear that NATO forces would in fact have little alternative to adopting such tactics. However, a major Warsaw Pact attack would involve thousands of tanks and other armoured vehicles, probably trying to achieve a number of breakthroughs simultaneously. Thousands of ER war-heads would be required to blunt attacks such as these, and very large areas of West Germany, certainly in excess of 10 per cent of its territory, could expect to irradiated.[79] It should also be noted that the military efficacy of TNWs would be reduced wherever the terrain affords protection to the targeted forces. Such protection, in the form of hills, woods, villages and the like, is indeed a feature of the central front, and this would necessitate the use of an even larger number of nuclear warheads.[80] We should note too that the inaccuracy of delivery systems, particularly at longer ranges, would also militate towards the use either of higher-yield warheads or of barrage nuclear attacks. For example, the Lance missile, for which ERWs were developed, has a high probability of missing its target by some distance.[81]

Arguments in favour of ERWs do appear to be undermined if one believes that the Soviet battlefield nuclear arsenal is generally of a higher yield and 'dirty'; that is, prone to leave behind long-term radiation. It is presumably for this reason that the proponents of the ERW have sought to convince their antagonists, and perhaps themselves, of the possibility that the Soviet arsenal may in fact consist of lower-yield and 'cleaner' nuclear weapons than is generally assumed. It would seem that the best Cohen can do, however, is to quote an American major-general who in 1976 said, 'Early Soviet tactical nuclear systems were apparently high-yield weapons. We are much less certain about the systems introduced in recent years'.[82] To be fair, Cohen does go on to present a quite convincing case that the Soviet Union has every incentive to limit the average yield of its TNWs and indeed to be restrained in their use, but this cannot alter the fact that we do not know a great deal about Soviet capabilities in this area,[83] and those who remain unconvinced of the 'humanity' of the use of low-yield nuclear weapons even by the NATO side may not be reassured by the logical possibility that any Soviet retaliation might be unexpectedly low-yield too.

For all the opposition to ERWs, no one has argued that the large-scale use of fission warheads would somehow be more acceptable than an equally massive use of neutron bombs. Thus the horror that greeted the proposed introduction of ERWs into Europe was based in part on emotional reaction to this 'capitalist' weapon and in part on the view that the reluctance to use ERWs might be less. In other words, the ERW issue underscored once again the continuing lack of consensus on the location of the nuclear threshold and the old ambiguities in the relationship between defence and deterrence. These are issues already dealt with in these pages, and in any case their relationship to the ERW debate can perhaps best be appreciated in the context of a consideration of NATO's handling of the ERW affair, which in itself seemed to contribute to the furore. It was not simply that the diplomacy was clumsy or insensitive, although in many instances it was. The central failing was that the Carter administration was determined to fully consult and involve the Allies in any decision to develop and deploy ERWs. Alas, the Europeans — both governments and societies — were found wanting. Indeed, the whole affair revealed just how difficult is Washington's role as the physically distant but military and political leader of an alliance of democratic states. Whether one adheres to the view that European governments have actually sought co-responsibility with the US for the major decisions relating to the Alliance, as some have claimed they have,[84] or whether, as has been argued elsewhere, 'it had always been accepted that it was for the Americans to exercise leadership', especially in nuclear matters,[85] there can be little doubt that the course of the neutron bomb debate had a profound effect on subsequent Alliance decision-making. For this reason, if for no other, it is worth dwelling a little on the events surrounding the proposed development and deployment in Europe of ER warheads.

President Carter gave his personal support to the 'neutron bomb' lobby in a letter he wrote to Senator John Stennis[86] in which he noted that 'We are not talking about some new kind of weapon, but of the modernisation of nuclear weapons', and argued that ER weapons would both enhance deterrence and would 'minimise damage and casualties to individuals not in the immediate target area' should their use nevertheless occur. The president also made it clear, especially during a televised press conference on 12 July 1977, that he had little confidence in controlled nuclear war fighting. Although the proponents of the 'neutron bomb' had never regarded Europe as the only or even the most advantageous theatre for deployment, Carter nevertheless realistically anticipated that Europe was the most significant and likely host for the new warheads. As we have seen, however, the controversy in Europe was if anything even more ferocious than that which was taking place in the United States, and for both these reasons Carter decided towards the end of 1977 that any decision to produce the weapon would be contingent on a commitment by the NATO allies to deploy it. The shift of the focus to Europe provided an altogether unhappy experience for individual NATO governments and for the Alliance as a whole. Not surprisingly, it was the German government which had the greatest difficulty, and indeed it did all it could to avoid committing itself either way. Although Chancellor Schmidt was to claim later that he had in fact informed Washington of Bonn's willingness to accept 'neutron bomb' deployment, the public stance of the West German government was a fence-sitting one. In essence, Schmidt's position was that the decision to produce the weapon was an American one, that a public German commitment to deploy it might follow, but that the 'neutron bomb' should first be introduced into the Mutual and Balanced Force Reduction Talks in Vienna as a 'bargaining chip' in an attempt to bring about a reduction in Warsaw Pact tank levels, and that in any case Germany could not be expected to be the only NATO ally to allow its deployment. [87]

The American and other NATO governments had also expressed interest in the arms-control idea, and indeed it featured in Carter's controversial decision of April 1978 to delay production of the weapon. In his statement the president said that any ultimate decision on production and deployment 'will be influenced by the degree to which the Soviet Union shows restraint in its conventional and nuclear arms programmes and force deployments', [88] and he promised continued discussions with the Allies concerning any arms-control initiatives which might be taken. Although the German and British governments — in fact NATO as a whole — offered their support for the decision, they did so in the most lukewarm of terms, and made it known that they felt Carter had caused them to make enormous political gambles at home only to be left hanging. Many of those congressmen and senators who had initially opposed the 'neutron bomb' now criticised Carter's decision for the impression of weakness and irresolution that it created. Europe's conservative political circles had something of a field day. In characteristically colourful language, Franz-Josef Strauss described the decision as the first instance since 1945 'where an American president openly and recognisably submitted to a Russian Tsar'. This remark found its echo in London, where the Conservative shadow defence spokesman exclaimed, 'It now seems that the Kremlin has virtually the right of veto over weapons that NATO is allowed to deploy'.[89] Moscow's behaviour during the imminent debate on NATO's long-range theatre weapons modernisation suggests that the Soviets drew similar conclusions.

In fact, Carter put more substance into his decision in October 1978 when he ordered the production and separate stockpiling of two components of the ER warhead.[90] All that was left to do was to combine the two parts, and this the Reagan administration ordered in August 1981. The new administration seemed to have made up its mind to proceed with production soon after its inauguration, but deployment in Europe could still not take place without the consent of Europe's governments. At the time of writing, this consent remains withheld. Although the Reagan administration's production decision was greeted with a predictable outrage from Europe's peace movements, its governments were more restrained in their response. Chancellor Schmidt reiterated Bonn's insistence that deployment would not take place in Germany alone, and that any decision to deploy should be a NATO rather than a bilateral decision.

NATO, then, has arrived at the seemingly bizarre situation wherein the United States is busily producing and stockpiling ER weapons for delivery systems chiefly deployed in Europe and in accordance with a 'strategy' designed primarily for Europe, whereas the official position of the Europeans is that such warheads should not be deployed on their soil. The Alliance has contrived to reach this state of affairs as a result of two factors which have bedevilled any consideration of the role and purpose of NATO's tactical nuclear weapons since their initial introduction thirty years ago. First, European, and especially German, public opinion has remained profoundly apprehensive about the prospect of being defended by a nuclear arsenal so large and so destructive that it raises the question of whether it is worth being defended at all. As Helmut Schmidt, hardly a 'peace' activist, noted as long ago as 1962, 'When the defence of Europe is seen to entail its nuclear destruction, the European incentive to permit the use of nuclear weapons on its soil diminishes rapidly'.[91] The proponents of the neutron bomb have so far failed to convince much of European public opinion that the reduced collateral damage which would result from the introduction of the weapon would make a difference so significant as to render acceptable the prospect of a battlefield nuclear war. Of course, the peace movement has shown a tendency in the past to wane, but equally it has shown a tendency to wax. There is no reason to suppose that it will not return, perhaps with even greater numbers, more electoral success, and with a still more adverse affect on the cohesion of the Alliance and the stability of its governments. The second factor contributing to NATO's eccentric position on the neutron bomb is the continued absence of an acceptable or even plausible strategy for the use of the battlefield nuclear arsenal. This in part reflects the special attachment Europeans hold to the contribution they make to deterrence and the persisting unwillingness of Europeans to fashion a strategy for the Alliance based on what it would actually make sense to do once the deterrent has failed. It reflects too the partly related disagreement on whether a battlefield nuclear war could be fought in a controlled, survivable and 'purely military' fashion, even if it was regarded as desirable to develop such a strategy. Again, the 'neutron bomb' debate simply formed part of the overall lack of consensus on the role of tactical nuclear weapons in Europe. As one observer has put it, 'ERW are new pieces in an old and as yet unresolved puzzle'.[92]

TOWARDS A SMALLER PILE

It was not surprising that the rather random way in which NATO's TNW stockpile built up in Europe from the early 1950s onwards resulted in an overall total which was not closely related to any coherent definition of military need. The estimated imbalance in TNWs in Europe, which by the mid-1970s stood at 2 to 1 in NATO's favour,[93] seemed a rather generous margin for the purposes of deterrence too. Attempts made in the early 1960s to bring down these numerical levels appear to have foundered on the combined opposition of the US military, the European allies, and a State Department in Washington highly sensitive to the political symbolism represented by the warheads abroad.[94] It was also not surprising, however, that commentators should continue to query the relevance of the figure which, of course, stood at around 7,000, and to suggest alternative, lower ceilings. For example, the former assistant secretary of defence, Alain C. Enthoven, thought that just 1,000 warheads would be sufficient, divided between surface-to-surface missiles and artillery shells.[95] A reputable Brookings Institution study published in 1974 suggested a figure of 2,000.[96]

James Schlesinger, the defence secretary, was, as we have seen, strongly committed to reshaping the stockpile to render it more usable. This not only involved a reduction in yields, better command and control, and better protection, but it also suggested a numerical reduction. As Schlesinger somewhat cautiously put it, the 7,000 figure was, 'under certain circumstances', too large and could be reduced.[97] This could involve, for example, a withdrawal of those systems with excessively high yields, or which were too vulnerable or posed particularly acute command and control difficulties. A series of press articles which appeared during 1974 implied a rather stronger commitment to reductions on Schlesinger's part than his rather cagey comments to the Senate Committee had implied, and strengthened too the impression that the defence secretary himself believed that the threat of a substantial first use of nuclear weapons by NATO lacked credibility. Once again, however, the State Department and the nervous European allies obstructed any major review of the stockpile actually occurring.[98]

However, whilst some elements of the Pentagon continued to fret over the disutility of much of the TNW stockpile, a barely perceptible change in attitudes towards the size and make-up of the stockpile has been taking place in Europe too. This has stemmed in part from an awareness of the damage the shorter-range systems could cause to their own territories; in part from a recognition that, as the US would at least attempt to control and limit any escalatory process, the link between these shorter-range systems and the US strategic arsenal had become rather tenuous; and stemming too from the re-arousal of public concern about the role of nuclear weapons in NATO's strategy. All this led to the adoption of more relaxed attitudes towards any proposals to reduce the size of the stockpile. The age of some of the warheads, and the inaccuracy of some of their delivery systems, has been an additional factor, itself boosted by the increasing availability of conventional alternatives. A good example of this is the conventionally-tipped Patriot surface-to-air missile, which constitutes an ideal replacement for the less accurate and excessively destructive nuclear headed Nike-Hercules anti-aircraft missile. Just as imperceptible as the shift in European perspectives has been the policy process which resulted in the NPG annexing to the final communiqué of its October 1983 meeting at Montebello, near Ottawa, an announcement of its decision to withdraw 1,400 warheads from the stockpile over the following five to six years.[99] In fact, this proposal can be traced back to a series of decisions made by the North Atlantic Council at its May 1977 summit in London.[100] Here, task groups were established to consider the needs of Alliance strategy in each of ten specified areas. The Montebello annex sought to hold the TNW stockpile 'to the minimum number necessary for deterrence', and promised that 'appropriate consideration will be given to short-range systems'. In March 1985, the NPG meeting in Luxembourg discussed the proposals SACEUR had devised as a result of Montebello.[101] SACEUR's plan, to be achieved by 1988, 'embraces reductions in a variety of warheads', although at the time of writing no further details appear to have emerged. The NPG also undertook to consider SACEUR's recommendations aimed at ensuring 'the maintenance of a survivable, responsive and effective nuclear force structure', although it is not clear whether any decisions were made to this end.

When added to the immediate withdrawal of 1,000 warheads as part of the 1979 LRTNF modernisation decision, the stockpile will have reduced by 2,400 by 1988 from the approximately 7,000 figure which had been maintained from the mid-1960s to the late 1970s. In addition, the 1979 decision determined that for each GLCM or Pershing II deployed, one existing warhead would be removed. The generally lower-yield, longer-range and smaller TNW arsenal that will result is perhaps more accurately represented as a functional rationalisation rather than as an indication of a significant change in strategy. Nevertheless, in the context of the often snail-like pace at which NATO's doctrine and, even more so, its force capabilities evolve, there does now appear to be a greater consensus than it has been possible to identify for many years on the need to raise the nuclear threshold. This inevitably means an improved conventional-force posture. Before turning to developments in this arena, the French attitude towards TNWs has to be considered.

THE FRENCH AND TNWS

Like the British, the French have the capacity to use battlefield nuclear weapons on their own initiative. Unlike the British, however, the French have presented their strategy, in this and other respects, as distinct and independent from that of NATO as a whole. Yet Paris initially shared with other European capitals a suspicion of the faith Americans seemed so often to have in the possibility of using nuclear weapons in a tactical and militarily rational way. Thus General Ailleret, in the lecture he gave in 1964 to which we have already referred, argued that although 'The use of nuclear fire on the battlefield and in the rear. . .is likely to block an invasion fairly quickly', the dispersion of the aggressor's forces would mean that success would require 'the continuous firing of a very great number of low-power nuclear weapons or a small number of very high-power weapons'. Thus, he concluded, 'even a purely tactical nuclear exchange would completely wipe out Europe over a depth of 1,800 miles from the Atlantic to the Soviet frontier'.

By the late 1960s, French policy had incorporated TNWs, which at that time consisted only of free-fall bombs, but only to the extent that they could provide a warning to an aggressor of an imminent resort to the strategic *force de frappe*. [102] Interestingly, the 'shot across the bows' idea was also one which had found favour elsewhere in Europe, as we have noted, and was for example included as an option in the Anglo-German proposals of 1969. American scepticism, however, has prevented it becoming a prime role of NATO's TNWs, and instead it has been relegated to an oft-criticised option among many more acceptable ones. [103]

For a while the Giscard government seemed in the mid-1970s to contemplate the use of TNWs in a broader context. This was associated with the so-called 'enlarged sanctuary' concept, discussed in speeches by the chief of staff of the armed forces, General Mery, as well as by his president, and which implied that France no longer saw French security as in some way detachable from that of her neighbours. [104] As the Preamble to the 1976 Military Programme, apparently written by Giscard himself, put it, 'It would indeed be illusory to hope that France could maintain more than a reduced sovereignty, if her neighbours had been occupied by a hostile power or were simply under its control. The security of Western Europe as a whole is therefore essential to France'.[105] Under the new concept, the French would participate in any war before French territory had actually been violated, and would consider the use of her TNWs in a war-fighting role rather than as simply a means to demonstrate resolve. Since the arrival of the first short-range Pluton surface-to-surface missiles in 1974, Paris was in fact in a better position to consider TNWs in this way. On the other hand, that there were never more than thirty Pluton missiles, each with a 15–25 kiloton warhead, and a maximum of sixty fighter bombers each equipped to carry just one small 10–15 kiloton bomb, suggested severe limits to the French ability to conduct a battlefield nuclear exchange of any duration. Bonn, predictably welcomed the possibility that they might be brought forward into West Germany in the event of a war, given the Pluton's 75-mile range.[106] However, such was the furore which greeted the new proposals that the Giscard administration retreated from them,[107] and with the accession of the socialist government of President Mitterrand, a veil once again fell over the role of TNWs.[108]

Yet recent changes in the French battlefield nuclear capability have implications which cannot be ignored, regardless of any vagueness the declaratory policies which envelop them may possess. A new tactical nuclear missile, the Hades, has been planned to replace the Pluton by 1992. It will possess a range two or three times that of its predecessor, which means that it will not detonate on West German territory even if fired from within France. Perhaps more interesting, however, is the fact that the 120 Hades missiles, each with a single 150-kiloton warhead, will be placed under the direct command of the French president.[109] Even so, the precise role these systems are to play remains obscure and, as with almost all aspects of French defence policy, is being subjected to increased questioning.[110] Whatever the role the French envisage for their TNWs, the Mitterrand government remains unwilling to discuss with Bonn the circumstances in which they might be used.[111] Furthermore, the French have been pursuing an ERW programme of their own. Apparently, feasibility studies were begun in 1976,[112] research and experimentation has continued since, and that a test had been conducted was admitted by the French defence minister in June 1983. As yet no decision has been made to produce ERWs, and as Hernu put it, 'If the decision to construct the neutron bomb is taken, we will consider it as a tactical weapon which would not change our strategic conception'.[113] Presumably this implies a continuing attachment to the 'warning shot' idea rather than a conversion to battlefield nuclear war-fighting, even with ERWs. Apparently, it will be possible to fit the Hades missile with ER warheads,[114] and it could be that any future French production and deployment of the warheads would be confined to it. Given presidential control, a range sufficient to reach Eastern Europe but not the USSR, the number to be produced and the relatively high yield, deciphering the function these missiles are to perform is not easy, but it is unlikely to be nuclear war-fighting in the sense that Washington and other states of NATO understand that concept. For France, it would still appear, nuclear weapons are instruments of deterrence, or in Mitterrand's words, the French objective remains 'to assure the defence of its territory by nuclear deterrence'.[115] The role of existing and future French TNWs seems to be to make the 'trip wire' just a little less taut.

8 Below the Nuclear Threshold

Recent years have seen a torrent of literature based on the twin premises that NATO now has no alternative to increasing its non-nuclear military capabilities and that there is Alliance-wide recognition of this fact. In other words, it is now widely argued that a new consensus is developing around the need to reduce reliance on nuclear weapons, to raise the nuclear threshold. There is certainly no disputing the existence and intensity of the debate. Although there is no likelihood of NATO adopting a declared no-first-use policy as a result of this debate, there do appear to be trends which favour the creation of a *de facto* no-first-use posture. For example, the present SACEUR, General Bernard W. Rogers, who has been an active participant in the recent debate on NATO's conventional strength, has argued that, with the completion of current improvement programmes, the 'general nuclear' and 'deliberate nuclear escalation' responses which form part of the strategy of flexible response, remain credible. [1] However, NATO's preferred response, he contends, is (or ought to be) 'direct defence' with conventional forces, which would aim either 'to defeat an attack, or place the burden of escalation on the enemy'. What he seeks is 'a sufficient capacity to provide a *reasonable prospect* of frustrating a conventional attack', utilising this preferred response. In other words, General Rogers seeks an overall deterrent posture which does not necessarily rely for its effectiveness on a resort to nuclear weapons. He is rejecting not just an early use but, if possible, any first use of nuclear weapons. Quite consistently, he has dismissed the adoption of a declared no-first-use policy because direct, conventional, defence could fail; because the possibility of a battlefield use of nuclear weapons would require Warsaw Pact armies to disperse, thus blunting their attack; and because the continued residual possibility of a NATO resort to nuclear weapons strengthens the deterrent, not least to Soviet first use. Clearly, though, his preferred 'action' policy would be to avoid nuclear use, and in this his thinking is in line with that of every American defence secretary since Robert McNamara, albeit with varying degrees of insistency.

One reason why General Rogers is seeking to reduce NATO's reliance on nuclear responses is because of his belief that the use even of small, battlefield nuclear weapons could immediately escalate to the use of strategic weapons. [2] This, as we have seen, is a not uncommon assessment, especially in Washington — where it is also a particularly worrying one. But insofar as there is now a much wider realisation within NATO that the Alliance's dependence on nuclear weapons is excessive, it cannot entirely be explained by a recognition of the vulnerability of the American homeland to strategic nuclear retaliation. This is a circumstance which has been with us for over twenty years, as, for example, the highly influential report produced in 1977 by two American senators, Sam Nunn and Dewey F. Bartlett, noted. [3] It formed the backdrop for McNamara's initial presentation of flexible response in 1962. Of course, 'vulnerability' has during this period transformed itself into 'parity' and, some would say, Soviet strategic superiority, but these are measurements of overkill, and Americans were not slow even whilst still ahead of the Soviet Union in strategic weaponry to point out to Europeans both the physical and doctrinal consequences of America's vulnerability. Perhaps there is now a more determined American desire to wriggle off the hook of 'extended deterrence'. Certainly David M. Abshire, the US permanent representative to the North Atlantic Council, thinks so. In a call for improved conventional forces, he implored Europeans 'to understand American politics in the nuclear age'. He went on:

Some in Europe continue to believe that an extended tripwire is the best way to sustain the American commitment to defend Europe, whilst others also see a nuclear defence, for which they do not have to pay, as a means of getting defence on the cheap. Increasingly however, Americans are unwilling to live with this situation [4]

Thus, although European governments may for over two decades have been willing to base NATO's strategy on an ultimate American willingness to commit suicide on their behalf, it could be that such interest as they now show in providing non-nuclear alternatives stems from a new sense that Americans may mean what they have long been saying about the incredibility of such a posture.

Other factors are at work, too, however. The unease many Europeans have felt since the anti-nuclear movements of the 1950s concerning the consequences of a nuclear defence of their homelands has also come to a head in recent years. Of course, there are numerous complicating factors here. Some anti-nuclear protesters are in fact anti-defence altogether, [5] and the focus has in any case been less on strategic nuclear systems than on American-controlled nuclear capabilities in Europe. [6] Nevertheless, European NATO governments, and especially Bonn, have increasingly felt themselves under pressure from their electorates to devise a NATO posture which does not seem to necessarily involve nuclear war-fighting in Europe. Then, again, since the mid-1970s there has been a sharpened perception that the Warsaw Pact spent much of the détente era enhancing its conventional capabilities, and that in relative terms NATO's conventional leg may now be in worse shape than it has ever been. Yet another contribution to the renewed interest in conventional defence has come from recent technological developments — or 'emerging technology' (ET). The greater battlefield lethality ET offers seem to some observers to present NATO with a better opportunity than it has had for some time of mounting a serious conventional defence by exploiting the West's technological lead over the Soviet Bloc. Simultaneously, it has been argued that these new conventional weapons can efficiently perform the battlefield tasks hitherto allotted to nuclear warheads, and should be substituted for them.

This chapter, then, is concerned with the way in which pressures from Washington, from public opinion, from the Warsaw Pact force build-up, and from the advance of technology, seem to have converged to force the Alliance to look again at its conventional force capabilities. [7] It will trace the evolution of these force levels on the central front, consider how serious are NATO's supposed deficiencies in this area, and delve (rather shallowly) into some of the various suggestions which have been forwarded to improve matters. So muddied are these waters, however, that caution must be our guide, and we should be thankful that space permits us only to touch upon the issues. There is, alas, no agreement on how chronic NATO's conventional weaknesses are, what is the nature of the threat it faces and what it should do in the non-nuclear field to meet it. [8]

DETERMINING THE BALANCE

As good a place as any to start our investigation of the evolution of NATO's conventional forces on the central front is, once again, with General Bernard Rogers. He is adamant that the explanation for the current malaise lies in the fact that 'nations in the Alliance have never fully met their commitments to conventional force improvements'. [9] David Abshire has, with less delicacy, observed that for this reason, 'flexible response, while a sound strategy, has never been fully implemented'. [10] Indeed, Rogers himself has likened the actual strategy NATO's force structure enables him to implement, as a 'delayed tripwire', [11] a reference to the strategy which, of course, preceded the adoption of flexible response. It is appropriate at this juncture, then, to investigate the conventional-force balance on the central front as it has evolved over the years.

We noted earlier in this volume how, in the early years of the Alliance, NATO convinced itself that the Soviet Bloc possessed an overwhelming and, it seemed, unbridgeable advantage in ground-troop strength. In particular, the Soviet Union alone was credited with a quite phenomenal 175 divisions. This total was not reconsidered until the early 1960s, even though Soviet armed manpower seems to have fluctuated substantially during this period. In fact, thirty-five of these 'divisions' may not have existed at all. [12] The real challenge to the 175 figure, however, came from the systems analysts employed by the Kennedy administration. [13] They found that NATO had an overall active manpower superiority over the Pact, which incorporated a lead in ground strength. They found too that at least half of Moscow's divisions were essentially 'paper divisions' with manning levels of perhaps 10 per cent and with a below-complement stock of usually out-dated hardware. Furthermore, they also discovered that a fully mobilised American division was almost three times the size of a fully mobilised Soviet division, and that Western divisions in general were larger than their Warsaw Pact counterparts. The Pentagon analysts asked similarly penetrating but, in retrospect, rather obvious questions where tactical air forces were concerned too. Thus they disputed a joint US—West-German Air Force study which concluded that NATO air forces would no longer be able to contest with the Pact after three days of battle owing to the latter's numerical superiority. Here the analysts pointed out that the study counted only those aircraft formally committed to NATO, that large numbers were presumed to be withheld for nuclear missions, and that reinforcement from the US was held to be limited. None of these debilitating assumptions were applied to the Pact side. The upshot of all this questioning was that it had become clear by 1967 that there was a rough parity on the ground and that, if anything, NATO enjoyed aerial superiority.

The reconsiderations of the NATO—Warsaw-Pact balance which took place in Washington during the 1960s highlighted a number of problems involved in force comparisons, particularly in Central Europe.[14] First, there is the problem of who to count, which, on the NATO side, revolves largely around the position of France in the Alliance. Then, there is the dilemma of what to count; for example, which US forces would be available for reinforcement of Europe in a crisis, or for the Pact, would all or any of the forces in the western military districts of the Soviet Union be mobilised and brought to bear in Central Europe? Third, there is the especially complex issue of the quality of forces. This refers not just to human factors such as morale or training but also to assessments of the adequacy of military hardware. A notable manifestation of the 'quality' problem has been the identification of first-, second- and third-category Pact forces. Whereas a premobilisation category III division may consist of just 25 per cent of its manpower and equipment, a category I unit will exceed 75 per cent of its fully mobilised complement. Finally, and crucially, assumptions have to be made about the timing and relative rates of mobilisation of the two sides' forces. In short, comparisons can consist of static bean-counts through to dynamic, complex assessments. During the 1960s the civilian analysts at the Pentagon confronted the existing static balances, which favoured the Soviet Bloc, with their own more complex multi-faceted assessments, which tended to rectify perceptions of the balance more in NATO's favour. It is now rarely disputed that, in the early years of the Alliance, as the US defence secretary,

Donald Rumsfeld, conceded in 1977, 'The size of the Soviet conventional forces oriented toward Europe was over-estimated'.[15]

A SHIFTING BALANCE

In fact, some now look back on the mid-1960s as almost a golden age for NATO's conventional forces, and argue that the balance since the adoption of flexible response, with its supposed emphasis on non-nuclear strength, has, if anything, moved against the Western Alliance.[16] The divisional balance of forces, at least since the mid-1960s, appears not to have deteriorated. During that period NATO has added one division to reach a current total of twenty-seven active divisions (this figure includes the three French divisions based in West Germany but not those in France), whilst the Pact division count has remained unchanged at fifty-seven — a ratio, that is, of around 2:1.[17] The overall figure for NATO divisions in Europe has increased from seventy-nine in 1970 to eighty-four today, whilst the Pact has added seven divisions and now has 173.[18] We have already seen how the concept of a 'division' can be quite nebulous, and for this reason the Pentagon has devised a system of weighting the capabilities of weapons systems to arrive at a measurement known as an 'armoured division equivalent' (ADE). Although the number of ADEs on each side has not been made available, the ratio has been revealed to give the Pact a mere 1.2:1 advantage, even less impressive than the 2 : 1 advantage the East enjoys in simple active divisions.[19]

Manpower trends, on the other hand, do suggest a deterioration in NATO's circumstances. Senator Sam Nunn has observed that 'It is one of the paradoxes of recent history that NATO today maintains far fewer men under arms than it did during the era of massive retaliation'.[20] Certainly there has been a decline in NATO force levels since the adoption of flexible response, but the imbalance between the Pact and NATO which now exists in Central Europe is rather more a result of Soviet Bloc increases. Thus, since 1965, there has been a 50,000 reduction in NATO's ground force personnel and a 150,000 increase in the Pact's, transforming a small NATO numerical superiority into a current 20 per cent Pact lead.[21] A large part of the Pact increase was due to the invasion of Czechoslovakia in 1968. This manpower ratio in Central Europe of around 1.2 : 1 [22] is not an unhealthy one for NATO, given that an attacking force is usually regarded as needing at least a 3 : 1 advantage over the defender. Furthermore, if all French ground forces are included, NATO retains a slight lead. [23] The situation would have been worse for NATO if it were not for the fact that West Germany maintained its force build-up, notably during the late 1960s, to make up for the decline in the Central European deployments of nearly all the other NATO members. [24] In fact, in the early 1960s the Federal Republic overtook the US in the provision of armed personnel in Western Europe and has maintained its position as NATO's major contributor of armed strength in Europe ever since. [25]

THE MOBILISED BALANCE

These are rather static comparisons, yet they do not suggest that NATO is in a chronically bad shape *vis-à-vis* the Warsaw Pact. Figures such as these enabled James Schlesinger to feel in 1974 that there was 'an approximate balance' on the central front [26] and Donald Rumsfeld three years later to believe that 'At present, the United States and its allies in NATO have sufficient active forces to maintain an acceptable ratio of defence to offence'. [27] It may be more instructive, however, to take the mobilisation potentials of the two alliances into account when comparing their relative strengths. At this juncture, of course, most of the pitfalls involved in conventional-force measurement make their appearance, and it is therefore not surprising that differing assumptions and assessments abound. Until 1977 NATO assumed that the Warsaw Pact would take a month to ready itself for a major war in Central Europe. [28] This would involve calling up reservists to flesh out the below-strength divisions, releasing military hardware from depots and maintenance stations and making it available to the units, and moving forces from their peacetime deployment locations to the battle zone. [29] Indeed, a Pact mobilisation period of one month was probably a realistic basis around which NATO should plan. [30] It was further assumed for planning purposes that NATO's mobilisation would begin one week later, on the assumption that it could take seven days for Western intelligence to identify that an unambiguous Warsaw Pact mobilisation had indeed begun, and for the requisite political authority for NATO forces to follow suit to be granted. What would then follow would be a reinforcement and mobilisation 'race' during which mobilised force ratios could continually alter as forces were readied and moved forward into battle positions at differential rates. Given that, as the defensive alliance, NATO mobilisation would always be a few days behind that of the Pact, it was essential that at no point during the 'race' should the Soviet Bloc be allowed to attain a particularly favourable force ratio, as this could tempt Moscow to attack before full mobilisation had been completed, and could hinder NATO's continuing preparation. Assumptions made about the rates and extent of mobilisation which would be carried out by the two sides vary so much that, rather than provide yet another tabulation of a hypothetical mobilisation race, it should be more instructive to consider the bases on which these assumptions are made. [31]

The first problem we are faced with when considering NATO's potential to resist a Warsaw Pact assault is an imponderable, yet vital, one. Would NATO's political authorities set in train their mobilisation procedures in time? If NATO were to delay ordering its own mobilisation for say, a week or more after the beginning of a Pact mobilisation, then it would probably find itself faced with dangerously unequal force ratios at each point in the process. [32] There is little reason to assume that NATO intelligence would be at fault, [33] and major NATO commanders would be likely to declare a state of 'military vigilance'. But 'simple', 'reinforced' or 'general' alert states require political approval, and in certain circumstances dissension on the NATO Council is quite imaginable. [34] It would be difficult to prove that a Pact mobilisation was aimed at starting a war rather than fighting one should it nevertheless break out, or to know that the objective was to attack NATO rather than, say, to put down an East German revolt. Alternatively, Greece and Turkey might be unwilling to become involved in a crisis hitherto centred exclusively on Norway, and vice versa. In short, there could be circumstances in which some NATO capitals would regard mobilisation as itself a provocative act which could transform a crisis into an otherwise avoidable war.

Another seemingly unanswerable but nevertheless crucial set of questions relates to the extent of the mobilisation which each alliance would carry out. In this respect it is worth noting that, whereas the Pact has since 1970 increased its total available active armed strength from 4.3 million to 5.7 million, NATO's has reduced from 5.6 million to 4.4 million, almost an exact reversal. However, if the forces of France and NATO's most recent member, Spain, are added, the NATO figure increases by over 800,000 and the 'gap' becomes insignificant. As Bonn has pointed out, during this period the US has reduced its overall manpower totals by just over a million and thus, almost alone, accounts for the NATO decline, whereas Moscow has increased its forces by around 800,000, thus contributing over half of the Pact's force increases. [35] Of course, what proportion of these forces would be brought to bear in a European crisis is anybody's guess. How lightly attended would the Soviet Union be prepared to leave the Sino-Soviet border, for example? Similarly, would Washington redeploy to Europe in a crisis those forces at present located in the Far East?

Another complicating factor are the reservists; that is, those citizens who have undergone some military training as a result of their country's conscription system and who are still liable to call up. In this category the Warsaw Pact has a clear numerical advantage, with well over 6.5 million reservists available compared to NATO's under 5.5 million. [36] The Soviet Union alone has 3 million ground-force reservists. [37] The chief explanation for the Pact lead, despite the fact that NATO countries have a combined population over half as large again as the Pact, is that Great Britain, Canada and, since the early 1970s, the United States, do not have conscription and thus have a smaller pool of trained manpower on which to draw. As an illustration of this, the strength of reserve US ground forces alone declined by around 70,000 during the 1970s. [38] On the positive side, Bonn alone can call on 850,000 trained men and claims that it can use these reserves to augment its half-million-strong active force by around 700,000 in just three days. [39] On the other hand, reservists can sometimes take a very long time to prepare for combat, [40] and the economic impact of a full mobilisation of reservists would be substantial. Nevertheless, it is perfectly feasible that at least some mobilisation of reservists would take place within both NATO and the Warsaw Pact. West German reservists could make a substantial and very early impact on force ratios soon after mobilisation began, and the Soviet Union and its allies rely heavily on reservists to bring their low-category divisions up to wartime strength. Again, though, the extent to which reservists would be called up is highly scenario-dependent and thus unpredictable.

Then we have to consider perhaps the most important and complicated factor of all, the relative speed at which the two sides could mobilise. Chiefly because US divisions have to first cross the Atlantic, in some cases bringing their equipment with them, and would then have to be moved to their wartime deployment zones in Europe, some have argued that NATO would be at its most vulnerable between one and two weeks after Pact mobilisation began, but that the balance would be redressed thereafter as American forces stationed in the US in peacetime began to arrive.[41] Even so, most analysts conclude that, over a thirty-day mobilisation period and, assuming that the gap between mobilisation start dates is less than a week, then at no time during that period would the Pact enjoy significantly more than a 2 : 1 manpower-ratio advantage. In this period, indeed, matters may have actually improved somewhat since the mid-1960s.[42] Given that a 2 : 1 advantage is generally regarded as insufficient to overwhelm a prepared defender, and given too that the longer the period of mobilisation so the more the attacking force would lose the advantages of surprise, it is generally agreed that the Soviet Bloc does not possess a manpower advantage sufficient to give it a high degree of confidence of success.

THE HARDWARE ARMS RACE

Thus far, our analysis of the non-nuclear military balance in Central Europe has focused largely on the manpower ratios achieved there. However, the Pact has also made what has been described as an 'extraordinary effort' to improve both the quality and quantity of its military hardware. By contrast, 'NATO's response has been laconic'.[43] The result is that in almost every category of military equipment, the Pact enjoys advantageous force ratios which are often equal to or greater than those obtaining where manpower is concerned and which have been improved substantially in the Pact's favour since the adoption by NATO of flexible response.[44] Inevitably, the figures arrived at depend enormously on assumptions made, and some variation is to be found. But the similarities are more compelling than the differences, and the trends seem beyond dispute. It has been calculated that since 1965 over 80 per cent of the overall increase in armament levels in Central Europe is accounted for by the Warsaw Pact, or, put another way, for every one new weapon NATO has added, the Pact has introduced 4.4 new weapons.[45] To offer just one all-important example, the Pact has increased its main battle tank inventory by over 4,000 since 1965, giving the Pact a ratio advantage in excess of 2 : 1; furthermore, NATO can be far from confident that it has retained its former qualitative edge.[46] In 1984 Soviet production of main battle tanks alone far exceeded that of NATO as a whole, and overall Pact tank production was double that achieved by NATO.[47] Nor can NATO claim either a quantitative or even qualitative lead over the Pact in anti-tank systems.[48] A comparison of the European hardware deployments of the two superpowers is especially instructive. Almost half of all new weapons introduced into Central Europe since 1965 have been Soviet; only 7 per cent have been American; the Central European deployment ratio between the superpowers for main battletanks is 18 : 1.[49] In fact, just as seems to be the case with manpower in Central Europe, the Warsaw Pact is being increasingly 'Sovietised', whereas NATO has become more 'European' in the make-up of its forces in Central Europe.

FORWARD DEFENCE: POLITICAL NECESSITY AND MILITARY COMPLEXITY

In the early 1960s NATO formally accepted a commitment to a defence as far forward in West Germany as military feasibility will allow. Although it was evident to the West's military authorities even in the late 1940s and early 1950s that defence in West Germany was both militarily necessary and politically desirable, it was only out of deference to Bonn's sensibilities—and even then only as a result of very active lobbying — that a defence as close to the inner German border as possible was incorporated into NATO's military planning. West German insistence on forward defence is entirely explicable. Thirty per cent of the population and 25 per cent of the Federal Republic's industrial capacity is within 100 kilometres of the inner German border. As Bonn has put it, 'This fact denies the Federal Republic of Germany any alternative to forward defence', which is taken to mean 'cohesive defence near the border with the objective of preventing any loss of ground and limiting damage'.[50] Although the 1979 West German White Paper incorporated 'the recapture of lost territory' in its definition of forward defence,[51] the 1983 White Paper conceded that should territory be lost to an invading force, any attempt to retake it would not only result in massive devastation of the area being fought over but would also be a militarily formidable and costly task.[52]

The narrowness of West German territory, and the fact that NATO's informal lines of communication, especially since the 'loss' of France, run on a north–south axis and are often quite close to the East German border, constitute additional disincentives to the conduct of a more mobile defence-in-depth which would involve trading territory.[53] As a very eminent group of German generals once put it, 'the battle of Europe would already be lost if the forces of the Allied 'shield' had to withdraw to the Vosges and the Ardennes'.[54] In other words, there are sound military reasons intermingled with the political ones for NATO to fight shy of adopting defensive tactics which envisage a ready sacrifice of territory. Any such sacrifice could become permanent.

Just how forward defence should be effected, however, has not only varied over time but also varies from one sector to another of the inner German border. Before the early 1960s, of course, NATO's ground strategy was best described as 'fallback',[55] and consisted of delaying the speed at which West German (or, perhaps, West European) territory was gobbled up by the advancing communist hordes pending the collapse of their will and ability to continue the campaign as a result of the strategic bombardment of their homelands. Even the adoption of 'trip wire' in the late 1950s and forward defence in the early 1960s did not produce either a commitment or capability to hold every inch of German soil. In fact, again as we have already noted, the role of NATO's conventional forces was an altogether minimal one during this period. It was not truly until the adoption of 'active defence' in the mid-1970s that a firmer commitment to maintaining the territorial integrity of West Germany can be properly identified. Even 'active defence', in some respects akin to the concept of 'mobile defence' with which the West Germans themselves have often professed sympathy,[56] envisaged an initial trading of space for time. 'Active defence' provides first of all for a heavy covering force located right on the border, the aim of which would be to slow the pace of advance of the attacking force. The second stage consists of a continuous, entrenched heavily armed defensive line preventing breakthroughs, further breaking the momentum of the attacking force and wearing it down. Then, essential if the coherence of West German territory is to be preserved, comes the counter-attack, a concept which is predictably and especially dear to the Bundeswehr.

It is possible to offer a number of criticisms of active and indeed of any form of manoeuvre defence,[57] although many of them depend on how much space it is assumed would be traded. Of course, any set of tactical rules which envisage sacrificing territory, albeit temporarily, is risky, for regaining even small pockets of territory could involve enormous expenditure of men and material. Furthermore, if the fighting retreat of the defender's covering force became a rout, breakthroughs in the defence may occur anyway. This, of course, is a problem with any basically linear defence; the line might be broken. And the less linear 'forward defence' in Germany is planned to be, the less 'forward' is that defence, and the more West Germany territory is covered by fighting. This also explains why NATO, but especially Bonn, has been keen, at least in its rhetoric, to provide sufficient operational reserve strength to back up the forward defensive line, so as to plug gaps and smother breakthroughs.[58]

It is, in truth, enormously difficult if not impossible to maintain a country's territorial integrity without adopting pre-emptive tactics. It is this realisation which guides Israeli defence policy, and it was a consideration not unappreciated by Western military leaders before West Germany joined the Alliance. Indeed, it has even been suggested that the capability for mobile defence, with its strong emphasis on the counter-offensive, which has been acquired by the Bundeswehr carries with it pre-emptive and thus destabilising implications.[59] Accordingly, a debate has recently emerged in the US on the desirability and feasibility of NATO conducting pre-emptive conventional strikes into Eastern Europe during a crisis. Perhaps the most notable contribution to this debate has been that provided by the respected American scholar Samuel P. Huntington.[60] Believing that NATO's defensive strategy in Central Europe 'almost ensures military defeat', he seeks to make 'forward defence more forward' by contemplating retaliatory offensive attacks against weak points in the Soviet military chain; for example, a Pact attack on the north German plain could be countered by a NATO offensive into southern East Germany and Czechoslovakia. Less dramatic but of greater significance has been the development by the US Army in conjunction with the US Air Force of the Airland Battle doctrine, as incorporated into the 1982 version of the Army's Manual, FM 100–5.[61] Airland Battle seeks to replace the basically reactive nature of much US Army tactical doctrine with the spirit of the offensive, by seizing the initiative and, most importantly, by conducting a 'deep battle' against enemy forces up to 150 kilometres behind the immediate battle area. The emphasis is on aggression, rapidity, surprise. Although Airland Battle was developed as a purely US doctrine and is meant to apply globally rather than specifically or exclusively to Central Europe, and although General Rogers in his capacity as SACEUR has reiterated the convention that 'NATO policy does not permit ground attacks across its borders'[62] (i.e. by NATO ground forces), the relationship of US Army tactics to NATO tactics is complicated by SACEUR's additional role as commander-in-chief, USAREUR, and by the exact status as a military commander SACEUR would enjoy in wartime. In any case, the tone of recent US thinking is clear, and is part of a wider debate about how best to defend foward in Central Europe.

Discussion of any aspect of NATO strategy and force posture, including forward defence, are ultimately no more and no less than discussions of commitments made in peacetime. In essence SACEUR and his staff at SHAPE provide the focus for Allied planning and doctrinal discussion. All that SACEUR actually controls in peacetime are some nuclear forces and the air-defence network. Member states decide for themselves what forces they will make available to NATO in wartime and, as one observer has put it, 'how this might work under the duress of conflict is anyone's conjecture'.[63] Although these forces would then be under an integrated command structure, NATO's ground strength would nevertheless be made up of 'a group of armies with pronounced individual styles at the tactical level'.[64] Indeed, not only would styles differ but so would much of the equipment used. NATO's armies are deployed side by side in a 'layer cake' along the inner German border.[65] Thus SACEUR would have the responsibility in wartime of implementing forward defence using national armies each of which would be employing its own operational tactics in its sector of the front. In the Central Army Group region (CENTAG), the Bundeswehr would be conducting its mobile defence alongside a US Army which may be experimenting with its Airland Battle doctrine, or more cautiously carrying out an 'active defence' to which, or so it seems, SACEUR is still attached even though it has been discarded by the US Army itself. In the Northern Army Group region (NORTHAG), in addition to elements of the Bundeswehr and those US Army divisions which had already arrived from across the Atlantic, SACEUR would be conducting his defence with British, Dutch and Belgian forces all implementing their own quite distinct variants of area or positional defence — concepts altogether more cautious than those with which the Germans and Americans are infused.[66] Clearly it would be enormously difficult to synchronise counter-offensives, cover flanks and hold continuous defensive lines. Thus it is difficult in the circumstances to know what to make of Bonn's assertion in the context of a defence of 'forward defence' that 'There is not much room for divergent national concepts',[67] and it is easy to sympathise with those who argue that the credibility of 'forward defence' would be enhanced if these tactical differences could be reduced or eliminated.[68] Given the continued attachment to sovereign control over national armed forces, the prospects for much progress on this front must be rated as slim.

Operationally, forward defence today requires that the majority of NATO troops are allocated defensive positions in a belt between 20 and 40 kilometres wide along the border between the two Germanies.[69] Although the terrain along the border varies considerably, some have argued that it nevertheless offers as ideal a defensive line as Central Europe can offer, and for two reasons. First, the terrain is generally disadvantageous to the attack. Although the NORTHAG region is usually regarded as the most vulnerable part of NATO's front owing to its general flatness, it nevertheless features marshland, bogs, rivers, canals, urban sprawl and, in its south, the Harz mountains. Southern Germany, covered by CENTAG, is not only defended by NATO's best-equipped German and US forces but is also heavily forested, quite mountainous and again has numerous rivers and other obstacles. The so-called 'gaps' in this area, the Gottingen Corridor leading towards the Ruhr, the Fulda Gap pointing at Frankfurt, and the Hof Corridor leading towards Stuttgart, are in fact rather narrow and themselves somewhat obstacle-laden. Furthermore, at about 50 kilometres from the border the countryside opens up along almost its entire length, facilitating much greater mobility to an invading force and providing far fewer and more isolated strong points around which to anchor a defence.[70]

Related to these geographical factors are another set of considerations which tend to favour the present forward defensive line. These are concerned with what is known as the force-to-space ratio. Put simply, the shorter the defensive line, the smaller the force with which it can be defended successfully. The numerical balances with which we were concerned earlier represent aggregates only. The 3 : 1 or more advantage the attacking force is conventionally regarded as requiring to achieve a breakthrough may in fact be insufficient to penetrate a defence across a narrow front. In Central Europe a defensive line established deeper into West German territory would also be a longer line. NATO would find its forces more stretched, its defence less dense and, as a result, more easily breached. Not only has it been calculated that NATO's force-to-space ratios on the inner German border are far from unhealthy, but the combined effects of the terrain and the aggregate numerical balance of forces could make the task of the attacking force greater still. The terrain would tend to channelise any invading force in Central Europe, for it is simply not possible to attack equally across the whole front. Indeed, the Pact could only attain overwhelming force ratios if it concentrated on a few axes of attack. However, there is an upper limit on the density of an attack too; it would not be possible for the Pact to fit all of its attacking forces into a constricted channel. They would need to attack in waves, or echelons, which means that, at the actual point of engagement, they again would be denied the advantageous force ratios a breakthrough might require. On the other hand, the fewer axes

NATO found itself defending, the greater the proportion of its forces it could afford to employ as an operational reserve, located just behind the front line from where it could plug any gaps or smother any breakthroughs.[71]

SURPRISE ATTACKS: THE NEW THREAT?

The strategies each side employs to win a Central European battle could be of greater significance than any force imbalance, and over the past decade or so there have been indications that Moscow has adopted a strategy which does not require extensive mobilisation. In 1977 SACEUR concluded that it might take between one and two weeks for the Eastern Bloc to ready itself for an attack in Central Europe, rather than the one month which had previously been assumed.[72] At around the same time many were concluding that the Pact had so structured and equipped its forces as to make an unreinforced, 'standing start' attack on NATO a feasible and frightening option. Even SACEUR's more recent supposition regarding available warning time may have been wildly optimistic. The Nunn–Bartlett report was the most influential document outlining this point of view, and it appeared to envisage a 'standing start' attack consisting of up to fifty-eight divisions; that is, all Soviet and non-Soviet divisions in Eastern Europe.[73] This would appear to be a little excessive, and more recent studies have put the figure at thirty or less,[74] with only category I or even only Soviet divisions capable of such an enterprise. The bigger the attack, the less likely it would be that the Soviet Union and its allies would achieve surprise, and surprise would be the essence of such a venture.

The surprise attack option which some believe the Soviet Bloc now has is the result of years of incremental, undramatic but continuous improvements, especially in its forward-based, category I divisions in Central Europe. During the past two decades these forces have acquired an independence from long and vulnerable logistic chains; greater mobility and firepower; offensive tactical air capabilities for launching deep, devastating and demoralising strikes against NATO's nuclear weapons storage sites, ammunition dumps, airbases, C^3I installations and other high-priority targets; improved and formidable air defence; heliborne and airborne assault forces; and improved electronic counter-measures. [75] In short, the Soviets have built into their overall force structure a core of high-readiness, offensive divisions designed not to overwhelm NATO's defences by sheer weight of numbers but to pierce and fragment these defences before they had even moved fully into position and to disrupt any reinforcement taking place behind NATO's front lines. These are *Blitzkreig* rather than steamroller tactics, [76] and they appear to be associated with a 'new' concept in Soviet ground warfare which has recently been identified by Western observers of Soviet tactics, that of the so-called Operational Manoeuvre Group (OMG). [77] Although its precise make-up and role is still surrounded by controversy in the West, an OMG consists of a high-speed, heavy-firepower and combined-arms 'raiding force' created as the situation requires out of existing units and formations. It would be committed very early on in a battle, probably between days one and three, and would aim to pierce NATO's defences and penetrate deep into the rear to destroy or capture prime targets such as airfields, nuclear and conventional arms stores, and command posts, and to cause chaos and disorganisation. Clearly it is a concept which presupposes the material force improvements we have already discussed, and appears furthermore to have been designed specifically with NATO's defensive structure in mind. Ideally, as one analysis of OMGs put it, the result of the employment of the concept would be 'to induce the perception among NATO allies that continued resistance or nuclear escalation would be futile'. [78]

This is precisely the outcome that some Western analysts of the central front predict would result from an unreinforced Pact attack, with or without the use of OMGs. Tactics such as these do not rely on numerical advantage for their success, but on shock. In fact, given that NATO ostensibly maintains well over twenty active divisions on the central front, the Pact might not even achieve a 1 : 1 divisional ratio as a result of an unreinforced attack, and its manpower ratio could be worse still given the fact that Western divisions are generally larger than their Soviet Bloc counterparts. However, recent studies have revealed that the readiness of NATO's forward divisions is less than impressive, not least because not all of NATO's central front active divisions are actually located in peacetime in their forward defence positions. Only one of the total of six brigades donated by the

Netherlands for forward defence in Germany is, or ever has been, actually in the Federal Republic. As one observer put it, 'the greatest problem facing the Dutch will be getting to the war'.[79] No more than one of Belgium's two divisions earmarked for the inner-German border are actually in Germany, the other having been withdrawn in the mid-1970s,[80] and, notwithstanding the supposedly renewed NATO interest in its conventional deterrent, it was reported in the spring of 1985 that Brussels was considering pulling several hundred more soldiers out of NATO's front-line in West Germany as an economy measure.[81] Britain actually maintains in Germany only three of her active defence divisions,[82] with the fourth to be brought in in the event of mobilisation, possibly from Northern Ireland.[83] Even German and American forces are in peacetime often located at some distance from their wartime defensive positions along the inner-German border.[84] In fact, less than a quarter of NATO's seventy-one active forward defence brigades are located in peacetime within 50 kilometres of their forward defence positions.[85] In addition to the four US divisions based in the Federal Republic, there should by the end of 1985 be sufficient prepositioned equipment in the Federal Republic for another six divisions in the event of a crisis. It is expected, however, that these will not be ready to fight until around ten days after mobilisation.[86] As a result of factors such as these, the Belgian General Robert Close, who spent much of his military career within the NATO structure, reckoned that SHAPE would be able to count on just fifteen or sixteen divisions within the first few days following a Soviet Bloc surprise assault,[87] and that even under the most optimistic assumptions, combat positions necessary for an effective forward defence would not be manned until between ten and thirty hours after mobilisation had been ordered.[88] Elsewhere it has been calculated that it would take four days from mobilisation for NATO's forward defence structure to be in place, and even then much of the necessary defensive preparation — the creation of physical barriers, the enhancement of air defences for airfields and other vital installations, and so on — would hardly have begun.[89] Clearly, as a respected German commentator has noted, this combination of a lack of preparedness on the NATO side and the *Blitzkrieg* capability of the Pact may enable the latter in some circumstances to 'pre-empt NATO's defence preparations and thus prevent it from

even organising an effective initial forward defence'.[90] Even the
1 : 1 ratio which may be all the Pact could hope for if Moscow
chose to launch an unreinforced attack could be more than
sufficient to cause substantial chaos to the still-deploying defensive forces of NATO.[91] As the US defence secretary, Harold
Brown, put it, 'we still act as though we will have the time to
mobilise'.[92] There may not be time.

NATO's apparent lack of readiness is the result of a seemingly
incessant round of cuts, curtailments, stretched-out programmes,
unattained targets and unfulfilled promises. There may have been
an element of military thinking behind some of these reductions.
Certainly on the Pact side it would appear that Moscow has been
determined to emulate the generally larger and better-equipped
NATO divisions, and has pursued this policy so successfully that
today only US and German divisions on the NATO side are
comparably armed. NATO's armies, on the other hand, have
been drifting in the opposite direction, and have shed much of
their heavy firepower and cumbersome logistic support in the
attempt to increase their 'teeth-to-tail' ratios. They now more
nearly resemble the lighter, smaller, less self-contained Pact
divisions of the mid-1960s. Like the Pact, however, they did not
adjust the number of their divisions to take account of the new
organisational structure, with the result that the Pact has not only
been permitted to retain its division-ratio advantage but has also
been able to catch up and overtake NATO in combat capability
per division.[93]

It is, though, more convincing to argue that NATO's weaknesses have come about chiefly as a result of uncoordinated,
political and budget-inspired cost-cutting exercises which have
showed scant respect for military needs. General Robert Close
has offered an insight into the drift downwards in the military
preparedness of his own country. Thus a Belgian division today
has half the personnel and one-third the number of tanks of twenty
years ago; the country's armed forces in the early 1950s were
twice their present size; expenditure on defence then took up over
6 per cent of GNP, and now the figure is just over 3 per cent.[94] A
small but graphic—and not untypical example of the general
slackening which has taken place in NATO's armed forces is
provided by the fact that regular volunteers and NCOs in the
Belgian Army are awarded three days off duty if they mount

guard over a weekend! In fact, examples such as this give a better picture than can changes in force levels or variations in the proportion of the national economy devoted to defence, for short-term spending restraints tend to reduce training, diminish ammunition stockpiles, reduce terms of service and slow down re-equipment programmes.

The recent attention NATO's war reserve stockpiles has received provides a good illustration of this uncomfortable drift. To sustain combat for any significant period of time, reserve stocks are necessary — replacement weapons, spare parts, ammunition, fuel, and so on. The current level of NATO's war reserve stocks is classified, and in any case, because it is the responsibility of each NATO member to furnish its own stocks, the situation varies depending on the country and on the item. What is clear, however, is that the Europeans generally maintain lower levels than does the US,[95] and that the Nunn–Bartlett Report found that 'the disparity betwen authorised and actual levels of equipment maintained in US war reserve and prepositioned stocks is nothing short of a disgrace', that the US Army in Europe (USAREUR) possesses 'but a fraction of the ammunition it will need during the first thirty days of war' and that as a result 'deployed USAREUR combat units and initial reinforcements might not be able to sustain more than a few days of high-intensity combat'.[96] At least two US secretaries of defence, Donald Rumsfeld and Harold Brown, alluded to the precarious levels of US and Allied war reserve stocks too.[97] Although funds for improvements were requested, this did not prevent General Rogers from lamenting in 1982 that, worried as he is about the insufficient manpower base of the US Army, he would expect 'to run out of equipment to replace losses'[98] before running out of men, and that for these reasons 'we have built ourselves a short war'.[99] More recently still, a report by the very eminent British Atlantic Committee revealed that although NATO countries are supposed to possess one month's supply of stocks, in some vital areas they can only muster about seven days' worth. The report described this state of affairs as 'The most salient problem on land, lying at the heart of all NATO's inferiority'.[100] As things stand, it is difficult to see how a clash on the central front could turn itself into a long war of attrition, as some have argued.[101] On the other hand, things could be about to improve as NATO's Defence

Planning Committee (DPC), meeting at ministerial level in December 1984, 'determined to make a special effort' to make good shortfalls in ammunition war reserve stocks.[102] Some member states had already made improvements in this area on their own initiative. For example, West Germany planned to increase its expenditure on ammunition stocks by 13 per cent in real terms between 1981 and 1984, and intends to sustain the same rate of growth until 1987.[103] As the DPC communiqué reveals, however, there remains a long way to go before NATO achieves anything like the sustainability necessary for the nuclear threshold to be raised to General Rogers' satisfaction, or to match the estimated two to three months of conflict which Warsaw Pact stockpiles of ammunition, fuel and tactical pipe-laying equipment would permit it.[104]

FOLLOW-ON FORCES ATTACK AND 'EMERGING TECHNOLOGIES'

Many of the suggestions which have been made to improve NATO's conventional-force posture are quite undramatic.[105] War stocks are vitally in need of improvement if sustainability is to be achieved, and some have highlighted the importance of upgraded and expanded reserve organisations in this respect too.[106] The dearth of firepower, notably in the Dutch, Belgian and British sectors, has provoked comment.[107] Clearly, too, NATO's prospects of conducting a successful defence would be substantially enhanced if a bigger proportion of those forces earmarked for forward defence were deployed in peacetime rather closer to the inner-German border than is the case at present. After all, if the force ratios are not markedly unfavourable to NATO, then an improved initial defensive capability combined with enhanced sustainability, rather than any radical restructuring or massive build-up, would appear to be the more appropriate responses. Even if this is accepted, however, there is, given some limitation of resources, bound to be an element of trade-off between investment in the initial defence, on the one hand, and efforts made to ensure an improved durability, on the other. Those analysts who have expressed most scepticism regarding the likelihood of a successful 'surprise attack' by the Warsaw Pact forces are, not surprisingly, particularly inclined to propose improvements designed to enhance the staying power of NATO's forces in Central Europe.[108] Yet as early as 1976 the US Army Manual FM 100–5 stressed the view that 'the first battle of our next war could well be its last battle. . . the US Army must, above all else, prepare to win the first battle of the next war'.[109] Such a belief inevitably brings in its train preferences regarding the allocation of scarce resources.

Considerations such as these have coloured, though did not inspire, the Alliance's deliberations concerning and fascination with the promise of so-called 'emerging technologies' (ET), some of which, it must be said, have already emerged.[110] ET refers to various types of smart, highly accurate conventional weapons systems.[111] Of course, technology progresses incrementally, and the current debates about ET in many ways reflect earlier debates about 'precision-guided munitions' (PGMs),[112] and this term is in fact sometimes applied to describe the newer weapon systems. 'ET' is still controversial. Some have doubted whether much of it will actually work in the typical conditions of a Central European battlefield;[113] there are differences of opinion concerning the financial cost of many of the new systems;[114] there are disputes about whether ET favours the offence, the defence or whether, perhaps as always with technology, ET is 'neutral'[115] in this respect; and there are fears that because of the American lead in research and development of ET, the future might see a 'one-way street' in NATO's arms trading, with Europeans being obliged to become increasingly dependent on 'off the shelf' purchases from the US. Whatever the future holds, NATO governments and military authorities have begun to show interest in the application of ET to the European battlefield.[116]

In November 1984, NATO's DPC agreed a Long-Term Planning Guideline relating to the concept known as Follow-on Forces Attack (FOFA). The FOFA concept is one of the more concrete spin-offs from ET. It emerged from an investigation set up by General Rogers in 1979 into the task of 'reducing to a manageable ratio with conventional weapons the number of enemy forces arriving at our General Defensive Position', by targeting Pact forces behind the first attacking wave. Such forces could, of course 'stretch from just behind the troops in contact to as far into the enemy's rear as our target acquisition and conventional weapons systems will permit'.[117] which would suggest that it both incorporates highly salient aspects of Airland Battle and simultaneously envisages deeper strikes.[118] As such, FOFA applies both to OMGs and other forward elements of an unreinforced attack, and to forces, bases and installations much deeper into East European territory and essential to a more substantial Pact mobilisation. As General Rogers has been at pains to point out, 'deep strike' into the enemy's rear is hardly a newly acquired NATO requirement, but it has hitherto been a task allotted chiefly to NATO's increasingly vulnerable, expensive and scarce manned aircraft. More recently, however, alternative conventional weapon systems, such as runway cratering munitions, remotely deliverable mines and the Multiple Launch Rocket System, have become or are becoming available; the same is true of the improved target-acquisition resources which are vital for locating and identifying mobile targets. Many of these systems would serve as substitutes for elements of NATO's existing TNW arsenal — the conventionally armed Lance missile, for example — and FOFA can also be seen as part of a wider attempt to raise the nuclear threshold and enhance 'the conventional option', in addition to its contribution to the reinvigoration of forward defence.

TOWARDS A MORE CONVENTIONAL FUTURE?

General Rogers has repeatedly stated that it would require an average annual real defence spending increase of 4 per cent per annum throughout the Alliance if NATO is to establish a conventional capability sufficient to implement flexible response by the end of the 1980s. To achieve force goals already agreed by NATO would require the same 4 per cent real increase, according to SACEUR. But, as he has noted, 'past commitments often become overdue promissory notes as we witness slippages, reductions and cancellations of essential programmes'.[119] He has cited as evidence the widespread failure of member states to achieve the 3 per cent real increase they committed themselves to in 1977. It was calculated that by 1981 only five countries had achieved an average increase of 3 per cent in the four years since 1977 — the United States, much of whose spending increase was not on conventional forces; the insignificant example of Luxembourg;

France, which does not even sit on the DPC from where the 3 per cent commitment emanated; and Norway and Portugal. West Germany and Belgium exceeded 2.5 per cent; Greek defence spending, on the other hand, actually declined in real terms. [120] In 1981 itself, eight NATO countries met or surpassed the 3 per cent figure, whereas in 1982 only the UK, Norway and Luxembourg managed to repeat the performance, and even here the British figure is largely explained by the Falklands conflict rather than by increased NATO-related expenditure. [121] Even so, in June 1983 NATO's defence ministers once again reaffirmed the 3 per cent commitment, although it was only to apply to the following two years. Most states have not met the target. Of course, there are many flaws in setting spending goals in this way. There is no guarantee that the extra resources made available will be wisely spent; nor spent in such a way as to recognisably enhance military capacity. In the UK, for example, a 'catching up' pay rise for the armed services ate up some of the larger budget. There is no little scope for disagreements about how the increases should be measured, and what it relates to. This can provide opportunities for 'creative accounting', and there is little doubt that countries have endeavoured to boost their reputations within the Alliance by using such ploys. [122]

The genesis of this so-called '3 per cent solution' is also instructive. As a report made by the US defence secretary, Caspar Weinberger, to the US Congress in March 1984 noted, whereas real US defence spending during the 1970s actually declined by 7 per cent, that of Washington's European allies increased by 23 per cent. [123] The average real increase for the Europeans had been above 2 per cent per annum and often had exceeded 3 per cent, whereas for the US it had fallen by over 1 per cent, and between 1971 and 1976 by 2 per cent per annum on average. [124] In fact the pledge formed not only a response to a seemingly enhanced Soviet threat but was also part of a larger argument about burden-sharing — the Weinberger report already noted was itself produced as a result of congressional pressure which sprang from the widespread belief that the Europeans were not pulling their weight. This is an aspect of relations between NATO's member states which has never been absent, which may now be developing into a major cause of Allied dissension but which falls outside the scope of this book. The Americans may now be spending more than formerly, and all may be spending more than they would have done in the absence of the 3 per cent commitment, a commitment which has undoubtedly proved useful in domestic disputes with other spending ministries. Nevertheless, the European members are not spending a bigger percentage of their GNPs on defence now than they were before the 3 per cent solution was adopted. [125] Furthermore defence spending continues to consume a substatially smaller portion of NATO's collective GNP than it did during the 1950s and 1960s, and there are few signs as yet of a return to those heady days. With SACEUR we must question, for all the rhetoric, the extent of NATO's renewed passion for conventional forces. Although improvements — in war stocks, mobilisation rates and other aspects of readiness — are taking place, it is too early to declare that NATO is, at last, on the verge of providing the forces which would in a conflict offer NATO's military commanders options beyond the implementation of that 'trip wire' strategy which was officially discarded two decades ago.

THE NATIONAL AND ALLIANCE ROLES OF FRENCH CONVENTIONAL FORCES

Before concluding our remarks about NATO's non-nuclear posture, it is worth considering the French position. NATO's renewed concerns about its non-nuclear strength has inevitably refocused attention on the contribution France makes. For their part, the French too have become aware of the development of the Warsaw Pact's ground forces over the years. Accordingly, Paris has been reconsidering the role its conventional forces might play not only within the context of national defence policy but also as part of a wider Alliance effort. It cannot be said, however, that French attitudes in this area are noticeably less opaque than those which colour her nuclear policies; indeed, to treat French conventional-force policy in isolation from nuclear strategy would be artificial. At the core of overall French security policy is the apparent refusal to declare in peacetime what France would do in the event of war. Yet the very choices Paris makes in its procurement of defence forces cannot help but hint at what the country's preferences are likely to be. So it has been recently.

Even at the time of France's withdrawal from the military structure of the Alliance, the break was never complete. Not only did France continue to station troops in West Germany, (though now based on a bilateral understanding with Bonn) but a set of guidelines was drawn up with General Lemnitzer, NATO's Supreme Allied Commander, which outlined the terms of future co-operation between French forces and those of the rest of the Alliance. Covering training exercises, manoeuvres and war games, it has also been suggested that they incorporated contingency plans for French participation in war alongside other NATO armed forces, although this was never admitted openly. [126] On the other hand, whatever the precise details, French withdrawal has ever since complicated SHAPE's task. NATO's military authorities have been unable to draw up plans predicated on the certainty of French participation. In some respects, the loss of French territory and of guaranteed access to her air-space was an even bigger blow than the withdrawal of her forces — General Lemnitzer was himself apparently of this view — for it forced NATO to locate bases, storage dumps and lines of communications in more forward and hence more vulnerable positions. [127] It has also been argued that, as NATO did not have the capacity to properly implement flexible response anyway, the withdrawal of French forces from SACEUR's wartime domain made little real difference. [128] As for the Alliance's commitment to forward defence, the French had declined to move their rearward forces into more suitable locations even before 1966, [129] so on this score, at least, their withdrawal probably made little difference.

However, the tampering which took place, first in the late 1960s but more dramatically in the mid-1970s, with France's variant of 'massive retaliation', inevitably percolated down to the non-nuclear forces. By the late 1960s Paris was much more open that hitherto in its willingness to consider co-operation with its NATO allies at the conventional level; the French were also much more direct than were their European allies regarding their lack of enthusiasm for and inability to sustain a long campaign. [130] The Giscard government was more explicit still, with General Mery, the chief of staff of the armed forces, prepared to note the compatibility between 'a second-echelon participation in the first battle' (i.e. in Germany) and the defence of France itself. [131] During the same period the French also launched a reorganisation of their armed forces which, in line with the trend elsewhere in NATO, cut their overall size, created smaller army divisions but offered them more mobility and firepower.[132] There was also a 10,000-man reduction in the German deployment. The socialist government of President Mitterrand has not only continued along these lines but has made innovations which in themselves have aroused considerable speculation. A five-division, 47,000-strong rapid deployment force (FAR) has been created, part of which consists of a helicopter force designed for an anti-tank role.[133] More sensationally, perhaps, the defence minister, Charles Hernu, has conceded that in a European battle, the FAR would come under SACEUR's command and would depend on NATO's integrated air support and logistics.[134] The mobility, deployment and anti-tank profile of the FAR would appear to suit it admirably for the role of combating in West Germany OMGs which have broken through NATO's forward defences, and it has indeed been suggested that this would be its task.[135] In an interview with *Le Monde* in January 1983, General Rogers said:

Our goal is to do the maximum in time of peace so that if the French authorities decided to put their forces at the side of the Allies in the defence of Western Europe, we would not lose either time or effort and the two forces could join battle in a co-ordinated plan.[136]

The assessment of one analyst is that 'the FAR may represent a watershed in French planning for conventional commitments in Central Europe'.[137]

It is not simply the FAR which hints at a greater French role in any conflict in Germany, for the Mitterrand government has also planned to increase the number of tanks deployed with French forces in the Federal Republic and to take measures aimed at speeding up mobilisation. With ten ready divisions to add to the FAR's five, and with fourteen reservist divisions which would theoretically at least be available within forty-eight hours, the French would be in a position to make a not insubstantial contribution to NATO's overall ground capability. Although Paris continues to insist that its conventional forces are designed for a short war only, and although the French are believed to have war reserve supplies which would last for just two weeks of warfare, they are hardly in any worse a position in this respect than some of the European allies who are meant to be committed to a strategy which envisages a longer period of war than that the French foresee. It is also the case that a fairly high degree of practical integration and co-operation of French forces with those under NATO command has been built up over the years.[138] There may still be a resentment felt elsewhere in NATO that the French position serves only to weaken the Alliance's overall deterrent but, as *Pravda* has pointed out, France's 'non-participation in the military disposition of the Atlantic organisation does not have any importance owing to the fact that the engagements contracted by Paris have the same value as those of the other North Atlantic countries'.[139]

One final and interesting aspect of the French relationship with her Western partners is what appears to be a burgeoning 'special relationship' with West Germany. We have already noted the bilateral basis for the continued stationing of French forces on German soil. Similarly, the Germans maintain military storage sites inside France.[140] On a number of occasions, and usually with a laudable delicacy, Germans have raised the issue of a greater French co-operation with NATO and a firmer commitment to participate in any conflict.[141] In 1982, at a summit meeting between Chancellor Kohl and President Mitterrand, it was agreed that a Franco-German military commission be established. It meets every three months and includes matters of a generally strategic nature on its agenda.[142] Although much of the commentary and the very scantiness of detail on the proceedings of these meetings would both suggest that little of substance has resulted, the French prime minister, Laurent Fabius, has recently seen fit to describe the Franco-German strategic dialogue as 'historic'.[143] Whether there is or is not an element here of hyperbole, it may well be that the time is fast approaching when — with, it seems, Moscow — NATO may come to regard the French contribution as no less valuable and no less reliable than that offered by those countries who in peacetime agree to earmark forces for SACEUR.

9   Conclusion

An American student of NATO, David Calleo, once remarked, 'It is fair to say that if the Russian Army ever does advance into Europe, it will be the most elaborately anticipated and least expected invasion in Europe's history'.[1] It is indeed important to keep the life-and-death issues with which security policy is concerned in perspective. Few in NATO believe, or have ever believed, that a Soviet Bloc assault is, or has been, imminent. Assumptions that Soviet strategy may be essentially defensive in its orientation, or that Moscow tends to overinsure in its provision of force capabilities, have widespread currency — perhaps too widespread. Yet it has not been easy to relax in the face either of Soviet behaviour and attitude or of the post-war arrangements in Europe, for which Moscow bears much of the responsibility. It is not simply, or even particularly, the case that once some kind of Soviet threat to Western Europe and Western interests had been identified, then 'worst case analysis' took over and came to dominate the choice of response. It also seems apparent both that intentions are rarely divorced entirely from capabilities, and Moscow has never left itself devoid of somewhat worrying capabilities; and that a dynamic exists in military relations between East and West which creates pressures for both sides not to let their guards slip. Political face, and a European political context, have to be preserved, and the maintenance of armed forces organised in some sort of purposeful fashion has become a symbol of the determination of each side not to lose points in this political competition.

NATO clearly labours under some disadvantages in this Central European stand off. Its governments are at the electoral mercy of populations who are not only unconcerned on a day-to-day basis about military matters, but who have perfectly legitimate economic and welfare requirements on which they can effectively insist and which eat up scarce resources. To convince of the need to maintain a viable military strength when it is openly admitted that no attack is deemed to be imminent, or during periods of broader political relaxation and détente, is no easy task. It is complicated still further by the advent of nuclear weapons when, with the overdramatisation and simplification which inevitably characterises debate in the market place for political support, even those who think seriously about the issue might easily conclude that defeat and occupation is better than death. That avoidance of either of these evils may require a willingness to elaborately and expensively prepare to cause, and suffer, the latter, is not likely to be an argument which resonantly strikes political chords.

The exigencies of democracy have not been the only factors identified within these pages which have served to divert the Alliance from the creation of a militarily more cohesive posture. The very make-up of NATO, as a voluntary gathering of sovereign entities, has also tended to impurify the logic of the West's military position. Geography, historical experience, political preferences, economic circumstances and cultural make-up are not shared or identical within the Alliance, and that there have been areas of disagreement should come as no surprise. The central thesis of this volume has been that the 'flexible response' formally adopted in 1967 was not the same concept as that introduced by the US secretary of defence, Robert McNamara, half a decade earlier. Furthermore, it seems at least debatable whether NATO's current overall posture is substantially different from that which Washington sought to replace in the early 1960s. This is not a markedly radical or novel interpretation, for it is a view held in varying degrees by some of those who hold or have held some of the highest official positions within the Alliance. Nor is it an insignificant observation, however, for the basis for Washington's earlier revisionism remains intact, for all the relaxation in the American approach to its European allies. The underlying unease or malaise which this has fostered has been fuelled in recent years by a resurgence of Europe's 'peace movements'. At the time of writing, pressure from this source has lessened. But it will return when the Alliance next seeks to revise its doctrine or adjust its military capabilities in some substantial way. In a world in which justice and logic enjoyed a more intimate relationship, it would be those European governments which have so effectively thwarted Washington's underlying desire to reduce NATO's dependence on nuclear responses which were finding themselves under attack from the vociferously pacifistic elements in their own populations. Instead, it has been the Alliance leaders across the Atlantic who have incurred the wrath. It is they who, primarily through the insufficiency of the non-strategic elements of NATO's military power, have been required to flirt so publicly, interminably and speculatively with scenarios of nuclear war. The point here is that for all its power, the US has not been able to ensure the adoption of an Alliance posture more to its liking, or even to ensure that this is clearly understood.

With the ancient Greeks we can profess that knowledge cannot be compartmentalised, but, alas, our age forces specialisation upon us. A focus on the military relationships between states does not readily permit the analysis of economic, cultural and other areas of international exchange. Yet behind — or beneath — the day-to-day business of NATO affairs lies the shifting sand of economic and social changes which are barely susceptible to the short-term manipulations of policy-makers, however astute and politically representative these may be. The recent traumas through which NATO has been dragged have been marked by an antipathy among some sections of European opinion towards American governments and the system which produces them.[2] The Reagan administration has been singled out for particular hostility, yet its domestic popularity has been undoubted. This is a phenomenon which seems to have been most prevalent in the Federal Republic of Germany. Possibly, hopefully, such trends as these will in time be seen to be shallow and temporary. On the other hand, those societal changes of which they are manifestations may continue apace, only to emerge more forcefully, and destructively, at some future date. Emphatically, there is no desire nor reason, yet, to join with so many others and once again sound the death-knell of the Alliance. Yet NATO must be careful not to allow itself to become an empty husk, with form and outline but little of substance.

Notes

1. NATO BORN, GERMANY REBORN

1. Rothschild, 1982, p. 19.
2. Reid, 1980, p. 12.
3. Bohlen, 1973, p. 267.
4. For a fuller discussion, see Baylis, 1982.
5. For the text of the Brussels Treaty, see *NATO: Facts and Figures*, 1971, pp. 266–8.
6. Furniss, 1960, pp. 8–10.
7. Backer, 1978, pp.134–5.
8. Quoted in Ireland, 1981, p. 68. Ireland's book contains numerous illustrations of the French fear of a resurgent Germany.
9. It is not within the scope of this book to furnish an account of the origins of the Cold War. The bibliography for this is endless, but from more recent works the following are recommended: Gaddis, 1972; Paterson, 1973; Davis, 1974; Yergin, 1980.
10. See, for example, his telegram to President Truman, as quoted in Ismay, 1954, pp. 3–4.
11. As quoted in Achilles, Part I, 1979, p. 11.
12. Quoted in Henrikson, 1980, p. 16.
13. Henderson, 1982, p. viii.
14. Reid, 1980, p. 16; Henrikson, 1980, p. 10.
15. For accounts of this 'threat', see Reid, 1980, pp. 16–17; Henrikson, 1980, pp. 11–12; Henderson, 1982, pp. 11–12.
16. Reid, 1980, p. 17; Henderson, 1982, pp. 11–12; Rendel, 1979, pp. 16–18.
17. Reid, 1980, p. 13; Henderson, 1982, pp. 24–5.
18. For a discussion of Senator Vandenberg's contribution, see Ireland, 1981, pp. 80–114; Williams, 1985, pp. 12–14, 17–24; for the text of the Resolution, see *NATO: Facts and Figures*, 1971, p. 269.
19. Reid, 1980, p. 12.
20. For a discussion of Bevin's early thoughts, see Rendel, 1979.
21. Quoted in Henrikson, 1980 p. 19.
22. Achilles, 1979, Part 2, p. 16.
23. For a brief but interesting discussion of how history and technology combined to elevate a reluctant Iceland to a position of strategic signifi-

cance, see Egilsson, 1983, pp. 24—31.

24. Nogueira, 1980, pp. 8—13; see also Henderson, 1982, pp. 78, 110—11.
25. For more detailed accounts of the negotiations pertaining to Scandinavia, see Henderson, 1982, pp. 83—6; Henningson, 1979 and 1980; Vaerno, 1981.
26. Henderson, 1982, p. 87.
27. *Ibid.*, pp. 77, 105.
28. For more on the arguments surrounding Italian participation, see *ibid.*, pp. 55—6, 68—9, 80—1, 95—7; Ortona, 1981, Parts 1 and 2. Ortona, a senior diplomat at the Italian embassy in Washington during the negotiation, makes more of British opposition to Italian membership than does the British diplomat, Henderson. Ortona also has some interesting things to say about Italian lobbying inside the US.
29. Achilles, 1979, Part 1, p. 14.
30. For a discussion of the Treaty, see Ireland, 1981, pp. 37—41.
31. For the text of this proposed treaty, see Henderson, 1982, pp. 115—17.
32. Acheson, 1970, p. 365.
33. Ireland, 1981, pp. 110—11; Henderson, 1982, pp. 89—91; Williams, 1985, pp. 17—20.
34. Acheson, 1970, pp. 369—70.
35. Ibid., p. 376.
36. Henderson, 1982, pp. 69—70, 99—100.
37. Achilles, 1979, Part 2, p. 18.
38. Henderson, 1982, p. 82.
39. Quoted in Delmas, 1980, p. 24.
40. Harrison, 1981, p. 11.
41. Keesings 10143.
42. Quoted in Ireland, 1981, p. 134.
43. Quoted in Reid, 1980, pp. 14—15.
44. For a discussion of the treatment of foreign arms assistance prior to the ratification of the North Atlantic Treaty, see Ireland, 1980, pp. 122—30.
45. Schilling et al., 1962, p. 191.
46. Ismay, 1954, p. 9; Hilsman, 1959, p. 14.
47. According to Ireland, 1981, pp. 146—7.
48. Quoted in *ibid.*, p. 142.
49. Keesings 10008.
50. By Hammond in Schilling *et al.* 1962, p. 334; for details of the hearings, see Ireland, 1981, pp. 153—63; Williams, 1985, pp. 27—35; Keesings 10008.
51. Osgood, 1962, p. 47.
52. Keesings 10008.
53. Quoted in Ireland, 1981, p. 189.
54. *Ibid.*, pp. 166—7.
55. *Ibid.*, pp. 185—6; see also pp. 4—6, 54—5, 59.
56. *Ibid.*, p. 169.
57. Sticker, 1965, pp. 297—9; see also Fursdon, 1980, pp. 78—9; McGeehan, 1971, pp. 54—5.
58. Delmas, 1980, p. 24.
59. Quoted in Harrison, 1981, p. 14.

60. For an excerpt from the text of this statement, see Fursdon, 1980, p. 70.
61. Quoted in ibid., p. 64.
62. See, for example, McGeehan, 1971, pp. 3, 9.
63. Quoted in Fursdon, 1980, p. 68.
64. Quoted, for example, in Van Der Beugal, 1966, p. 260.
65. This is a major theme of Ireland's book, especially pp. 183–220. The following passages are based substantially on Ireland's findings.
66. McGeehan, 1971, p. 31, footnote.
67. For fuller details of the Plan and its origins, see Fursdon, 1980, pp. 86–90; McGeehan, 1971, pp. 62–5. The following discussion of the negotiations on the Plan is based on these two sources.
68. Keesings 10944.
69. For a portrayal of the enthusiasm which US officials, and particularly the US secretary of state, Dulles, displayed towards the EDC, see Van Der Beugal, 1966, pp. 273–96.
70. The following passages are based on Fursdon, 1980, pp. 310–336.
71. Quoted in Kirby, 1977, p. 103.

2. THE ROOTS OF NATO STRATEGY

1. Wolfe, 1970, p. 10.
2. McGeehan, 1971, p. 7.
3. Wolfe, 1970, p. 10.
4. Ismay, 1954, pp. 112–13.
5. Enthoven and Smith, 1971, pp. 132–42.
6. Keesings 10865.
7. Ismay, 1954, pp. 112–13.
8. Keesings 10450.
9. Richardson, 1981, p. 38.
10. Keesings 10869.
11. Ismay, 1954, p. 102.
12. *Ibid.*, p. 108; Keesings 13640.
13. See McGeehan, 1971, p. 7.
14. *NATO: Facts and Figures*, 1971, p. 195.
15. Ismay, 1954, p. 102.
16. Keesings 11679.
17. Wolfe, 1970, pp. 10–11, footnote.
18. Mackintosh, 1967, p. 66; Ismay, 1954, p. 29.
19. Keesings 10290.
20. *Ibid.* 10450.
21. *Ibid.* 11423.
22. *Ibid.* 11679.
23. Ismay, 1954, pp. 112–13.
24. These figures are taken from Kaufmann, 1964, p. 3.
25. Ismay, 1954, p. 4.
26. Keesings 9840.
27. Ismay, 1954, p. 4.

28. *Ibid.*, pp. 40, 110−12.
29. *NATO: Facts and Figures*, 1971, p. 89.
30. Keesings 10008.
31. *Ibid.* 10038.
32. Ismay, 1954, p. 133.
33. McGeehan, 1971, p. 237.
34. For a deeper discussion of this issue, see Foot, 1981, especially pp. 28−53.
35. Keesings 11978.
36. *Ibid.* 11357.
37. Huntington, 1961, pp. 314−15.
38. Ismay, 1954, p. 44; Foot, 1981, pp. 41−7.
39. Hilsman, 1959, pp. 15−17.
40. *Ibid.*, pp. 21−2.
41. Quoted in Osgood, 1962, p. 76.
42. Foot, 1981, p. 44.
43. For recent assessments of this document, and an insight into controversies which still surround it, see Wells, 1979; Gaddis and Nitze, 1980. The full document, declassified by Henry Kissinger in February 1975, was reproduced in *The Naval War College Review* (May/June 1975), 6.
44. Schilling *et al.*, 1962, pp. 400−6; Huntington, 1961, pp. 62−9; Osgood, 1962, pp. 87−91.
45. 'US Security Issues in Europe', *93rd Congress, 1973*, p. 13.
46. Heisenberg, 1973, p. 1.
47. Keesings 13357.
48. Ismay, 1954, p. 108.
49. Leitenberg, 1978, p. 126.
50. Keesings 13758.
51. Leitenberg, 1978, p. 111.
52. For further details of the TNW inventory in Europe, see the tables provided by Leitenberg, 1978, pp. 130−6; also see the disclosures by the US secretary of defence, James Schlesinger, in 'Nuclear Weapons and Foreign Policy', *93rd Congress, 1974*, p. 201.
53. Walter Whitman, quoted in Gilpin, 1968, pp. 114, 118.
54. For a further examination of these views, see Oppenheimer, 1953.
55. York, 1976, p. 135.
56. Quoted from the text of the report, reprinted in *ibid.*, p. 152.
57. Gilpin, 1968, p. 115.
58. Quoted in Rosenberg, 1983, p. 30; for more information on Project Vista, see Gilpin, 1968, pp. 117−20; Gavin, 1958, pp. 132−5.
59. Gilpin, 1968, pp. 124−5.
60. Heisenberg, 1973, p. 34.
61. Keesings 11903.
62. Zuckerman, 1982, p. 60.
63. Gavin, 1958, pp. 113−14.
64. *Ibid.*, p. 135.
65. Rosenberg, 1983, p. 27; see also Rosenberg, 1982, which also offers an insight into the role Eisenhower played in these early years.
66. Figures given in Rose, 1980, p. 57.

67. *Ibid.*, p. 62.
68. Osgood, 1962, p. 68; see also Leitenberg, 1978, p. 10.
69. Leitenberg, 1978, p. 10.
70. Keesings 11903.
71. Rose, 1980, pp. 83–4.
72. *Ibid.*, p. 87.
73. Rosenberg, 1983, pp. 29–30.
74. Gavin, 1958, p. 136.
75. *Ibid.*, p. 139.
76. Keesings 13061; Ismay, 1954, p. 106.
77. Ismay, 1954, p. 105.
78. Gavin, 1958, p. 139.
79. *Ibid.*, p. 153.
80. *Ibid.*, p. 265.
81. Richardson, 1981, p. 38.
82. Taylor, 1959, p. 174.
83. Rose, 1980, p. 32.
84. Quoted in Kaufman, 1964, p. 21.
85. Quoted in McNamara, 1983, p. 262; for further treatment of the economic motivations behind the New Look, see Schilling *et al.*, 1962, pp. 379–524.
86. Schilling *et al.*, 1962, p. 439.
87. Quoted in Osgood, 1962, p. 105.
88. Quoted in *ibid.*, p. 109.
89. Keesings 15336.
90. Schilling *et al.*, 1962, pp. 454–60.
91. Quoted in Rosenberg, 1983, p. 13.
92. *Ibid.*, pp. 14–15.
93. Schwartz, 1983, Ch. 2.
94. Rosenberg, 1983, pp. 22–3.
95. *Ibid.*, p. 31.
96. Quoted in Gaddis, 1982, p. 149.
97. Quoted in Huntington, 1961, p. 80.
98. Keesings 13640.
99. Quoted in Kaufmann, 1964, p. 25.
100. Rosenberg, 1982, p. 31.
101. 'US Security Issues in Europe', *93rd Congress, 1973*, p. 13.
102. Wikner, 1983.
103. 'Nuclear Weapons and Foreign Policy', *93rd Congress, 1974*, p. 37.
104. *Ibid.*, p. 85.
105. *Ibid.*, pp. 197–8.
106. *Ibid.*, pp. 18–19.
107. Kaufmann, 1964, p. 29.
108. 'Nuclear Weapons and Foreign Policy', *93rd Congress, 1974*, p. 132.
109. Rosenberg, 1982, p. 43.
110. Cochran *et al.*, 1984, p. 15.
111. Rosenberg, 1982, p. 55.
112. Reprinted, for example, in Ambrose and Barker, 1972, pp. 61–3.
113. Rosenberg, 1982, pp. 27–8.

114. *Ibid.*, p. 43.
115. *Ibid.*, pp. 42–3, 48–9.
116. Gaddis, 1982, p. 167.
117. Quoted in ibid., p. 175.
118. Quoted in Osgood, 1962, p. 109.
119. By Snyder, in Schilling *et al.*, 1962, p. 496.

3. OBVIATING THE NECESSITY

1. 'The modernisation of NATO's Long-Range Theatre Nuclear Forces', *96th Congress, 1980*, p. 12.
2. For an in-depth consideration of this and related points, see Heilbrunn, 1965.
3. Pierre, 1972, pp. 75–7.
4. Keesings 12054.
5. *Ibid.* 11978.
6. Greenwood, 1977, p. 178; figures putting British defence spending at a little under 10 per cent are cited in this article, p. 186.
7. Osgood, 1962, p. 88.
8. Greenwood, 1977, pp. 185–6.
9. Quoted in Groom, 1974, p. 95.
10. *Ibid.*, p. 62.
11. Schilling *et al.*, 1962, pp. 388–9.
12. Huntingdon, 1961, p. 118.
13. Cmnd. 9075, p. 5.
14. *Ibid.* 9391, p. 6.
15. Quoted in Groom, 1974, p. 109.
16. Kirby, 1977, p. 107; Mulley, 1962, p. 133.
17. Cmnd. 124, pp. 2–3.
18. *Ibid.* 363, paras. 4–5.
19. Groom, 1974, pp. 60, 122.
20. *Ibid.*, p. 66.
21. Baylis, 1977, p. 77.
22. Groom, 1974, p. 67.
23. Mulley, 1962, pp. 144–5; see also Groom, 1974, p. 262; and Pierre, 1972, p. 167.
24. Osgood, 1962, p. 134.
25. Cmnd. 363, para. 12.
26. Groom, 1974, p. 211.
27. Quoted in *ibid.*, p. 74.
28. Quoted in *ibid.*, p. 86.
29. Quoted in *ibid.*, pp. 83–84.
30. Keesings 15724.
31. *Ibid.* 15726.
32. Groom, 1974, p. 291.
33. *Ibid.*, p. 566.
34. Healey, 1959, p. 220.

35. *Ibid.*, p. 212.
36. *Ibid.*, p. 218.
37. Keesings 10886.
38. *Ibid.* 12050.
39. Harrison, 1981, p. 34.
40. Keesings 10886.
41. *Ibid.* 11044.
42. Harrison, 1981, p. 33.
43. Keesings 12878.
44. Harrison, 1981, p. 33.
45. *Ibid.*, pp. 34–5.
46. Mulley, 1962, pp. 151–2.
47. Harrison, 1981, pp. 34–5.
48. For a fuller exposition of these arguments, see *ibid.*, pp. 37–43.
49. Beufre, 1967, p. 52.
50. Harrison, 1981, pp. 21–2.
51. Beufre, 1967, pp. 33–46.
52. Harrison, 1981, pp. 12–13, 16–20.
53. Beufre, 1967, p. 29.
54. Kohl, 1971, pp. 30–3.
55. Harrison, 1981, p. 36.
56. Kohl, 1971, p. 42; see also pp. 37–47.
57. Harrison, 1981, pp. 34–5.
58. Groom, 1974, p. 61.
59. Osgood, 1962, p. 132.
60. Kelleher, 1975, p. 282.
61. Fursdon, 1980, p. 117.
62. Kelleher, 1975, p. 16.
63. Craig, 1959, pp. 240–1.
64. Kelleher, 1975, p. 33.
65. For the account which follows, see *ibid.*, pp. 43–9; see also Keesings 15094. For the background to Radford's proposals, and the leaks, see Taylor, 1959, pp. 39–43.
66. Craig, 1959, p. 243.
67. *Ibid.*, pp. 244–54.
68. Kelleher, 1975, pp. 45–8.
69. *Ibid.*, pp. 53–4, 61, 76–7, 84–5, 87, 160, 214–17.
70. For what follows, see Keesings 15723.
71. Keesings 16006.
72. Mulley, 1962, pp. 132–3.
73. *Ibid.*, p. 130.
74. McGeehan, 1971, p. 237.
75. Richardson, 1966, p. 76.

4. NUCLEAR CONTROVERSIES

1. The following passage is based on Kelleher, 1975, pp. 78–9; Osgood, 1962, p. 118; and Schwartz, 1983, pp. 71–3.

2. Kelleher, 1975, p. 95; Richardson, 1966, p. 50.
3. Kelleher, 1975, p. 55.
4. Schwartz, 1983, pp. 57–9.
5. For a useful treatment of the British origins of the concept, see Groom, 1974, pp. 55–91.
6. *Ibid.*, pp. 132, 261–2.
7. Mulley, 1962, p. 75.
8. Van Cleave and Cohen, 1978, p. 15.
9. Kissinger, 1965, pp. 97–8.
10. 'US Security Issues in Europe', *93rd Congress, 1973*, p. 16.
11. Quoted in Kelleher, 1975, pp. 111–12.
12. Craig, 1959, pp. 247–8.
13. Kelleher, 1975, pp. 113–14; Richardson, 1966, p. 57, footnote.
14. The following passage is based on Craig, 1959, pp. 245–7.
15. Kelleher, 1975, p. 114.
16. *Ibid.*, pp. 115–16.
17. Quoted in *Ibid.*, p. 114.
18. Osgood, 1962, p. 389, footnote.
19. Quoted in Craig, 1959, p. 244.
20. For details of the TNW arsenal, see Leitenberg, 1978; Cochran *et al.*, 1984.
21. Miller, 1970, reprinted in 'Nuclear Weapons and Foreign policy', *93rd Congress, 1974*, pp. 213–14.
22. Richardson, 1981, p. 40.
23. Zuckerman, 1982, pp. 64–5.
24. Enthoven and Smith, 1971, p. 128.
25. For further details, see Steinbruner, 1974, pp. 176–7, 182–8.
26. *Ibid.*, p. 242.
27. Schwartz, 1983, pp. 63–7.
28. *Ibid.*, p. 74.
29. Quoted in Kaufmann, 1964, p. 213.
30. Schwartz, 1983, pp. 64–5.
31. *Ibid.*, pp. 69–70; see also Kohl, 1971, pp. 35–41; and Harrison, 1981, p. 36.
32. Schwartz, 1983, pp. 69–70.
33. *Ibid.*, pp. 73–74.
34. *Ibid.*, pp. 70–71.
35. Quoted from his book, *Defence and Retaliation* (1961), in 'The Modernisation of NATO's Long-Range Theatre Nuclear Forces', *96th Congress, 1980*, p. 8.
36. For a recent consideration of Soviet thinking behind the Cuban missile deployments, see Weinland, 1984, especially p. 18.
37. For a full discussion of US plans for a nuclear strike against the Soviet Union in the event of war, see Rosenberg, 1983; and Brown, 1978.
38. The following account is based primarily on the detailed study of the MLF saga contained in Steinbruner, 1974, pp. 153–342; see also Kissinger, 1965, pp. 127–59; Buchan, 1964; Boulton, 1972; for a detailed account of the Federal Republic's MLF policies, see Kelleher, 1975, pp. 228–69.
39. Quoted in Williams and Reed, 1971, p. 173. Pierre gives an interesting

account of British tactics, pp. 243–51, 275–84.
40. For this distinction, see Buteux, 1983, particularly pp. 7–11.
41. Kohl, 1971, p. 19.
42. *Ibid.*, p. 46.
43. For a discussion of the Fourth Republic's programme, see *ibid.*, pp. 16–29.
44. For good general discussions of de Gaulle's approach to questions of security and international relations, see Harrison, 1981, pp. 49–71; Kissinger, 1965, pp. 41–64; and Grosser, 1980, pp. 183–6.
45. Kohl, 1971, pp. 61–2.
46. Bertrand Goldschmidt, *L'Aventure atomique* (Paris: Arthéme Fayard, 1962), p. 143, and quoted in Kohl, 1971, p. 82.
47. Kohl, 1971, pp. 44–7.
48. *Ibid.*, pp. 49–50.
49. Quoted in Harrison, 1981, p. 98.
50. The memorandum is reproduced in full in Grosser, 1980, pp. 186–7.
51. For an account of this, see Kohl, 1971, pp. 70–81; and Harrison, 1981, pp. 86–101.
52. This passage is based on Kohl, 1971, pp. 50–4; and Harrison, 1981, pp. 77–81.
53. Also see Osgood, 1962, pp. 225–6, and footnotes 24–6.
54. Harrison, 1981, p. 22.
55. Quoted in Kohl, 1971, pp. 66–7.
56. Quoted in *ibid.*, p. 90.
57. See Neustadt, 1970, pp. 30–55, for an account of this deal.
58. The Nassau communiqué is reproduced in MacMillan, 1973, pp. 553–5.
59. Harrison, 1981, p. 80.
60. Kohl, 1971, pp. 217–24.
61. For an account and an analysis of these events, see *ibid.*, pp. 229–38.
62. *Ibid.*, pp. 93–5.
63. *Ibid.*, p. 91; for a discussion of the steps leading to the French departure from NATO, see Harrison, 1981, pp. 134–40, on which the following passage is based.

5. FLEXIBLE RESPONSE

1. For two brief but useful discussions of strategic thought in the 1950s, see Moulton, 1973, pp. 27–35; and Mandelbaum, 1979, pp. 54–68.
2. Quoted in Gaddis, 1982, p. 219.
3. Ball, 1980, p. 190; for nuclear targeting during the 1950s, see also Rosenberg, 1983; and Brown, 1978.
4. See Kissinger, 1957, especially pp. 174–202.
5. For details of Moscow's tactical and theatre nuclear capabilities, see Meyer, *Adelphi Papers* 188 (1983/4).
6. For a brief account of the campaign, see Moulton, 1973, pp. 35–41.
7. For details of the developments in Soviet nuclear capabilities during this period, see Berman and Baker, 1982, pp. 45–9.

8. Ball, 1980, p. 55.
9. McNamara, 1968, p. 60; this work affords a valuable insight into McNamara's thinking; see also Kaufmann, 1964. Kissinger, 1965, especially pp. 91−125, is more critical.
10. Quoted in Kaufmann, 1964, p. 75.
11. Cleveland, 1970, p. 80.
12. Quoted in Kaufmann, 1964, p. 97.
13. Quoted in *ibid.*, p. 215.
14. Quoted in Kissinger, 1965, p. 102.
15. Quoted in Kaufmann, 1964, p. 128.
16. Quoted in *ibid.*, p. 76.
17. Quoted in *ibid.*, p. 112.
18. Quoted in Kissinger, 1965, p. 104.
19. McNamara, 1983, p. 263.
20. *Ibid.*, p. 270.
21. Kelleher, 1975, p. 159.
22. Schwartz, 1983, p. 151.
23. For this, see *ibid.*, pp. 153−6; Kelleher, 1975, pp. 158−62; Kaufmann, 1964, pp. 105−13.
24. Schwartz, 1983, p. 156; the quotations used in this text are taken from Schwartz, who reproduces large chunks of the speech, declassified in 1979, pp. 157−68.
25. Quoted in Williams and Reed, 1971, p. 254.
26. For the full text of the communiqué, see *NATO: Final Communiqués, 1949−1974*, pp. 195−98.
27. Cleveland, 1970, pp. 80−1.
28. See Nailor, 1981, p. 173.
29. McNamara, 1983, p. 264.
30. Nailor, 1981, p. 173.
31. This distinction is offered by Schwartz, 1983, p. 190.
32. For excerpts from Norstad's speech, see Keesings 17845.

6. EXTENDING DETERRENCE

1. Kissinger, 1980, p. 8.
2. Quoted in Williams and Reed, 1971, p. 142.
3. For a treatment of the incorporation of ideas such as these into American strategic doctrine, see Freedman, *The Evolution of Nuclear Strategy*, 1981, pp. 227−56.
4. This shift is described in Ball, 1980, pp. 179−211; Friedberg, 1980, pp. 47−53; and constitutes a major theme of Moulton's book.
5. Quoted in Friedberg, 1980, p. 51, from the US DoD Annual Report, 1965, p. 12.
6. McNamara, 1968, p. 67.
7. Quoted in Kaufmann, 1964, p. 115.
8. Enthoven and Smith, 1971, p. 175.
9. For an account of the US strategic build-up during this period, see Ball, 1980.

10. *Ibid.*, p. 57.
11. For these and other figures relating to the Soviet strategic build-up, see Berman and Baker, 1982.
12. US DoD Annual Report, 1975, p. 33.
13. US DoD Annual Report, 1981, p. 66.
14. Quoted in Davis, 1975/76, p. 2.
15. Cordesman, 1982, p. 13.
16. Quoted, for example, in US DoD Annual Report, 1975, p. 35.
17. Quoted in Sloss and Millet, 1984, p. 21.
18. Cordesman, 1982, pp. 13–14, 17–18; Davis, 1975/76, pp. 5–6; for a more detailed consideration of the force requirements and difficulties of a limited flexible nuclear options strategy, see Davis, pp. 14–22.
19. Ball, 1975, p. 214.
20. For an excerpted text of Brown's speech, see *Survival* 22 (Nov./Dec., 1980), 6.
21. For a brief consideration of US strategic nuclear policies during the 1970s, see Schilling, 1981.
22. US DoD Annual Report, 1983, pp. 17–19.
23. Ball, 1981, pp. 35–8.
24. US DoD Annual Report, 1978, pp. 83–4.
25. See Brown's speech as cited above.
26. See 'The Effects of Nuclear War', Office of Technology Assessment, 1979, p. 94; see also Schilling, 1981, p. 64; Ball, 1983, p. 20.
27. See, for example, Clark, 1982, and my review of this book in *The Journal of Strategic Studies* (June 1984), 2: 214–15.
28. For example, Cordesman, 1982; Ravenal, 1982.
29. Rosenberg, 1983, pp. 14–15.
30. This figure is given in Berman and Baker, 1982, p. 43.
31. Keesings 17845.
32. Portugalov, 1981, p. 41.
33. See Meyer, *Adelphi Papers* 188, 1983/84, pp. 7–9; see also Meyer's *Adelphi Papers* 187, 1983/84, for an analysis of Soviet nuclear weapons doctrine with regard to the European theatre from the beginning of the nuclear age up to the present.
34. Ball, 1983.
35. The Soviet figures given throughout this chapter are taken from Meyer's *Adelphi Papers* 188, 1983/84, or from Berman and Baker, 1982.
36. Lautenschlager, 1980, p. 17.
37. Meyer, *Adelphi Papers* 188, 1983/84, p. 29.
38. For an analysis of the Soviet decision to develop and deploy the SS-20, see Garthoff, 1983.
39. Bundy, 1982.
40. For a full discussion of the military characteristics of the SS-20, see Meyer, *Adelphi Papers* 188, 1983/84, pp. 26–9.
41. See the statement by Richard R. Burt, reproduced in *Survival* 26 (Mar./Apr. 1984) 2:90.
42. See *The Times*, 'Moscow Accuses US of Juggling Missile Numbers', 13/10/1984.

43. See *The Times*, 'Russia Deploying More Missiles Claims US', 15/3/1985.
44. See *The Times*, 'More SS-20s in Europe Bush Says', 29/6/1985.
45. Meyer, *Adelphi Papers* 188, 1983/84, p. 26.
46. Schmidt, 1971, p. 113.
47. For the text of the speech, see, for example, *Survival* 20 (Jan./Feb. 1978), 1.
48. A point made by Joffe, 1983, pp. 21–6.
49. Burt, *Survival*, 1976; see also Burt, 1977.
50. Holm and Peterson, 1983, p. 9
51. See *Strategic Survey*, IISS, London, 1976, p. 17.
52. Thomson, 1984, p. 603.
53. US DoD Annual Report, 1978, p. 56.
54. Quoted in 'The Modernisation of NATO's Long-Range Theatre Nuclear Forces', *96th Congress, 1980*, p. 16.
55. Thomson, 1984, pp. 603–4.
56. Quoted in Joffe, 1983, p. 33.
57. 'The Theatre Nuclear Force Posture in Europe', Schlesinger, 1975.
58. 'Nuclear Weapons and Foreign Policy', *93rd Congress, 1974*, pp. 151–211; for a description of the relationship between the GSP and the SIOP, see p. 163; for a further discussion of NATO's deployment rationales, see Sigal, 1984, pp. 24–53.
59. 'The Modernisation of NATO's Long-Range Theatre Nuclear Forces', *96th Congress, 1980*, p. 19.
60. See 'The Theatre Nuclear Force Posture in Europe', Schlesinger, 1975, p. 29, for the Poseidon decision; and *Strategic Survey*, IISS London, 1976, p. 123, for the F1-11 announcement.
61. Thomson, 1984, p. 605.
62. *Ibid.*, pp. 606–7.
63. *Ibid.*, p. 609; see also 'The Modernisation of NATO's Long-Range Theatre Nuclear Forces', *96th Congress, 1980*, pp. 20–3.
64. Thomson, 1984, p. 610.
65. Quoted in 'The Modernisation of NATO's Long-Range Theatre Nuclear Forces', *96th Congress, 1980*, p. 34.
66. Buteux, 1983, pp. 173–4.
67. See 'The Modernisation of NATO's Long-Range Theatre Nuclear Forces', *96th Congress, 1980*, pp. 29–31 for the work of the SG.
68. *Ibid.*, pp. 37–8; for the December communiqués, see pp. 65–70.
69. Quoted in Thomson, 1984, p. 609.
70. Moore, 1981, p. 404.
71. Garthoff, 1983, footnote 12, p. 119.
72. US DoD Annual Report, 1983, pp. 71–2.
73. Quoted in Millet, 1981, p. 4.
74. Ball, 1983, pp. 15–17.
75. Quoted in Millet, 1981, p. 8.
76. Quoted in 'The Modernisation of NATO's Long-Range Theatre Nuclear Forces', *96th Congress, 1980*, p. 51.
77. Quoted in *ibid.*, p. 52.

78. Portugalov, 1981, pp. 40–3.
79. See the comments he made in an interview he gave to *Der Spiegel*, as excerpted in *Survival* 24 (Jan./Feb. 1982), 1.
80. Sigal, 1984, pp. 54–104, offers a useful account of the impact of the LRTNF modernisation decision on the European political scene.
81. The term is Richard Burt's; see Burt, 1981, p. 52. For a broader discussion of Soviet attitudes to NATO's 'Eurostrategic' missiles, see Garner, 1983.
82. Reproduced in *Survival* (Nov./Dec. 1964), 6.
83. Quoted in Harrison, 1981, p. 78.
84. Quoted in Kohl, 1971, p. 103.
85. *Ibid.*, p. 198.
86. For details of the Mirage IV force, see *ibid.*, pp. 179–83.
87. For these details, see Kolodziej, 1982, pp. 190–2; Davis, 1984, pp. 166–7; and Ross, 1983, p. 30.
88. Berger, 1981, p. 44.
89. Kolodziej, 1982, pp. 190–2.
90. Ross, 1983, p. 30.
91. Excerpts from which were published in *Survival* 26 (Nov./Dec. 1983) 6.
92. See Rudney, 1984, for a general analysis of Mitterrand's 'Atlanticism'.
93. Howarth, 1984, pp. 588–90.
94. See Malone, 1984, pp. 156–89, for a discussion of this shift in Washington's, and Europe's, perspectives.
95. For a statement of rationales, see Pym, 1980.
96. See Malone, 1984, pp. 106–28, for a detailed account of the Trident decision.
97. Most notably David Greenwood; see Greenwood, 1982, for example. Malone, 1984, pp. 129–55, offers a good discussion of the cost of the system and its likely consequences for the British defence budget generally.

7. THE NUCLEAR BATTLEFIELD

1. Quoted in Kelleher, 1975, p. 165.
2. *Ibid.*, p. 213.
3. Quoted in *ibid.*, pp. 346–7, footnote 37; see also p. 173.
4. For a full account of the Berlin Crisis of 1958–62, see Richardson, 1966, pp. 245–336.
5. Kelleher, 1975, pp. 212, 243.
6. Quoted in *ibid.*, p. 40.
7. *Ibid.*, p. 176.
8. *Ibid.*, pp. 206–7.
9. Von Hassel, 1965.
10. Kelleher, 1975, p. 209.
11. Quoted in *ibid.*, p. 213.
12. *Ibid.*, p. 217; see pp. 203–20 for a discussion of the evolution of West German policy during this period.

13. For a discussion of these developments, see Groom, 1974, pp. 55–91.
14. Healey, 1969.
15. See Groom, 1974, pp. 513–19.
16. For a brief description of the TNW capabilities of France and the UK, see Leitenberg, 1978, pp. 64–73.
17. Ailleret, 1964.
18. Quoted in Yost, 1984, p. 8.
19. For an analysis of the 'European' attitude towards flexible response in the early and mid-1960s, see Kissinger 1965, pp. 91–125.
20. Buteux, 1983, is by far the best source of information on the NPG, and the following pages are based on it. See pp. 39–68 for an account of the origins of the NPG.
21. For a discussion of the 'host-country veto' issue, see *ibid.*, pp. 64, 104–6, 231.
22. Alford, 1981, p. 80; a figure of 370 has more recently been cited, in Segal, 1984, p. 157.
23. For a brief account of the visit and the associated furore in West Germany, see Kelleher, 1975, pp. 215–18.
24. 'The Theatre Nuclear Force Posture in Europe', Schlesinger, 1975, p. 18.
25. SIPRI, 1978, pp. 151, 239.
26. Kelleher, 1975, p. 303.
27. A point made during Senate Hearings in 1974; see 'Nuclear Weapons and Foreign Policy', *93rd Congress, 1974*, p. 203. For coverage of the NPG's deliberations on ADMs, on which the treatment here has been based, see Buteux, 1983, pp. 54–5, 72–4, 106, 110, 115–21, 135–6, 241.
28. 'Nuclear Weapons and Foreign Policy', *93rd Congress, 1974*, p. 204.
29. US DoD Annual Report, 1983, p. 74.
30. For an outline of the Healey–Schroeder proposals, see Buteux, 1983, pp. 90–1.
31. *Ibid.*, pp. 222–7, for the demonstration use of TNWs issue.
32. Morton Halperin, in 'Nuclear Weapons and Foreign Policy', *93rd Congress, 1974*, p. 44.
33. For a discussion of the overall European attitude to TNWs, see Bracken, 1983, pp. 158–64; for a concise statement of the German position, see Davidson, 1974.
34. See Bundy *et al.*, 1982, and the reply from Kaiser *et al.*, 1982. For a broader analysis of the NFU issue, see Steinbruner and Sigal, 1983.
35. Henry Kissinger, 'End the Nuclear War Paralysis', *The Sunday Times*, 3/3/1985.
36. Joffe, 1983, p. 33.
37. US DoD Annual Report, 1975, p. 82.
38. 'Nuclear Weapons and Foreign Policy', *93rd Congress, 1974*, pp. 151–211.
39. US DoD Annual Report, 1978, pp. 83–4.
40. *Ibid.*, p. 13.
41. US DoD Annual Report, 1980, p. 18.

42. A point made by Schlesinger in his 1975 report, 'The Theatre Nuclear Force Posture in Europe', p. 22.
43. Most notably Colin Gray, who is, in fact, British born. To be fair, his comments relate chiefly to intercontinental exchanges. See Gray, 1979; and Gray and Payne, 1980.
44. Two relatively recent and worthwhile critiques of the use of TNWs in Europe are Thomson, 1983; and Frye, 1980. See also Bracken, 1980; and Record, 1974.
45. 'Nuclear Weapons and Foreign Policy', *93rd Congress, 1974*, p. 199.
46. Bracken, 1983, p. 165.
47. Schlesinger described the release procedures in 'Nuclear Weapons and Foreign Policy', *93rd Congress, 1974*, p. 157; for a diagrammatic representation, see his 1975 report, 'The Theatre Nuclear Force Posture in Europe', p. 21.
48. Leitenberg, 1978, p. 43.
49. *Ibid.*, see also Bracken, 1983, pp. 170–1.
50. Leitenberg, 1978, p. 129.
51. Bracken, 1983, pp. 168–9.
52. 'The Theatre Nuclear Force Posture in Europe', Schlesinger, 1975, p. 27.
53. See Buteux, 1983, pp. 209–10.
54. Steinbruner, 1974, p. 182.
55. 'Nuclear Weapons and Foreign Policy', *93rd Congress, 1974*, p. 155.
56. *Ibid.*, p. 202.
57. *Ibid.*, p. 209.
58. *Ibid.*, p. 198.
59. For extensive quotation from the article, see Cohen, *The Neutron Bomb*, 1978, p. 35.
60. According to Leitenberg, 1982, p. 355.
61. Quoted in Cohen, *The Neutron Bomb*, 1978, p. 35.
62. Quoted in *ibid.*, p. 37.
63. Quoted in Vardamis, 1978, p. 43.
64. Quoted in Cohen, *The Neutron Bomb*, 1978, p. 36.
65. Sommer, 1977.
66. In an article in *Vorwarts*, 17/7/1977, and quoted in Joffe, 1981, p. 84. The following passage is based on this article.
67. See Vermaat, 1981.
68. For an insight into the legalistic and moralistic basis of Kruisinga's (and many of his compatriot's) opposition to the ERW, see his statement in *The Bulletin of Atomic Scientists* (Oct. 1981) 8:59–60.
69. Quoted in Cohen, *The Neutron Bomb*, 1978, p. 36; see pp. 43–7 for Soviet behaviour during the crisis.
70. See Freedman, 'The Neutron Bomb Returns', 1981.
71. The following technical explanation follows Kaplan, 1978, pp. 44–51; see also Kaplan, 1981, pp. 6–7; Cohen, *The Neutron Bomb*, 1978, pp. 66–70; Cohen, 'Enhanced Radiation Warheads', 1978, pp. 9–17.
72. Quoted in Cohen, *The Neutron Bomb*, 1978, p. 47.
73. Quoted in Cohen, 'Enhanced Radiation Warheads', 1978, p. 13.

74. See Kistiakowsky, 1978, pp. 25–9, for this argument; see also Kaplan, 1978.
75. See Cohen, 'Enhanced Radiation Warheads', 1978, pp. 15–16.
76. For this argument, see Wisner, 1981, pp. 246–51.
77. Leitenberg, 1982, makes this point strongly; see especially p. 347.
78. Shreffler, 1978, p. 962.
79. See Leitenberg, 1982, p. 344.
80. See Wisner, 1981, p. 249 for this point.
81. See Shreffler, 1978, p. 961, and the retort by Cohen and Van Cleave annexed to the article, p. 970.
82. Quoted in Cohen, *The Neutron Bomb*, 1978, p. 73, and Cohen, 'Enhanced Radiation Warheads', 1978, p. 14.
83. See Schlesinger's comments in 'Nuclear Weapons and Foreign Policy', *93rd Congress, 1974* p. 159.
84. Leitenberg, 1982, pp. 353–4.
85. Buteux, 1983, p. 160.
86. Reprinted in full in Cohen, *The Neutron Bomb*, 1978, pp. 94–5.
87. See Leitenberg, 1982, pp. 356–7, too, for the German position.
88. Quoted in Cohen, *The Neutron Bomb*, 1978, p. 51.
89. Quoted in *ibid.*, p. 53.
90. See Leitenberg, 1982, p. 359; the following passages are based on this article.
91. Quoted from Schmidt's *Defence or Retaliation*, 1962, p. 82, by Freedman, 'The Neutron Bomb Returns', 1981.
92. Wisner, 1981, p. 251.
93. According to Schlesinger in 'Nuclear Weapons and Foreign Policy', *93rd Congress, 1974*, p. 159.
94. See Alain C. Enthoven's testimony in *ibid.*, p. 133.
95. *Ibid.*, p. 74.
96. Record, 1974, p. 70.
97. 'Nuclear Weapons and Foreign Policy', *93rd Congress, 1974*, p. 163.
98. For a brief summary of this, see Leitenberg, 1978, pp. 38–9.
99. For excerpts from both the communiqué and annex, see *Survival* 26 (Jan./Feb. 1984), 1:36–7.
100. Buteux, 1983, p. 156.
101. For excerpts from the final communiqué, see *Survival* 27 (May/June 1985), 3:129–30.
102. Yost, 1984, pp. 8–10.
103. See the exchange between Senator Symington and Stanley Hoffman in 'Nuclear Weapons and Foreign Policy', *93rd Congress, 1974*, p. 44.
104. See *Survival* 17 (Sept./Oct. 1975), 17; and *Survival* 18 (Sept./Oct. 1976), 5, for statements of the French position from President Giscard, Prime Minister Chirac and General Mery, head of the armed forces.
105. Quoted in Yost, 'The French Defence Debate', 1981, p. 20.
106. These details are taken from Kolodziej, 1982, p. 203. The range of the Pluton seems to be a matter of some uncertainty. Ross, 1983, gives it a 60-mile reach, whilst a report in *The Guardian*, 21/4/1983, entitled 'French Raise Spending on Nuclear Arms', puts it at just 45 miles.

107. See Yost, 1984, pp. 12–13.
108. For a broader consideration of French defence policy under Mitterrand, see Rudney, 1983 and 1984; for differences of opinion within the French Socialist Party, see Howarth, 1984.
109. Davis, 1984, p. 169.
110. For an outline of contemporary French security debates, see Yost, 'The French defence debate', 1981; Davis, 1984.
111. Dvis, 1984, p. 173.
112. Yost, 'The French Defence Debate', 1981, p. 25.
113. Quoted in *The Guardian*, 27/6/1983, 'French Neutron Blast'.
114. Rudney, 1984, p. 89.
115. Quoted in Rudney, 1983, p. 25.

8. BELOW THE NUCLEAR THRESHOLD

1. This section is based on Rogers, *Strategic Review*, 1983; see also the text of his lecture at the Royal United Services Institute in London in September 1982, in *RUSI Journal*, 1982.
2. See his response to a question put by Senator Goldwater during Senate Hearings on 'Department of Defence Authorisation for Appropriations for 1983', *97th Congress, 1982*, pp. 4335–6.
3. 'NATO and the New Soviet Threat', 1977 (hereafter referred to as the Nunn–Bartlett Report), p. 7.
4. Abshire, 1984, p. 10; also see comments made by George Ball and Albert Wohlstetter in Hampson, 1983–84, pp. 57–58; also Cordesman, 1982; and Ravenal, 1982.
5. There is no shortage of material on the 'peace movement;' for a sample of the analysis of two influential Germans, see Worner, 1982; and Hofmann, 1984.
6. For an analysis of this phenomenon as it related to LRTNF, see Freedman, 1982.
7. See Stewart, 1985, for a similar list of motivations drawn up by a NATO official; see also the Report of the European Security Study (hereafter referred to as ESECS), 1983, p. 8.
8. For a consideration of the various proposals for alternative conventional postures, see Strachan, 1985.
9. Rogers, 1983, p. 13.
10. Abshire, 1984, p. 8.
11. In Rogers, 1983, p. 16; see also his testimony in 'Department of Defence Authorisation for Appropriations for 1983', *97th Congress, 1982*, p. 4335.
12. See Jukes, 1982, p. 96.
13. Enthoven and Smith, 1971, pp. 132–64.
14. See Shisko, 1981, on which the following passage is based.
15. US DoD Annual Report, 1978, p. 81.
16. Karber, 'The Battle of Unengaged Military Strategies', 1983; see also Schemmer, 1976.

17. This figure is taken from Karber, 'To lose an Arms Race', 1983, p. 34. For slightly different totals, see Fischer, 1976, p. 8. *The Statement on the Defence Estimates* for 1985 issued by the British Ministry of Defence allows thirty-three NATO divisions to the Pact's fifty-seven (p. 50).
18. See the West German *Defence White Paper*, 1983, p. 84; the current figures given here are those officially given by NATO; see *NATO and the Warsaw Pact: Force Comparisons*, p. 7.
19. Mearsheimer, 1982, p. 8.
20. In the forward to the book by the Belgian Army General, Robert Close, 1979, p. ix.
21. Karber, 'To Lose an Arms Race', 1983, p. 34.
22. See the calculations in Fischer, 1976, p. 15.
23. A point made by Mearsheimer, 1982, p. 7, footnote 15.
24. Karber, 'To Lose an Arms Race', 1983, pp. 35−6.
25. See the graph representing US and West German force levels in Europe, 1948−83, in Sloan, 1983, p. 51.
26. US DoD Annual Report, 1975, p. 88.
27. US DoD Annual Report, 1978, p. 109.
28. Betts, 1981, pp. 140−1; also Nunn−Bartlett Report, 1977, p. 18.
29. See Fischer, 1976, pp. 15−25, for a discussion of mobilisation and reinforcement.
30. Schemmer, 1976, p. 30.
31. See Hampson, 1983−84, pp. 66−7, for a table comparing Pact/NATO force ratios under various mobilisation scenarios; see Fischer, 1976, and Shishko, 1981, for alternative Pact/NATO comparisons; Mako, 1983, p. 54, provides a table showing available NATO combat units at various junctures during a ninety-day mobilisation; Posen, 1984−85, contains a useful discussion of Pact and NATO mobilisation rates (pp. 62−70).
32. Mearsheimer, 1982, p. 9; and 1983, p. 168.
33. Posen, 1984−85, p. 67; Mearsheimer, 1983, p. 166; Fischer, 1976, p. 16, footnote 36.
34. For a consideration of these problems, see Betts, 1981; the following passage is, broadly, based on this source.
35. West German Defence White Paper, 1983, p. 59; for a detailed account of the evolution of US ground-troop levels in Europe since the Second World War, see Mako, 1983, pp. 3−30.
36. According to *The Military Balance*, IISS, 1983−84, p. 138; a 'reservist' here is defined as someone who has received military training within the last five years.
37. *Soviet Military Power*, Washington, 1985, p. 66.
38. Mako, 1983, p. 9.
39. West German Defence White Paper, 1983, pp. 125−6; see also Mako, 1983, p. 49.
40. For a general consideration of the relationship between reserve forces and readiness, see Betts, 1983, pp. 29−31.
41. Shishko, 1981, pp. 20−1; Betts, 1981, p. 141; Mako, 1983, p. 58; also

see Mako, pp. 52–3, for some observations on the complexities of US reinforcement of Europe.

42. Karber, 'The Battle of Unengaged Military Strategies', 1983 pp. 213–14.
43. Karber, 'To Lose an Arms Race', 1983, p. 80.
44. For some examples, see *ibid.*, p. 81; British Defence Estimates, 1985, p. 50; West German Defence White Paper, 1983, pp. 85–96; *The Military Balance*, IISS, 1983–84, pp. 138–9.
45. Karber, 'To Lose an Arms Race', 1983, p. 40; this is by far the best source on the shifting armaments balance in Europe.
46. *Ibid.*, pp. 42–6.
47. *Soviet Military Power*, Washington, 1985, p. 75.
48. Karber, 'To Lose an Arms Race', 1983, pp. 49–53.
49. *Ibid.*, pp. 85–8; Karber provides figures for other weapons categories too.
50. West German Defence White Paper, 1983, pp. 142–5.
51. *Ibid.*, 1979, p. 126.
52. *Ibid.*, 1983, pp. 158–62.
53. See Mearsheimer, 1981–82, for a critique of mobile defence.
54. Quoted in Yost, 1984, p. 59.
55. For a diagrammatic representation of the evolution of forward defence and a brief discussion of each of its stages, see Karber, 1984, p. 28.
56. See, for example, the West German Defence White Paper, 1983, p. 144; see also Stratman, 1983, p. 163. For a brief description of active defence, see Karber, 1984, pp. 42–6.
57. Mearsheimer, 1981–82; Depuy, 1979.
58. Stratman, 1983, pp. 163–71; Canby, 1983, pp. 120–3.
59. Mearsheimer, 1981–82, pp. 120–1.
60. Huntingdon, 1983–84; for a critique of Huntington's arguments, see Dunn and Staudenmaier, 1985.
61. For the genesis and contents of Airland Battle and its relationship to SHAPE's Follow-on Forces (FOFA) concept, see Rogers, 1984; Sutton *et al.*, 1984, and Gessert, 1984.
62. Rogers, 1984, p. 7.
63. Cotter, 1983, p. 213; see also Greenwood's comment, 1984, p. 12.
64. Dinter and Griffiths, 1983, p. 120.
65. For diagrammatic representations of NATO's 'layer cake' deployments, see Karber, 1984, p. 32; West German Defence White Paper, 1983, p. 143; Mako, 1983, p. 33; and Mearsheimer, 1982, p. 11.
66. For brief discussions of the variety of tactics employed, see Dinter and Griffiths, 1983, pp. 33–42; Karber, 1984, p. 42; Blackwell, 1984, pp. 141–7.
67. West German Defence White Paper, 1983, p. 160.
68. Dinter and Griffiths, 1983, especially p. 120; Blackwell, 1984, p. 147.
69. Lindner, 1984, p. 112.
70. Mearsheimer, 1982, pp. 20–6; Karber, 1984, pp. 28–34.
71. Force-to-space ratios are discussed in Mearsheimer, 1982, pp. 26–30;

Karber, 1984, pp. 34–6.
72. Betts, 1981, p. 141.
73. Nunn–Bartlett Report, 1977, pp. 1–7.
74. ESECS, 1983, pp. 15–16; Mearsheimer, 1982, p. 5, footnote 7.
75. For details, see Schemmer, 1976; ESECS, 1983, p. 15; see also the Nunn–Bartlett Report, 1977; and Close, 1979.
76. See Mearsheimer, 1983, pp. 23–64, for a consideration of *Blitzkrieg* tactics.
77. See Donnelly, 1982; Donnelly, 1983; Hines and Peterson, 1983; in fact, far from being a new concept, the OMG seems to be based on traditional force structuring ideas; for this, see Donnelly, 1984.
78. Hines and Peterson, 1983, p. 1395.
79. Blackwell, 1984, p. 142.
80. West German Defence White Paper, 1983, p. 105.
81. 'Money-Saver', *The Times*, 19/4/1985.
82. West German Defence White Paper, 1983, pp. 105–6.
83. Garrett, 1984, p. 69.
84. Nunn–Bartlett Report, 1977, p. 12.
85. Karber, 1984, p. 36.
86. West German Defence White Paper, 1983, p. 84.
87. Close, 1979, p. 163.
88. *Ibid.*, p. 175; see pp. 165–78 for a graphic description of a surprise attack scenario in Europe.
89. Karber, 1984, pp. 36–7.
90. Stratman, 1983, p. 171.
91. Karber, 'The Battle of Unengaged Military Strategies', 1983, p. 222.
92. US DoD Annual Report, 1980, p. 18.
93. This is a central thesis of Karber, 'To Lose an Arms Race', especially pp. 80–4.
94. Close, 1979, pp. 106–8.
95. For example, see the exchange between US Army General Kroeson and Senator Levin in 'Department of Defence Authorisation for Appropriation for 1983', *97th Congress, 1982*, p. 2759.
96. Nunn–Bartlett Report, 1977, pp. 13–14
97. US DoD Annual Report, 1978, p. 109; 1980, pp. 19, 102.
98. 'Department of Defence Authorisation for Appropriations for 1983', *97th Congress, 1982*, p. 4348.
99. *Ibid.*, p. 4335.
100. British Atlantic Committee, 1984, p. 36.
101. Dinter and Griffiths, 1983, especially p. 21.
102. For the communiqué of the meeting, see *NATO Review* (Dec. 1984), 6:24–6.
103. According to the *Defence Estimates*, 1985, p. 15.
104. *Ibid.*, p. 49.
105. See Posen, 1984–85, p. 47, footnote 1, for a brief but useful categorisation of proposed reforms; see also Strachan, 1985.
106. Canby, 1983, pp. 120–2; Alford, 1980, p. 21; Stratman, 1983; Garrett, 1984.

107. Garret, 1984, pp. 67–8; Mearsheimer, 1982, p. 37.
108. See, for example, Mearsheimer, 1982; Alford, 1980; and Posen, 1984–85.
109. As quoted in Mearsheimer, 1982, pp. 13–14.
110. See ESECS, 1983; British Atlantic Committee, 1984; and excerpts from a Senate report by Sam Nunn, reproduced in *Survival* 24 (Sept./ Oct. 1982), 5:234–6, for some influential examples of this fascination.
111. See Gordon, 1984, and Cotter, 1983, for brief but useful summaries of the new technologies.
112. See Burt, 'New Weapons Technologies', 1976; Kemp *et al.*, 1975; and Digby, 1975.
113. Greenwood, 1984.
114. Cotter, 1983, and Komer, 1984, err on the affordable side; Williams and Wallace, 1984, are less sure.
115. For various points on this offence/defence spectrum, see Mearsheimer, 1983, pp. 189–202; Mearsheimer, 1979; Goure and McCormick, 1980; Karber, 1984, pp. 47–9; Brown, 1982; and Hampson, 1983–84.
116. For a brief account of progress so far, see Stewart, 1985.
117. See Rogers, 1984, pp. 1–2; see also his article in *NATO's Sixteen Nations* (Feb./Mar. 1983), 1.
118. For comparisons of FOFA and Airland Battle, see note 61 above.
119. Rogers, 1981, p. 3.
120. Sloan, 1983, p. 46.
121. *Ibid.*, p. 14.
122. Examples are given in Foreign Policy Research Institute, 1981, and Greenwood, 1981. Both of these sources give good accounts of the genesis of the '3 per cent solution'.
123. *Allied Contributions to the Common Defence*, Washington, 1984, p. 1.
124. Greenwood, 1981, p. 253.
125. See *NATO Review* (Dec. 1984), 6:31. This shows defence spending expressed as a percentage of GNP for each NATO state since 1974.
126. For a discussion of these matters, and also of the allied evacuation of France and the alternative arrangements made, see Harrison, 1981, pp. 148–63.
127. Yost, 1984, pp. 59–61.
128. For this view, see Hunt, 1966, and Yost, 1984, p. 1.
129. Yost, 1984, p. 39.
130. *Ibid.*, pp. 8–10.
131. *Ibid.*, pp. 11–12.
132. *Ibid.*, pp. 22–5.
133. For details of the FAR and other aspects of the recent reforms, see *ibid.*, pp. 29–33; Ross, 1983, pp. 31–4.
134. Rudney, 1984, p. 90.
135. Howorth, 1984, p. 595, footnote 79.
136. Quoted in Rudney, 1983, p. 32.

137. Yost, 1984, p. 91.
138. For these points, see Ross, 1983, pp. 34–5.
139. Quoted in Rudney, 1984, p. 96. For a deeper analysis of Soviet attitudes and for a reinforcement of the view put forward here that Moscow barely differentiates between France and the rest of NATO where conventional forces are concerned, see Laird, 1985.
140. Yost, 1984, p. 73.
141. *Ibid.*, p. 3; Rudney, 1983, p. 30.
142. Howorth, 1984, p. 595, footnote 77.
143. For an edited text of the speech, see *Survival* (Nov./Dec.), 26:6.

9. CONCLUSION

1. Calleo, 1970, p. 30.
2. Grosser, 1980, is a good source for the wider aspects of the transatlantic relationship, including the cultural aspect.

Bibliography

The reading material on the various aspects of NATO's affairs is endless. The bibliography provided below consists solely of those items referred to in the text, and is thus far from exhaustive.

BOOKS, ARTICLES AND MONOGRAPHS

Abshire, David M. 'NATO's Conventional Defence: The Need for a Resources Strategy', *NATO Review* (Oct. 1984), 5.

Acheson, Dean. *Present at the Creation. My Years in the State Department* (Signet: New York, 1970).

Achilles, Theodore C. 'US Role in Negotiations that Led to Atlantic Alliance: Part I', *NATO Review* (Aug. 1979), 4; 'Part II', *NATO Review* 27 (Oct. 1979), 5.

Ailleret, General Charles. 'Flexible Response: A French View', *Survival* (Nov./Dec. 1964), 6.

Alford, Jonathan. 'NATO's Conventional Forces and the Soviet Mobilisation Potential', *NATO Review* 28 (June 1980), 3.

—— 'Tactical Nuclear Weapons in Europe', *NATO's Fifteen Nations* 2, 1981.

Ambrose, Stephen E. and Barber, James Alden (eds.), *The Military in American Society* (The Free Press: New York, 1972).

Backer, John. *The Decision to Divide Germany* (Duke University Press: Durham NC, 1978).

Baker, John C. See BERMAN and.

Ball, Desmond. 'Deja Vu: The Return to Counterforce in the Nixon Administration', in *The strategic Nuclear Balance*, ed. Robert O'Neill (Australian National University Press: Canberra, 1975).

—— *Politics and Force Levels: The Strategic Missile Programme of the Kennedy Administration* (University of California Press: Berkeley and London, 1980).

—— 'Can Nuclear War Be Controlled?', *Adelphi Papers* 169 (IISS: London), Autumn 1981.

—— 'Targeting for Strategic Deterrence', *Adelphi Papers* 185 (IISS: London), Summer 1983.

Barber, James Alden. See AMBROSE and.

Baylis, John. 'The Anglo-American Relationship in Defence', in *British Defence Policy in a Changing World*, ed. John Baylis (Croom Helm: London, 1977).

—— 'Britain and the Dunkirk Treaty: The Origins of NATO', *The Journal of Strategic Studies* (June 1982), 2.

Berger, Peter J. 'The Nuances of French Defence Policy', *Parameters* 11, 3.

—— 'The Course of French Defence Policy', *Parameters* 12 (Sept. 1983), 3.

Berman, Robert B. and Baker, John C. *Soviet Strategic Forces: Requirements and Responses* (The Brookings Institution: Washington DC, 1982).

Betts, Richard K. 'Surprise Attack: NATO's Political Vulnerability', *International Security* (Spring 1981), 4.

—— 'Conventional Forces: What Price Readiness?', *Survival* 25 (Jan./Feb. 1983), 1.

Beufre, General André *NATO and Europe* (Faber and Faber: London, 1967).

Blackwell, James A., Jnr. 'Conventional Doctrine: Integrating Alliance Forces', in *Conventional Deterrence: Alternatives for European Defence*, eds. James R. Golden, Asa A. Clark and Bruce E. Arlinghaus (D.C. Heath and Co.: Lexington and Toronto, 1984).

Bohlen, Charles E. *Witness to History, 1929–1969* (Norton: New York, 1973).

Boulton, J. 'NATO and the MLF', *Journal of Contemporary History*, July/October 1973.

Bracken, Paul 'Collateral Damage and Theatre Warfare', *Survival* 22 (Sept./Oct. 1980), 5.

—— *The Command and Control of Nuclear Forces* (Yale University Press: New Haven and London, 1983).

British Atlantic Committee, *Diminishing the Nuclear Threat: NATO's Defence and New Technology* (London, 1984).

Brown, Anthony Cave (ed.), *Operation World War III: The Secret American Plan 'Dropshot' for War with the Soviet Union* (Arms and Armour Press: London, 1978).

Brown, Harold. 'American Nuclear Doctrine', *Survival* 22 (Nov./Dec. 1980), 6.

Brown, Neville. 'The Changing Face of Non-nuclear War', *Survival* 24 (Sept./Oct. 1982), 5.

Buchan, Alistair. 'The Multilateral Force: An Historical Perspective', *Adelphi Papers* (IISS: London), October 1964.

Bundy, McGeorge. 'America in the 1980s: Reframing Our Relations with Our Friends and among Our Allies', *Survival* 24 (Jan./Feb. 1982), 1.

—— Kennan, George F., McNamara, Robert S. and Gerard Smith. 'Nuclear Weapons and the Atlantic Alliance', *Foreign Affairs* (Spring 1982), 4.

Burt, Richard. 'New Weapons Technologies: Debate and Directions' *Adelphi Papers* 126 (IISS: London, 1976).

—— 'The Cruise missile and Arms Control', *Survival* 18 (Jan./Feb. 1976), 1.

—— 'The SS-20 and the Strategic Balance', *The World Today* (Jan./Feb. 1977), 2.

—— 'The Hidden Nuclear Crisis: Problems in the Atlantic Alliance', in *NATO's Strategic Options: Arms Control and Defence*, ed. David S. Yost (Pergamon Press, Oxford and New York, 1981).

Calleo, David. *The Atlantic Fantasy: The US, NATO and Europe* (The Johns Hopkins Press: Baltimore and London, 1970).

Canby, Steven L. 'Military Reform and the Art of War', *Survival* 25 (May/June 1983), 3.

Clark, Ian. *Limited Nuclear War* (Martin Robertson: Oxford, 1982).

Cleveland, Harlan. *NATO: The Transatlantic Bargain* (Harper and Row: New York, Evanston and London, 1970).

Close, General Robert. *Europe without Defence? Forty-Eight Hours that Could Change the Face of the World* (Pergamon Press: Oxford and New York, 1979).

Cochran, Thomas B. Arkin, William M. and Hoenig, Milton M. *Nuclear Weapons Databook, Vol.1: US Nuclear Forces and Capabilities* (Ballinger Publishing: Cambridge, Mass., 1984).

Cohen, S.T. See VAN CLEAVE and

—— *The Neutron Bomb: Political, Technological and Military Issues* (Institute for Foreign Policy Analysis: Cambridge, Mass., and Washington DC) November 1978.

—— 'Enhanced Radiation Warheads: Setting the Record Straight', *Strategic Review* 6 (Winter 1978), 1.

Cordesman, Anthony H. 'Deterrence in the 1980s, Part 1: American Strategic Forces and Extended Deterrence', *Adelphi Papers* 175 (IISS: London), Summer 1982.

Cotter, Donald R. 'Potential Future Roles for Conventional and Nuclear Forces in Defence of Western Europe'. See ESECS.

Craig, Gordon A. 'Germany and NATO: The Rearmament Debate, 1950–1958', in *NATO and American Security*, ed. Klaus Knorr (Princeton University Press: New Jersey, 1959).

Davidson, Charles N. 'Tactical Nuclear Defence — The West German View', *Parameters* 4 (1974), 1.

Davis, Jacquelyn K. 'France Debates Its Defence Policy', *Air Force Magazine*, September 1984.

Davis, Lynn Etheridge. *The Cold War Begins* (Princeton University Press: Princeton, NJ, 1974).

—— 'Limited Nuclear Options: Deterrence and the New American Doctrine', *Adelphi Papers* 121 (IISS: London), Winter 1975/76.

Delmas, Claude, 'France and the Creation of the Atlantic Alliance', *NATO Review* 28 (Aug. 1980), 4.

Depuy, General William E. 'Technology and Tactics in Defence of Europe', *Army* (April 1979), 4.

Digby, James. 'Precision-Guided Weapons', *Adelphi Papers* 118 (IISS: London), 1975.

Dinter, Elmar and Griffiths, Paddy. *Not Over by Christmas: NATO's Central Front in World War III* (Anthony Bird: Chichester, Sussex, 1983).

Donnelly, C.N. 'The Soviet Operational Manouvre Group: A New Challenge for NATO', *International Defense Review* 15 (1982), 9.

—— 'Soviet Operational Concepts in the 1980s'. See ESECS

—— 'The Development of the Soviet Concept of Echeloning', *NATO Review* (Dec. 1984), 6.

Dunn, Keith A. and Staudenmaier, William O. 'The Retaliatory Offensive and Operational Realities in NATO', *Survival* 27 (May/June 1985), 3.

Egilsson, Olafur. 'An Unarmed Nation Joins a Defence Alliance', *NATO Review* (Jan. 1983), 1.

Enthoven, Alain C. and Smith, K. Wayne. *How Much Is Enough? Shaping the Defence Program, 1961–1969* (Harper and Row, New York, Evanston and London, 1971).

Report of the European Security Study (ESECS). *Strengthening Conventional Deterrence in Europe: Proposals for the 1980s*, (MacMillan: London, 1983).

Fischer, Robert Lucas. 'Defending the Central Front: The Balance of Forces', *Adelphi Papers* 127 (IISS: London), Autumn 1976.

Foot, Peter. 'Defence Burden-Sharing in the Atlantic Community, 1945–1954', *Aberdeen Studies in Defence Economics* (Summer 1981).

Staff of the Foreign Policy Research Institute. *The Three Per Cent Solution and the Future of NATO* (FPRI: Philadelphia, 1981).

Freedman, Lawrence. *The Evolution of Nuclear Strategy* (MacMillan: London, 1981).

_____ 'The Neutron Bomb Returns', *World Today* No.3 (Mar. 1981).

_____ 'Limited War, Unlimited Protest', *Orbis* 26 (Spring 1982), 2.

Friedberg, Aaron L. 'A History of the US Strategic Doctrine, 1945–1980', *The Journal of Strategic Studies* (Dec. 1980), 3.

Frye, Alton. 'Nuclear Weapons in Europe: No Exit from Ambivalence', *Survival* 22 (May/June 1980), 3.

Furniss, Edgar. *France: Troubled Ally* (Harper and Row: New York, 1960).

Fursdon, Major-General Edward. *The European Defence Community: A History* (MacMillan: London, 1980).

Gaddis, John Lewis. *The United States and the Origins of the Cold War, 1941–1947* (Columbia University Press: New York, 1972).

_____ and Nitze, Paul. 'NSC-68 and the Soviet Threat Reconsidered', *International Security* (Spring 1980), 4.

_____*Strategies of Containment: A critical Reappraisal of Post-war American National Security Policy* (Oxford University Press: New York and Oxford, 1982).

Garner, William V. 'Soviet Threat Perceptions of NATO's Euro-strategic Missiles', *The Atlantic Papers* 52–3, (The Atlantic Institute for International Affairs: Paris), November 1983.

Garrett, James M. 'Conventional Force Deterrence in the Presence of Theatre Nuclear Weapons', *Armed Forces and Society* 11 (Fall 1984), 1.

Garthoff, Raymond L. 'The Soviet SS-20 Decision', *Survival* 25 (May/June 1983), 3.

Gavin, Lt General James M. *War and Peace in the Space Age* (Harper: New York, 1958).

Gessert, Robert A. 'The Airland Battle and NATO's New Doctrinal Debate', *Journal of the Royal United Services Institute*, June 1984.

Gilpin, R. *American Scientists and Nuclear Weapons Policy*, (Princeton University Press: Princeton, 1968).

Gordon, Michael R. 'Technology and NATO Defence: Weighing the Options', in *Conventional Deterrence: Alternatives for European Defence*, eds. James R. Golden, Asa A. Clark, and Bruce E. Arlinghaus (D.C. Heath and Co: Lexington and Toronto, 1984).

Goure, Daniel and McCormick, Gordon. 'PGM: No Panacea',*Survival* 22 (Jan./Feb. 1980), 1.

Gray, Colin S. 'Nuclear Strategy: The case for a Theory of Victory', *International Security* (Summer 1979), 1.

_____ and Payne, Keith. 'Victory Is Possible', *Foreign Policy* 39 (Summer 1980).

Greenwood, David. 'Defence and National Priorities Since 1945', in *British Defence Policy in a Changing World*, ed. John Baylis (Croom Helm: London, 1977).

—— 'NATO's Three Per cent Solution', *Survival* 23 (Nov./Dec. 1981), 6.

—— 'The Trident Programme', *Aberdeen Studies in Defence Economies* 22 (Summer 1982).

—— 'Strengthening Conventional Deterrence: Doctrine, New Technology and Resources', *NATO Review* (August 1984), 4.

Griffiths, Paddy. See DINTER and.

Groom, A.J.R. *British Thinking about Nuclear Weapons*, (Frances Pinter: London, 1974).

Grosser, Alfred. *The Western Alliance: European-American Relations since 1945* (MacMillan: London, 1980).

Hampson, Fen Osler. 'Groping for Technical Panaceas: The European Conventional Balance and Nuclear Stability: A Review Essay', *International Security* 8 (Winter 1983–84), 3.

Harrison, Michael M. *The Reluctant Ally: France and Atlantic Security* (Johns Hopkins University Press: Baltimore and London, 1981).

Healey, Denis. 'Britain and NATO', in *NATO and American security*, ed. Klaus Knorr (Princeton University Press: Princeton, NJ, 1959).

—— 'NATO, Britain and Soviet Military Policy', *Orbis* 13 (Spring 1969), 1.

Heilbrunn, Otto. *Conventional Warfare in the Nuclear Age* (George Allen and Unwin: London 1965).

Heisenberg, Wolfgang 'The Alliance and Europe, Part 1: Crisis Stability in Europe and Theatre Nuclear Weapons', *Adelphi Papers* (IISS: London), Summer 1973.

Henderson, Sir Nicholas, *The Birth of NATO* (Weidenfeld and Nicolson: London, 1982).

Henningson, Sven. 'Denmark and the Road to NATO: Part 1', *NATO Review* (Dec. 1979), 6; 'Part II', *NATO Review* (Feb. 1980), 1.

Henrikson, Alan K. 'The Creation of the North Atlantic Alliance, 1948–1952', *Naval War College Review* 32 (May/June 1980), 3.

Hilsman, Roger. 'NATO: The Developing Strategic Context', in *NATO and American Security*, ed. Klaus Knorr (Princeton University Press: Princeton, NJ, 1959).

Hines, John G. and Peterson, Phillip A. 'The Warsaw Pact Strategic Offensive: The OMG in Context', *International Defence Review* (1983), 10.

Hofman, Wilfred. 'Is NATO's Defence Policy Facing a Crisis?', *NATO Review* 32 (Aug. 1984), 4.

226 Bibliography

Howorth, Jolyon. 'Consensus of Silence: The French Socialist Party and Defence Policy under Francois Mitterrand', *International Affairs* (Autumn 1984), 4.

Hunt, Brigadier Kenneth. 'NATO without France: The Military Implications', *Adelphi Papers* (IISS: London, December 1966).

Huntington, Samuel P. *The Common Defence: Strategic Programmes in National Politics* (Columbia University Press: New York and London, 1961).

——— 'Conventional Deterrence and Conventional Retaliation in Europe'. *International Security* 8 (Winter 1983/84), 3.

Ireland, Timothy P. *Creating the Entangling Alliance* (Greenwood Press: Westport, and Aldwych Press: London, 1981).

Ismay, Lord. *NATO: The First Five Years, 1949–1954* (Bosch: Utrecht, 1954).

Joffe, Josef, 'German Defence Policy: Novel Solutions and Enduring Dilemmas', in *The Internal Fabric of Western Security*, ed. Gregory Flynn (Croom Helm: London, and Osman and Co., New Jersey, 1981).

——— 'Allies, Angst and Arms Control: New Troubles for an Old Partnership', in *Nuclear Weapons in Europe: Modernisation and Limitations*, eds. Marsha McGraw Olive and Jeffrey D. Porro (D.C. Heath and Co., Lexington, 1983).

Jukes, Geoffrey, 'Western Assessments of Soviet Strength', in *Estimating Foreign Military Power*, ed. Philip Towle (Croom Helm: London, 1982).

Kaiser, Karl, Leber, G., Mertes, A. and Schulze, F.-J. 'Nuclear Weapons and the Preservation of Peace: a German Response to No First Use', *Foreign Affairs* 60 (Summer 1982), 5.

Kaplan, Fred M. 'Enhanced Radiation Weapons', *Scientific American* 238 (May 1978), 5.

——— 'The Neutron Bomb: What It Is, the Way It Works', *The Bulletin of Atomic Scientists* (Oct. 1981), 8.

Karber, Phillip A. 'The Battle of Unengaged Military Strategies', in *Soviet Power and Western Negotiating Politics, Vol.1: The Soviet Asset; Military Power in the Competition over Europe*, ed. Uwe Nerlich (Ballinger: Cambridge, Mass., 1983).

——— 'To Lose an Arms Race: The Competition in Conventional Forces Deployed in Central Europe, 1965–1980', *ibid.*

——— 'In Defence of Forward Defence', *Armed Forces Journal International* 121 (May 1984), 10.

Kaufmann, William W. *The McNamara Strategy*, (Harper and Row: New York, Evanston and London, 1964).

Kelleher, Catherine McArdle. *Germany and the Politics of Nuclear Weapons* (Columbia University Press: New York and London, 1975).

Kemp, G., Pfaltzgraff, R., Jnr, and Ra'anan, U. (eds.) *The Other Arms Race* (Lexington Books: Lexington, Mass., 1974).

Kirby, Stephen. 'Britain, NATO and European Security: The Irreducible Commitment', in *British Defence Policy in a Changing World* (Croom Helm: London, 1977).

Kissinger, Henry. *Nuclear Weapons and Foreign Policy* (Harper: New York, and Oxford University Press: London, 1957).

—— *The Troubled Partnership* (McGraw-Hill: New York, London and Toronto, 1965).

—— 'The Future of NATO', in *NATO: The Next Thirty Years. The Changing Political, Economic and Military Setting*, ed. Kenneth A. Myers (Westview Press: Boulder, Col., and Croom Helm: London, 1980.

Kistiakowsky, George. 'The Folly of the Neutron Bomb', *The Bulletin of Atomic Scientists* (Sept. 1978), 7.

Kohl, Wilfred L. *French Nuclear Diplomacy* (Princeton University Press: Princeton, NJ, 1971).

Kolodziej, Edward A. 'French Security Policy: Decisions and Dilemmas', *Armed Forces and Society* 8 (Winter 1982), 2.

Komer, Robert W. 'A Credible Conventional Option: Can NATO Afford It?', *Strategic Review* 12 (Spring 1984), 2.

Laird, Robbin F. 'Soviet Perspectives on French Security Policy', *Survival* 27 (Mar./Apr. 1985), 2.

Lautenschlager, Karl. 'Theatre Nuclear Forces and Grey Area Weapons', *Naval War College Review* 32 (Sept./Oct. 1980), 5.

Leitenberg, M. 'Background Information on Tactical Nuclear Weapons (primarily in the European context)'. See SIPRI.

—— 'The Neutron Bomb: Enhanced Radiation Warheads', *Journal of Strategic Studies* (Sept. 1982), 3.

Lindner, Philip R. 'Considerations of a Conventional Defence of Central Europe', in *Conventional Deterrence: Alternatives for European Defence*, eds. James R. Golden, Asa A. Clark and Bruce E. Arlinghaus (D.C. Heath and Co.: Lexington and Toronto, 1984).

McCormick, Gordon. See GOURE and.

McGeehan, Robert. *The German Rearmament Question: American Diplomacy and European Defence after World War II* (University of Illinois Press: Chicago and London, 1971).

Mackintosh, Malcolm. *Juggernaut: the Russian Forces, 1918–1966* (Macmillan: New York and London, 1967).

Macmillan, Harold. *At the End of the Day* (Macmillan: London, 1973).

McNamara, Robert S. *The Essence of Security: Reflections in Office* (Hodder and Stoughton: London, 1968).

—— 'The Military Role of Nuclear Weapons: Perceptions and Misperceptions', *Survival* 25 (Nov./Dec. 1983), 6.

Mako, William P. *US Ground Forces and the Defence of Central Europe* (The Brookings Institution: Washington, DC, 1983).

Malone, Peter, *The British Nuclear Deterrent* (Croom Helm: London, and St Martin's Press: New York, 1984).

Mandelbaum, Michael. *The Nuclear Question: The United States and Nuclear Weapons, 1946–1976* (Cambridge University Press: Cambridge, 1979).

Mearsheimer, John J. 'Precision-Guided Munitions and Conventional Deterrence', *Survival* 21 (Mar./Apr. 1979), 2.

——'Manouvre, Mobile Defence and the NATO Central Front', *International Security* 6 (Winter 1981/82), 3.

—— 'Why the Soviets Can't Win quickly in Central Europe', *International Security* 7 (Summer 1982), 1.

—— *Conventional Deterrence* (Cornell University Press: Ithaca and London, 1983).

Meyer, Stephen M. 'Soviet Theatre Nuclear Forces, Part I: Development of Doctrine and Objectives', *Adelphi Papers* 187; 'Part II: Capabilities and Intentions', *Adelphi Papers* 188 (IISS: London), Winter 1983/84.

Millett, Stephen M. 'Soviet Perceptions of the Theatre Nuclear Balance in Europe and Reactions to American LRTNF', *Naval War College Review* 34 (Mar./Apr. 1981), 2.

Millot, Marc Dean. See SLOSS and.

Moore, Robert A. 'Theatre Nuclear Forces: Thinking the Unthinkable', *International Defence Review* 14 (1981), 4.

Moulton, H. B. *From Superiority to Parity: The US and the Strategic Arms Race, 1961–1971* (Greenwood Press: Westport and London, 1973).

Mulley, F. W. *The Politics of Western Defence* (Thames and Hudson: London, 1962).

Nailor, Peter. 'Denis Healey and Rational Decision-making', in *Politicians and Defence: Studies in the Formulation of British Defence Policy*, eds Ian F. W. Beckett and John Gooch (University Press: Manchester, 1981).

Neustadt, Richard E. *Alliance Politics* (Columbia University Press: New York and London, 1970).

Nitze, Paul. See GADDIS and.

Nogueira, Albano. 'The Making of the Alliance: A Portuguese Perspective', *NATO Review* 28 (Oct. 1980), 5.

Oppenheimer, Robert J. 'Atomic Weapons and Foreign Policy', *Foreign Affairs* 31 (July 1953), 4.

Ortona, Egidio. 'Italy's Entry into the Atlantic Alliance, Part 1', *NATO Review* 29 (Aug. 1981), 4; 'Part II', *NATO Review* 29 (Oct. 1981), 5.

Osgood, Robert E. *NATO: The Entangling Alliance* (University Press: Chicago, 1962).

Paterson, Thomas G. *Soviet—American Confrontation: Postwar Reconstruction and the Origins of the Cold War* (Johns Hopkins Press: Baltimore, 1973).

Payne, Keith. See GRAY and.

Peterson, Phillip A. See HINES and.

Pierre, Andrew J. *Nuclear Politics: The British Experience with an Independent Strategic Nuclear Force, 1939—1970, (Oxford University Press: London, 1972).*

Portugalov, N. *'European Nuclear Balance — a Soviet View', NATO's Fifteen Nations* 26 (Oct./Nov. 1981), 5.

Posen, Barry R. 'Measuring the European Conventional Balance: Coping with Complexity in Threat Assessment', *International Security* 9 (Winter 1984/85), 3.

Prittie, Terence. *Adenaur: A Study in Fortitude* (Tom Stacey: London, 1972).

Pym, Francis. See 'Official Documents'.

Ravenal, Earl C. 'Counterforce and Alliance: The Ultimate Connection', *International Security* 6 (Spring 1982), 4.

Record, Jeffrey. *US Nuclear Weapons in Europe: Issues and Alternatives* (The Brookings Institution: Washington, DC, 1974).

Reed, Bruce. See WILLIAMS, Geoffrey, and.

Reid, Escott. 'The Miraculous Birth of the North Atlantic Alliance', *NATO Review* 28 (Dec. 1980), 6.

Rendel, Alexander M. 'The Alliance's Anxious Birth', *NATO Review* 27 (June 1979), 3.

—— 'Uncertainty Continues as Atlantic Treaty Nears Completion', *NATO Review* 28 (Apr. 1980), 2.

Richardson, James L. *Germany and the Atlantic Alliance: The Interaction of Strategy and Politics* (Harvard University Press: Cambridge, Mass., and Oxford University Press: London, 1966).

230 Bibliography

Richardson, Brigadier Robert C., III. 'NATO Nuclear Strategy: A Look Back', *Strategic Review* 9 (Spring 1981), 2.

Rogers, General Bernard W. 'Increasing Threats to NATO's Security Call for Sustained Response', *NATO Review* 29 (June 1981), 3.

—— 'NATO: The Next Decade', *Journal of the Royal United Services Institute* 127 (Dec. 1982), 4.

—— 'Greater Flexibility for NATO's Flexible Response', *Strategic Review* 11 (Spring 1983), 2.

—— 'Follow-on Forces Attack (FOFA): Myths and Realities', *NATO Review* 32 (Dec. 1984), 6.

Rose, John P. *The Evolution of US Army Nuclear Doctrine, 1945–1980* (Westview Press: Boulder, Col., 1980).

Rosenberg, David Alan. 'US Nuclear Stockpile: 1945–1950'. *The Bulletin of Atomic Scientists* 38 (May 1982), 5.

—— 'The Origins of Overkill: Nuclear Weapons and American Strategy, 1945–1960', *International Security* 7 (Spring 1983), 4.

Steven T. Ross, 'French Defence Policy', *Naval War College Review* 36 (May/June 1983), 3.

Rothschild, Baron R. 'Belgium and the Longest-Lasting Alliance', *NATO Review* (Feb. 1982), 1.

Rudney, Robert S. 'Mitterrand's Defence Concepts: Some Unsocialist Earmarks', *Strategic Review* 11 (Spring 1983), 2.

—— 'Mitterrand's New Atlanticism: Evolving French Attitudes Toward NATO', *Orbis* 28, (Spring 1984), 1.

Schemmer, Benjamin F. 'Soviet Build-up on Central Front Poses New Threat to NATO', *Armed Forces Journal International* 114 (Dec. 1976), 4.

Schilling, Warner R. 'US Strategic Nuclear Concepts in the 1970s: The Search for Sufficiently Equivalent Countervailing Parity', *International Security* 6 (Fall 1981), 2.

—— Hammond Paul Y. and Snyder Glenn H. *Strategy, Politics and Defence Budgets* (Columbia University Press: New York and London, 1962).

Schmidt, Helmut. *The Balance of Power: Germany's Peace Policy and the Superpowers* (William Kimber: London, 1971).

Schwartz, David N. *NATO's Nuclear Dilemmas* (The Brookings Institution: Washington, DC, 1983).

Shishko, Robert. 'The European Conventional Balance: A Primer', *RAND Paper* 6707 (The RAND Corporation: Santa Monica, 1981).

Shreffler, R. G. 'The Neutron Bomb for NATO Defence: An Alternative', *Orbis* 21 (Winter 1978), 4.

Sigal, Leon V. See STEINBRUNER and.

—— *Nuclear Forces in Europe: Enduring Dilemmas, Present Prospects* (The Brookings Institution: Washington, DC, 1984).

Sloan, Stanley R. *Defence Burden-Sharing: US Relations with NATO Allies and Japan*, Congressional Research Service, Report No. 83—140F, Washington, DC, 8/7/1983.

Sloss, Leon and Millot, Marc Dean. 'US Nuclear Strategy in Evolution', *Strategic Review* 12 (Winter 1984), 1.

Smith, K. Wayne. See ENTHOVEN and.

Sommer, Theo. 'The Neutron Bomb: Nuclear War without Tears?', reprinted from *Die Zeit* in *Survival* 19 (Nov./Dec. 1977), 6.

Staudenmaier, William O. See DUNN and.

Steinbruner, John D. *The Cybernetic Theory of Decision: New Dimensions of Political Analysis* (Princeton University Press: Princeton, NJ, 1974).

—— and Sigal, Leon V. (eds). *Alliance Security: NATO and the No-First-Use Question* (The Brookings Institution: Washington, DC, 1983).

Stewart, James Moray. 'Conventional Defence Improvements: Where is the Alliance Going?', *NATO Review* 33 (Apr. 1985), 2.

Stikker, Dirk. *Men of Responsibility* (Harper and Row: New York, 1965, and John Murray: London, 1966).

Stockholm International Peace Research Institute (SIPRI), *Tactical Nuclear Weapons: European Perspectives* (Taylor and Frances: London, 1978).

Strachan, Hew. 'Conventional Defence in Europe', *International Affairs'* 61 (Winter 1984/85), 1.

Stratmann, K. Peter. 'Prospective Tasks and Capabilities Required for NATO's Conventional Forces'. See ESECS.

Sutton *et al.*, Boyd D. 'New Directions in Conventional Defence?', *Survival* 26 (Mar./Apr. 1984), 2.

Taylor, General Maxwell D. *The Uncertain Trumpet* (Atlantic Books: London, 1959, and Harper and Row: New York, 1960).

Thomson, James A. 'Planning for NATO's Nuclear Deterrent in the 1980s and 1990s', *Survival* 25 (May/June 1983), 3.

—— 'The LRTNF Decision: The Evolution of US Theatre Nuclear Policy, 1975—1979', *International Affairs* 60 (Autumn 1984), 4.

Vaerno, Grethe. 'Norway and the Atlantic Alliance, 1948—1949', *NATO Review* 29 (June 1981), 3.

Van Cleave, William R. and Cohen S. T. *Tactical Nuclear Weapons: An examination of the Issues* (MacDonald and Jane's: London, 1978).

Van Der Beugal, Ernst H. *From Marshall Aid to Atlantic Partnership: European Integration as a Concern of American Foreign Policy* (Elsevier: Amsterdam, London, and New York, 1966).

Vardamis, Lt Colonel Alex A. 'The Neutron Warhead: Stormy Past, Uncertain Future', *Parameters* 8 (Mar. 1978), 1.

Vermaat, J. A. Emerson. 'Neutralist Tendencies in the Netherlands', *World Today* 37 (Dec. 1981), 12.

Von Hassel, Kai-Uwe. 'The Search for Consensus: Organising Western Defence', *Foreign Affairs* 43 (Jan. 1965), 2.

Wallace, William. See WILLIAMS, Phil, and.

Weinland, Robert C. 'The Evolution of Soviet Requirements for Naval Forces: Solving the Problems of the Early 1960s', *Survival* 26 (Jan./Feb. 1984), 1.

Wells, Samual F. 'Sounding the Tocsin: NSC-68 and the Soviet Threat', *International Security* 4 (Fall 1979), 2.

Wikner, N. F. 'Interdicting Fixed Targets with Conventional Weapons', *Armed Forces Journal* 120 (Mar. 1983), 8.

Williams, Geoffrey and Reed, Bruce. *Denis Healey and the Policies of Power* (Sedgwick and Jackson: London, 1971).

Williams, Phil. *The Senate and US Troops in Europe* (MacMillan: London, 1985).

—— and Wallace, William. 'Emerging Technologies and European Security', *Survival* 26 (Mar./Apr. 1984), 2.

Wisner, Kent F. 'Military Aspects of Enhanced Radiation Weapons', *Survival* 23 (Nov./Dec. 1981), 6.

Wohlstetter, Albert. 'The Delicate Balance of Terror', *Foreign Affairs* 37 (Jan. 1959), 2.

Wolfe, Thomas W. *Soviet Power and Europe, 1945–1970* (Johns Hopkins University Press: Baltimore and London, 1970).

Manfred Worner, 'The "Peace Movement" and NATO: An Alternative View from Bonn', *Strategic Review* 10 (Winter 1982), 1

Yergin, Daniel. *Shattered Peace: The Origins of the Cold War and the National Security State* (Penguin: Harmondsworth, 1980).

York, Herbert. *The Advisors: Oppenheimer, Teller and the Superbomb* (W. H. Freeman: San Francisco, 1976).

Yost, David S. 'The French Defence Debate', *Survival* 23 (Jan./Feb. 1981).

—— *France and Conventional Defence in Central Europe: EAI Paper No. 7*, (European–American Institute for Security Research: Marina del Ray, California), Spring 1984.

Zuckerman, Solly. *Nuclear Illusion and Reality* (Collins: London, 1982).

OFFICIAL DOCUMENTS, REPORTS, STATEMENTS, ETC.

NATO

NATO and the Warsaw Pact: Force Comparisons (NATO Information Service: Brussels, 1983).
NATO: Facts and Figures (NATO Information Service: Brussels, 1971).
NATO: Final Communiqués, 1949–1974 (NATO Information Service: Brussels, 1975).

United Kingdom
Statement on Defence, 1954, Cmd.9075, HMSO, London.
Statement on Defence, 1955, Cmd.9391, HMSO, London.
Defence: Outline of Future Policy, 1957, Cmd.124, HMSO, London.
Report on Defence: Britain's Contribution to Peace and Security, 1958, Cmd.363, HMSO, London.
The Future UK Strategic Nuclear Deterrent Force, Defence Open Government Document 80/23, July 1980, by Francis Pym.
Statement on the Defence Estimates, 1985, Cmd.9430–1, HMSO, London.

United States
'US Security Issues in Europe: Burden-Sharing and Offset, MBFR and Nuclear Weapons', *A staff Report for the Committee on Foreign Relations, US Senate, 93rd Congress* (GPO: Washington, DC), September 1973.
'Nuclear Weapons and Foreign Policy', *Hearings before the US Senate Committee on Foreign Relations, 93rd Congress* (GPO: Washington, DC), March/April 1974.
Annual Defence Department Report 1975, by James R. Schlesinger (GPO: Washington, DC), 4/3/1974.
'The Theatre Nuclear Force Posture in Europe', *A Report to the US Congress by Secretary of Defence James R. Schlesinger* (National Technical Information Service: Washington, DC, 1975).
'NATO and the New Soviet Threat', *Report by Senators Sam Nunn and Dewey F. Bartlett to the US Senate Committee on the Armed Services, 95th Congress* (GPO: Washington, DC), 21/1/1977.
Annual Defence Department Report 1978, by Donald H. Rumsfeld (GPO: Washington, DC), 17/1/1977).

Annual Defence Department Report 1980, by Harold Brown (GPO: Washington, DC), 25/1/1979).

'The Effects of Nuclear War', *Office of Technology Assessment* (GPO: Washington, DC), May 1979.

Annual Defence Department Report 1981, by Harold Brown (GPO: Washington, DC), 29/1/1980.

'The Modernisation of NATO's Long-Range Theatre Nuclear Forces', *A Report Prepared for the Sub-committee on Europe and the Middle East, of the House of Representatives Committee on Foreign Affairs, 96th Congress* (GPO: Washington, DC), December 1980.

Annual Defence Department Report 1983, by Caspar W. Weinberger (GPO: Washington, DC), 8/2/1982.

'Department of Defence Authorisations for Appropriations for 1983', *Hearings before the US Senate Committee on the Armed Services, 97th Congress* (GPO: Washington, DC), February/March 1982.

'Allied Contributions to the Common Defence', *A Report to the US Congress by Casper W. Weinberger* (Dept. of Defence: Washington, DC), March 1984.

Soviet Military Power (GPO: Washington, DC, 1985).

West Germany

Defence White Paper, 1979: The Security of the Federal Republic of Germany and the Development of the Federal Armed Forces, by the Federal Minister of Defence, Bonn, September 1979.

Defence White Paper, 1983: The Security of the Federal Republic of Germany, by the Federal Minister of Defence, Bonn, October 1983.

Index

Abshire, David M., 167, 169
Acheson, Dean, 9, 11, 12, 14
Achilles, Theodore C., 10
'active defence', 177−8, 180
Adenaur, Konrad, 16, 56, 57, 58, 67, 72, 129
Ailleret, Charles, 53, 119, 133, 163
Airland Battle, 179, 180, 189
Algerian War, 51, 52, 54
Ambassador's Committee, 11
anti-nuclear movements, protests, 56−7, 66−8, 117, 144, 148−52, 159, 160, 168, 196−7
'armoured division equivalent' (ADE), 171
'assured destruction', 95−8, 99
Athens address, McNamara's, 90−1, 128
Atlantic Nuclear Force (ANF), 73
Atomic demolition mines (ADMs), role of, 136−8
Attlee, Clement, 6, 18
Azores, 7

Bahr, Egon, 150
Ball, Desmond, 101
battlefield nuclear weapons. See nuclear weapons, tactical

Belgium:
armed forces of, 23−4, 35, 180, 184, 185−6, 187
and nuclear weapons, 35, 72, 114
'three per cent solution' and, 190
See also Benelux countries
Benelux countries, 4, 9, 59
Berlin:
blockade of, 1948−9, 5−6, 104
Crisis, 1958−61, 47, 128
Beufre, Andre, 52, 53
Bevin, Ernest, 5, 6, 7, 10
Blank, Theodor, 58
Bohlen, Charles, 3, 6, 79
Boll, Heinrich, 66
Bonnet, Henri, 13
Bradley, Omar, 15, 23, 24, 26, 28, 34
Brandt, Willy, 150
Brentano, Heinrich von, 59
Brezhnev, Leonid, 116, 151−2
British Army on the Rhine (BAOR). See Great Britain, military contribution to NATO by
British Atlantic Committee, 186
Brookings Institution, 161
Brown, Harold, 99, 101, 102−3, 142, 185, 186

Bruce, David, 50
Brussels Treaty, 4, 7, 9, 11, 12, 19–20
Bundeswehr. *See* West Germany, rearmament and armed forces of
Bundy, McGeorge, 85, 108
burden-sharing, 27, 190
Burt, Richard, 110
Bush, George, 108

Caffery, Lincoln, 12
Calleo, David, 195
Calmeyer, General, 59
Canada, 6, 7, 9, 10, 11, 174
Carney, Admiral, 34, 37
Carte Blanche exercise, 57, 66
Carter, Jimmy, 112, 152, 157–9
Central Army Group (CENTAG), 180–1
Christian Democrats (CDU), West German, 56, 66–7, 122
Churchill, Winston, 5, 45–6
Close, Robert, 184, 185
Cohen, S.T., 154, 156
Collins, J. Lawton, 24, 34, 37
Connally, Tom, 11
conventional forces:
  problems of measuring balance of, 21–6, 169–71
  balance of, 171–6
Cuban missile crisis, 72, 86, 107
Cyprus crisis, 147
Czechoslovakia, 5, 172, 179

Dean, Gordon, 32–3
De Gaulle, Charles, 53, 54, 71, 72, 73, 74–81, 119–20
Denmark:
  alliance and, 7, 8, 14

and nuclear weapons, 65, 72, 114
'dual key', 63, 77, 146–7
Dulles, John Foster, 19, 29, 37, 39, 57–8, 78
Dunkirk Treaty, 4

East Germany, 23, 179
Eden, Anthony, 19, 20, 46
Eisenhower, Dwight D., 17, 29, 33, 35, 37, 39, 40–2, 76, 77, 78
'emerging technology' (ET), 168, 188
Enhanced Radiation Weapons (ERWs), or 'neutron bombs', 110, 112
  controversy surrounding, 145–53, 157–60
  characteristics of, 153–5
  battlefield utility of, 155–7
Enthoven, Alain C., 69, 89, 161
Erhard, Ludwig, 129
Erler, Fritz, 56
European Defence Community (EDC), 17–19, 55
European Economic Community (EEC), 80
'extended deterrence', 54–5, 87, 94–5, 103–4, 107, 110, 122, 167

Fabius, Laurent, 121, 194
Falin, Victor, 116
Falklands campaign, 124, 190
Federal Republic of Germany. See West Germany
Fermi, Enrico, 32
Field Manual 100–5, US Army, 147, 179, 188
Field Manual 100–31, US Army, 35

'flexible response', *passim*
and introduction of, by US, 88, 90–2
and implementation of, by NATO, 92–3, 125–6, 166, 169, 196
West Germany and, 127–30
France and, 80, 81, 118–19, 133
Great Britain and, 132–3
Follow-on Forces Attack (FOFA), 188
Force Action Rapide (FAR), 193
force-to-space ratio, 181
Foreign Affairs, 129, 136
Foreign Minister's Conference, Four Power, 5, 7
'forward based systems', 104, 112
forward defence, 15–16, 60, 130, 134, 176–82, 183–5, 187, 192
France, *passim*
and attitude to, relationship with alliance of, viii, 8, 9, 10, 12–13, 27, 50–3, 76–81
and independent deterrent of, 54–5, 60–1, 65, 71–2, 74–81, 118–22
and Germany, 4, 15–16, 63–4, 164, 194
See also European Defence Community: Multilateral Force: nuclear weapons, tactical and: flexible response and
Frankfurter Allgemeine Zeitung, 137

Gaillard, Felix, 75
Gavin, James M., 33, 35, 36

General Strike Plan, SACEUR's, 112
Germany, 4. *See* East Germany: West Germany
Gilpatric, Roswell, 89
Gilson, M., 59
Giscard D'Estaing, Valery, 163–4
'Global Strategy Paper', 45–6
Gottingen Appeal, 66
graduated deterrence, 64, 130, 132
Great Britain, *passim*
and military contribution to NATO of, 19–20, 27, 44–7, 49–50, 58–9, 60, 61, 132
and independent deterrent of, 45–6, 75–9, 117–18, 122–5, 131–2
See also European Defence Community: Multilateral Force: flexible response and: nuclear weapons, tactical and
Greece, 5, 9, 34, 72, 147, 190
Greenland, 7
Groom, A.J.R., 49
Ground-Launched Cruise Missiles (GLCMs), Tomahawk, 72, 104–5, 111, 113–17, 162
Groves, Leslie R., 34
Gruenther, Alfred M., 24, 30, 37, 39, 42, 64

Haig, Alexander, 113, 154
Halperin, Morton, 40
Hassel, Kai-Uwe von, 129–31, 132, 136, 137
Hatfield, Mark, 150
Head, Anthony, 48
Healey, Denis, 49, 91, 95, 132, 138

Henderson, Sir Nicholas, 6
Hernu, Charles, 164–5, 193
Hiroshima, 31, 68
'host country veto', issue of, 135–6, 138
Huntington, Samuel P., 179

Iceland, 7, 8
Ikle, Fred, 111
Indochina:
France and, 51, 52
US and, 129
International Institute for Strategic Studies (IISS), 109, 110, 112
Ireland, 8, 10
Italy:
and alliance membership, 7, 8–10, 14, 19
and British force reductions, 59
and nuclear weapons, 71, 104, 114, 135

Johnson, Lyndon B., 90, 129

Kean, Major-General, 34
Kennan, George, 6
Kennedy, John F., 76, 78–9, 85, 86, 90, 100, 105, 129
Kissinger, Henry, 41, 65, 85, 94, 141
Kistiakowsky, George, 154–5
Kohl, Helmut, 194
Korean War, impact on NATO of, 16, 21, 24, 25, 28, 29, 45, 50, 52
Kruisinga, Rudolph, 151
Krushchev, Nikita, 23, 70, 72

Labour Party, British, 124
Leber, Georg, 141
Lemnitzer, Lyman L., 92, 192

Liddel Hart, Basil, 48
Lilienthal, David, 32
Lisbon force goals, 28, 29, 45, 55, 63
Lloyd, Selwyn, 58
'long haul', 29, 45
long-range theatre nuclear forces (LRTNF), NATO modernisation of, *See* nuclear weapons, theatre
Lovett, Robert, 6, 7, 13
Luxembourg, 190. *See also* Benelux countries

McMahon Act, 30, 45, 77, 78
Macmillan, Harold, 76, 77, 78
McNamara, Robert S., 128, 129, 133
and strategic nuclear detterrence, 87, 95–7, 99, 102
and tactical nuclear weapons, 39, 40, 88–9, 127, 135, 141
and 'no first use', 90, 141
and flexible response, 88–92, 167, 196
Marshall, George, 4, 5, 6, 7, 13, 17
Aid, 5
'massive retaliation', *see* New Look
Mayer, Rene, 12
MC-70, 63
Mery, Guy, 163, 192
military aid, US, 4–5, 8, 12–14, 16, 51
'military-industrial complex', 41
Military Review, 34
'missile gap' 86
Monde, Le, 16, 193
Mulley, Fred, 47–8, 51, 59

Multilateral Force (MLF), 70,
  73–4, 80, 110
Murray, Edward, 32
'mutual assured destruction'
  (MAD), 87, 89, 96

Nassau agreement, 78–9
Netherlands:
  and nuclear weapons, 72,
    114–15, 151, 152
  conventional forces of, 180,
    183–4, 187
  See also Benelux countries
'neutron bomb'. See Enhanced
  Radiation Weapons
New Look, 36, 39, 42, 46, 85,
  88, 117
New York Times, 116
Nixon, Richard M., 100
Norstad, Lauris, 64, 69–70,
  74, 93, 104
North Atlantic Treaty:
  need for, 4–7
  membership of, 7–10
  negotiation of, 10–12
Northern Army Group
  (NORTHAG), 180
Norway, 173, 190
  and alliance membership, 6,
    7, 8, 9, 14
  and nuclear weapons, 65, 172
Nott, John, 124
Nuclear Planning Group
  (NPG), 112, 134–8, 162
nuclear weapons, strategic or
  intercontinental, *passim*
  and Soviet development of,
    70
  and US and Soviet build-up
    of and parity in, 98–9
  and 'missile gap' in, 86
nuclear weapons, tactical or
  battlefield, *passim*

and military utility of,
  29–30, 31–5, 38–9,
  138–141
and definition of, 30–1
and conventional force levels
  and, 35–7, 128, 143–4
and production of, 39–41
and consequences of use of,
  41–2, 68–9, 88–9,
  129–31, 141–2, 144–5
and deployments in Europe
  of, 63–5, 160–2
and procedures governing use
  of, 135–8, 145–7
and France and, 53–4, 119,
  133–4, 163–5
and Great Britain and, 47–8,
  133
and West Germany and,
  66–8, 128–31, 135–9,
  140–1, 150–1, 158–9
See also Atomic demolition
  mines: Enhanced Radiation
  Weapons
nuclear weapons, theatre:
  Soviet capability in, 86,
    105–6
  proposed NATO-controlled
    force of, 69–70
  NATO capability in, 70–1,
    104–5, 110–11
  Soviet modernisation of,
    107–9
  NATO modernisation of
    (LRTNF), 109–15
  definition, perceptions, of,
    106–8, 115–17
  France and American-
    controlled, 71–2, 80,
    121–2
Nunn-Bartlett Report, 167,
  182, 186
Nunn, Sam, 171

Operational Manoeuvre Group (OMG), 183, 193
Oppenheimer, Robert J., 31, 32, 33
Osgood, Robert E., vii, 54–5

Pace, Frank, 34
'pause' concept, 64
'peace movements', *see* anti-nuclear movements
Permissive Action Links (PALs), 147
Pershing 11 missile, 72, 104–5, 113–17, 162
Pincus, Walter, 149–50
Pleven, Rene, 18, 51
   Plan, *see* European Defence Community
Poland, 5
Pompidou, Georges, 78
Portugal, 7, 8, 72, 190
Pravda, 151, 194
precision-guided munitions (PGMs), 188
Project Vista, 32

Quick Reaction Alert (QRA) aircraft, 147

I.I. Rabi, 32
Radford, Arthur, 58
   Plan, 57
RAND Corporation, 69
Richardson, Robert C., 36
Ridgway, Matthew:
   and 'Plan' of, 37
Rio Pact, 10–11
Rogers, Bernard W:
   assessment of NATOs conventional strength by, 166–7, 169, 186–7
   and relationship with France, 193

and FOFA, 179, 188–9
Rothschild, Baron Robert, 3
Runsfield, Donald H., 102, 142, 170–1, 172, 186
Rusk, Dean, 90

Salazar regime, 8
Sandys, Duncan, 46, 48
Schlesinger, James:
   and tactical nuclear weapons, 40, 137, 138, 142, 145, 147, 148, 161
   and strategic nuclear strike options, 99–101
   and theatre nuclear forces, 110–12
   and conventional force balance, 172
Schmidt, Helmut:
   and theatre nuclear forces, 72, 109–10, 111, 112
   and 'neutron bomb', 150, 158, 159
Schroeder, Gerhard, 129, 138
Schuman, Robert, 13, 16
second-strike capability, 95–6
Shinwell, Manny, 23
Single Integrated Operations Plan (SIOP), 99–100, 105, 112, 116
Slessor, Sir John, 46
Smith, K. Wayne, 69
Social Democratic Party, British (SDP), 124
Social Democratic Party, German (SPD), 56, 57, 66–7, 122, 136, 138, 150
Soviet Union, Bloc, *passim*
   and attitudes towards, 4–6, 29
   and conventional strategy of, 181–2

See also conventional forces: nuclear weapons, strategic and theatre: Enhanced Radiation Weapons, controversy surrounding; and etc.

Spain, 8, 9, 10, 174

Spiegel, Der, 115–16, 128

Sputnik, 70, 71, 76

Stalin, Josef, 4, 5, 16, 29, 52

Stampa, La, 116

Stennis, John, 157

'stepping stones', concept of, 7–8

Stikker, Dirk, 15

Strategic Air Command (SAC), US, 38, 65

Strategic Arms Limitation (SALT):
I, 99, 110
II, 116

Strategic Defence Initiative (SDI), 103

Strategic Rocket Forces, Soviet, 86

Strauss, Franz-Josef, 58, 73, 128–30, 158

Suez, 52, 71

Supreme Allied Command, Europe (SACEUR):
and control over tactical nuclear weapons, 65, 137, 146
and strategic nuclear forces, 70, 100, 112
and conventional forces, 179–90, 194
and NATOs air defence network, 81

Supreme Headquarters, Allied Powers Europe (SHAPE), 53, 64, 179, 192

Sweden, 8, 10

Symington, Stuart, 147

TASS, 116

Taylor, Maxwell D., 37, 88–90

Temporary Council Committee (TCC), 28, 50

'three percent solution', 189–91

Times, The, 48

Trettner, Heinz, 136, 137

'Triple Entente', 76

'trip wire' strategy, 63, 133, 165, 169, 177, 191

Truman, Harry, 11, 13, 14, 16–17, 27, 38
Doctrine, 4–5

Turkey, 173
alliance and, 5, 9
and tactical nuclear weapons, 34, 135–8,
and theatre nuclear weapons, 71–2, 104
and Quick Reaction Alert aircraft, 147

United Kingdom, *see* Great Britain

United States, *passim*
and early attitudes towards alliance of, 4–14
and troops in Europe of, 14–17, 23–4, 25, 57–8, 174, 176, 179, 180, 181
and nuclear strategy of, 85–7, 94–104

USSR, *see* Soviet Union

Vance, Cyrus, 112

Vandenberg, Arthur, 6, 11
Resolution, 6–7

Voigt, Karsten, 150

Warnke, Paul, 40
war reserve stocks,
 NATOs, 186–7, 193
 Soviet Bloc's, 187
Warsaw Pact, *see* Soviet
 Union, Bloc
Washington Post, The, 149–50,
 151
Weinberger, Caspar, 101, 115,
 190
West European Union, 6,
 19–20, 49, 58–9, 67
West Germany, *passim*
 and forward defence, 15–16,
 135, 176–9
 and rearmament and armed
 forces of, 15–20, 27,
 55–8, 59–60, 128, 172,
 178, 180, 181
 See France and: flexible
 response and: Multilateral
 Force: nuclear weapons,
 tactical, and
Wilson, Charles, 39
Wohlstetter, Albert, 96

Zagladin, Vadim, 116
Zeit, Die, 150
Zuckerman, Lord Solly, 33, 69